Sex and Pleasure
in Western Culture

Sex and Pleasure in Western Culture

Gail Hawkes

polity

First published in 2004 by Polity Press Ltd

Polity Press
65 Bridge Street
Cambridge CB2 1UR, UK

Polity Press
350 Main Street
Malden, MA 02148, USA

ISBN 0 7456 1670 4
ISBN 0 7454 1671 2   (pb)

A catalogue record for this book is available from the British Library and has been applied for from the Library of Congress.

Typeset in 10.5 on 12 pt Sabon
by SNP Best-set Typesetter Ltd., Hong Kong
Printed and bound in Great Britain by MPG Books, Bodmin, Cornwall

For further information on Polity, visit our website: www.polity.co.uk

The publisher has used its best endeavours to ensure that the URLs for external websites referred to in this book are correct and active at the time of going to press. However, the publisher has no responsibility for the websites and can make no guarantee that a site will remain live or that the content is or will remain appropriate.

Contents

Introduction

Death is an inevitable aspect of being human. So, in popular understanding, is sex. The inescapability of death is determined by our physicality. The inescapability of sex has a demonstrable social source. The inspiration for this book was to explore the mixed fear and fascination that the mere mention of 'sex' invariably provokes in the present. I have been interested in these mixed feelings for a long time, and earlier work suggested two things to me: first, that there was a set of ideas about sex and pleasure that persisted despite different social contexts and times; second (and more speculative), that this phenomenon suggested a strong link between sexual desire and the social order. These two ideas provide the foundation questions for this book. Why was sex considered a threat to social order, or, more simply, a 'social problem'? Did this apply to all 'sex'? Who defined it as such, and why? What were the consequences of this definition, and were they effective in reducing anxiety?

Since its birth, sociology has examined the interaction between the individual will and social forces. In this endeavour it has, until relatively recently, ignored the two most fundamental aspects for humankind – sex and death. Perhaps understandably, these two experiences have been shaded from scrutiny by the wide branches of biological definitions of both. Sex, like death, was primarily a biological fact. As such, neither was considered to yield much understanding of the ties that bind the individual to the social. A sociology of sex and of death began to emerge in the closing decades of the twentieth century. But much of this, especially the scholarship on sex, was to come from the tradition of interpretative sociology that emphasized the experiential over the structural. There was less recognition of an ideological dimension of sexual desire and pleasure that operated at a less conscious level and that linked sensual experience to social order.

The concept of 'social order' is not a fashionable one, either inside or outside walls of learning, for it seems to prioritize a mechanistic process over that of individual will and consciousness. Durkheim made much of the invisible forces that shape and influence the actions of individuals in society. These, he insisted, were social in origin, their role to contain the essential unruliness of human desires for gratification. Without these guiding forces, the bonds that tie individuals to each other, and ultimately to the 'whole', would disintegrate and chaos would result. However, what constitutes these bonds, how strong or flexible they are, is a topic for enquiry and explanation. Further, across time there is one feature that remains constant: the bonds that cement become identifiable only when they are challenged. They become more visible in order either to reinforce social norms or to adjust social bonds to the changed circumstances.

This book explores the social construction of ideas about sex, desire and pleasure, as part of the broader process of social order. It takes a broad sweep approach, rather than being inclusive of all cultural and historical variations and details. The intention is to provide a historical landscape whose signposts deal with the past and the present in each epoch. Theoretically there are three themes. First, as Marc Bloch demonstrated, the past can contribute much to an understanding of the present. Second, the sociological imagination, used in this way, can unearth and demonstrate the coexistence of change and continuity in social history. Third, the early Christian association between sin and sex kept the sexual body central to social control, where it remains today.

I begin by offering a 'bird's-eye view' of the sexual landscape of the new millennium, a term almost forgotten despite its huge currency at the close of the last century. The Prologue deliberately ignores scholarly work on sex and pleasure since this often barely impinges on the daily consumption of sexual desire and pleasure. Instead, examples from popular culture from the UK, Australia and North America are used to illustrate different 'levels of consciousness' about desire and pleasure against which individual choices and experiences occur. Looking more closely at this backdrop, which we largely take for granted, there is evidence of boundaries around modes of sexual pleasures even in a context where, at first glance, anything goes. This opening section 'flags up' three ideas for readers to keep in mind as they progress through the chapters. First, prevailing normative ideas are flexible. This allows the same acts to be viewed positively or negatively, depending on the context. Second, speaking about sex, whether encouraging or condemning, is endemic and apparently obligatory. Finally, there is a tacit recognition of the potentially disruptive potential of encouraging sexual desire.

Because the book deals with specific time periods, each chapter begins with a brief reminder about the key characteristics of the age. The first chapter reaches far back into time, to the distinctive association between sex pleasure and social order in classical Greece. In Plato's *Phaedrus* and *Symposium* I found obvious illustrations of this, as well as fascinating grounds for distinguishing between acceptable and unacceptable sexualities. The work of other classical scholars is used to summarize the distinctive features of sexual expression and their social roles for both men and women. Chapter 2 reviews the evolution of early Christian teachings about sex and the body. It emphasizes the early connection between sex and sin, and the danger represented by the irrational desiring body. Chapter 3 deals with the long era of the Middle Ages. While recounting the dominant role of the Church in controlling sexual behaviour, it also acknowledges the impact of secular ideas, especially from the spheres of medicine and both high and popular cultural practices. This expanded social context is continued in chapter 4, which discusses the ideas and influences of the Renaissance – the rebirth of knowledge, of secularism, of the love of the body and of its capability – on sexual mores and ideologies. Chapter 5 charts the twin developments of modernity and modern understandings of the sexual body. Sexual modernity made explicit what had been implicit throughout the account – sexual behaviour had profound implications for social life as well as for individual spiritual life. It also firmly established the sexual body as a legitimate object of attention for the modern medical profession. Chapter 6 identifies the twentieth century as the *sexual century*. This may seem counter-intuitive to the theme of this book, since all might be seen as sexual centuries. But it was in this period more than any previously that *natural* sex was deemed in need of proper *education*. Past anxieties had concentrated on identifying aspects of sexual desire and pleasure that were unnatural or abnormal. It was these characteristics that were a threat to the social order. But in the twentieth century 'normal' but uneducated heterosexuality was the subject of scrutiny and concern. The sexual century was also one of increasingly detailed and distinct discourses about sex from a *variety* of sources. This was also when sexuality became a political issue and a foundation for movements of liberation. By its close, sexual choice was a key marker for the self-identifying individual of late modernity.

The text ends with a review of the themes that have been recurrent and also reflects on the future implications of the fragmentation of categories that, still, normatively control sexual desire and sexual pleasure.

Prologue: The Sexual Landscape of the New Millennium

It is not the intention of this section to move directly into academic debates about sex and pleasure and their relationship to social order. The prologue follows an old theatrical tradition where a monologue sets the scene for the more structured performance that follows. In this respect I wanted first to draw the reader's attention to the *existence* of a sexual landscape and second to *display* its most distinctive features. Through this display, we are invited to look again at aspects of our social surrounds that we often take for granted. Especially this is the case in the fragmentation of discourses about sex. Our existence in the landscape often blurs our clarity of vision of the immediate surrounds. This effect is intensified in contemporary life by two aspects of late modernity. First, our social world is comprised of a rapidly increasing number of overlapping yet distinct spheres with which we all interact at varying levels. Second, the speed at which we are compelled to pass through these spheres blunts our critical faculties. In what follows we will retake the journey through the landscape, stopping to consider in more detail aspects of these sexual spheres that are not immediately obvious. We will focus on the presence of contradictions that are hidden by this fragmentation of spheres. In this way we will be identifying a key theme throughout the book: that the relationship between social construction and social order is often neither obvious nor direct. This becomes clearer in social contexts that are dominated by strong belief systems. In late modernity the secular belief system is dominated by the promotion of individual choice and individual authoring of self. Forms of social control, therefore, will be framed by this imperative and thus not appear overtly as control but rather the opposite – freedom. In the last half of the twentieth century, this word characterized much of what was said about sex. However, this was a freedom that was permitted, rather than being assumed or chosen.

The decades from 1960 to 1980 in the UK, the US and Australia were marked by the legalization of once illegal or stigmatized sexual behaviour. This included contraception to the unmarried; abortion; homosexuality between consenting adults; divorce on much less punitive grounds; and a relaxation of the censorship laws on explicitly sexual printed matter. Though the extent to which these were radical changes varied between states and between countries, there was an overall acceptance of the need to adjust levels of sexual morality in the post-war context. Second, there was a groundswell of movements for sexual liberation. Women, lesbians and gays demanded sexual freedom as an integral part of their democratic citizenship rights, using their desiring bodies to make a political as well as a personal statement. While these movements were effective in placing sexual rights on the political agenda, the extent to which they resulted in real freedom and autonomy was limited.

Sexual liberation was a double-edged sword. Certainly it alleviated the embarrassed secrecy that fed ignorance and discouraged open discussion about sexual matters. But it also fed campaigns by conservative movements about sexual promiscuity, the disintegration of the family and the corruption of youth. Talking about sex was not something that could be left to just anyone. The consequences might be the erosion of moral distinctions in sexual behaviour. Accordingly, specialized medical professionals retained their position of leadership, being the only legitimate outlet for sexual knowledge and sexual 'instruction'. In these professional discourses, and echoed in popular media, a number of key social norms were emphasized. First and foremost sex remained something one did in private and within the structure of a stable relationship, preferably marriage. It was, of course, heterosexual and coital. Positions or practices that increased pleasure were encouraged, but only insofar as they contributed to vaginal orgasm. Women's sexuality was nurtured and encouraged, their erotic training and expertise gradually over the century gaining an obligatory status. Clear normative distinctions were made between private and public sexual intimacy and expression. The 'proper place' for this exercise of 'sexual freedom' was behind closed doors, safely encased within the private and domestic sphere. Conversely, the experience of sexual pleasure and the expression of sexuality in public continued to be stigmatized and marginalized as morally corrupt and obscene.

In the last two decades of the twentieth century, this distinction became muddled, both conceptually and in reality. A number of features mark this change. First, sex and sexuality ceased to be the exclusive domain of the professional and the expert. The importance of official production and dissemination of sexual knowledge was replaced by the importance of choice and consumption of sex and sexuality. The detached expertise that was on offer in publications written by 'sexperts' was replaced by a new way of speaking about sex that inverted the priorities of the immediate past. Professional expertise was replaced by effectively marketing techniques of good sex by sexual entrepreneurs. Second, the once clear moral distinctions between sex in the private and the public sphere were dissolved. Anonymous sexual encounters, once marked as the defining feature of prostitution, began to be offered as entertainment and celebrated as the essence of a successful leisure experience. Advances in information technology drove the development of reality television that made good commercial use of offering voyeuristic opportunities to viewers while encouraging exhibitionist sexual displays between their contestants. Anonymously available erotic and pornographic material expanded with globalized access to internet technology.

This commodified eroticism breached the public–private divide in two senses. First, it offered the viewer a virtual entry into the intimacy of the bedroom – once the most private of spaces. Second, opening this space offered a legitimate context within which to condone sex disengaged from any commitment or emotional ties. Such sex, of course, has a very long history and remains formally defined as prostitution. But in the postmodern world this stigmatized connection has been severed by the fragmentation of contexts. This fragmentation defuses once clear moral boundaries around public and private sex. Indeed, any suggestion that the marketed commodified product is to be confused with 'real' sex – that is, heterosexual, and in stable relationships – is rejected as irrelevant.

New discourses of public and private pleasures

The distinction between 'the public and the private' is a fundamental one in sociology. As Norbert Elias has illustrated, what social activities fitted various categories differed depending on the historical period. This was most evident when comparing premodern and modern societies, where acts considered appropriate in the public sphere came to be inappropriate. In premodern times, Elias tells us, it was considered socially acceptable to share a bed at an inn with a total stranger of either sex. Similarly, public and intergenerational nakedness was not seen as immoral or, necessarily, associated with sexual desire. By contrast, in the family home of modernity, activities that took place within the four walls of 'the home' came to be seen by definition as private and intimate. Privacy became the key moral requirement as well as the key distinction between the private and public. Throughout the latter half of the twentieth century the search for profits fed an advertising industry growing in wealth and in its power to influence the self-perception of the all-important consumers. These new commentators of modern life made good use of the normative boundaries implied by the public–private divide. For example, advertisers avoided any direct acknowledgement that, in these private spheres, people had sex. The stereotype of the 'cornflake box family' required sex for its existence, but this was never acknowledged. Any reference to bodily functions, especially those that involved excretion, were sidestepped coyly, referred to only by inference or by elaborate euphemisms. So, for example, when after more than fifty years of use sanitary towels and tampons were considered acceptable advertising copy, the 'blood' they absorbed so efficiently was in fact blue water. Advertisements for lavatory cleaners in the UK were not permitted to show the bowl, only the cistern. Actors portraying characters in depictions of 'the family' were rarely, if ever, seen in bed together.

This construction of the home as the guardian of privacy and of modesty depended for its effectiveness on corresponding constructions in the public sphere. In premodern contexts urinating and even defecating in the public space was permitted. In the public sphere of modernity bodily functions were more or less outlawed or, at least, confined to clearly designated areas. The public toilet of modernity provided a designated socially acceptable context for a private act in the public space. Similarly the only acceptable context for public sex was within the walls of brothels. Sexual acts or images designed to induce sexual desire were morally demarcated in legally restricted spaces. Two examples will make the point. Erotic imagery is the mainstay of 'men's magazines'. Sealed in plastic from unsuitable eyes, these have an established presence in the newsagents and drugstores of modernity. Their purchase presented a social and moral challenge: the public admission of sexual needs. The act of choosing and of purchasing – in other words, the essential preliminary to consumption of sex in some form – involved exposing oneself to moral scrutiny and judgement. The request for condoms or for contraception in family planning clinics similarly makes a public statement about sexuality. As one research respondent commented to me about attendance at a family planning clinic, 'everyone knows why you're there'. 'You're there' because you desire sexual gratification and pleasure. But social mores make it difficult to acknowledge this need. Embarrassment results from crossing the threshold of intimacy and privacy with which acceptable sex was associated and by which it was defined. In late modernity the normative division between sex in private and in public has been eroded and even eradicated in some contexts. Instead, it has been replaced with intersecting yet distinct spheres that fragment both social meaning and normative judgement. Three examples from the sexual landscape will illustrate this claim: advertising sex, entertainment sex and unauthorized sex.

Advertising sex

Under the pressures of close competition for very similar products in the world market, globalizing capitalism recognized the necessity to use the power of sexual imagery in new ways. 'Traditionally', naked women's bodies were used to attract male attention to products related to blue-collar male work. The most famous of these were the Pirelli calendars that could be found on the walls of any car workshop, or indeed any workplaces with a preponderance of male employees. The association of such images with car tyres or power tools was clearly intended to encourage the guilty and secret enjoyment in a specific and enclosed context. This 'convention' contained erotic titillation within close and male-dominated confines, even before the challenges of feminism towards such commercialized objectification.

By contrast, from the 1990s explicit sexual imagery appeared on prime-time television, on billboards and hoardings in public thoroughfares and in mainstream magazines of all genres. The marketing targets likewise range across gender and age boundaries. The bodies are as likely to be men as women, in poses that conform to conventions of homoeroticism. The range of products they sell has expanded to include cars, chocolates, perfumes, food, drinks and clothing – especially underwear. But the most distinctive feature of advertising sex, apart from its wide range and increasing explicitness, is the appeal it makes to the active experience of sensuality. Cars are sold to both sexes not by their mechanical features but by the pleasurable sensations experienced through bodily contact with them. The carnality is conveyed by body language, facial expression and pounding music backgrounds. The Citroën Xsara campaign using Claudia Schiffer performing an elegant striptease and throwing her lace knickers out of the driver's window arguably began this trend. Similarly advertisements for ice-cream filmed in the bedroom directly associate the experience of eating the product with the experience of sexual pleasure and orgasm. Underwear and stocking advertisements freely enter what was once not only a private but also an intimate sphere of autoeroticism. All of these and many more present active and positive images of sexual pleasure outside of the conventional confines of relationships, and even sometimes heterosexuality, often making use of imagery that, two decades previously, would have been attacked for their sexist and exploitative messages. Women as well as men are targeted by these images, depending on the audience and potential buyers being addressed. Models are typically semi-clothed in underwear or in various stages of undress.

Many advertisements make direct references to sexual acts, usually coitus but sometimes also masturbation or oral sex. In the late 1990s in the UK, the British Sunday broadsheet *The Observer* ran a story on a new advertising campaign for Gossard Glossie – a new line in women's underwear. The advertisement shows a woman in a classically sexually available pose – eyes half-closed, mouth slightly open, arms flung back, waiting for sexual attention. The caption acknowledged women's sexuality and sources of pleasure – 'Who says a woman can't get pleasure from something soft?' However, the story was about the negative response to this ad, rather than the ad itself. The news story reported that the ad had drawn 800 complaints from the public in two weeks, but the Advertising Standards Authority (ASA) in the UK denied that the offence was 'widespread'. The ASA also refused to ban the Wonder Bra 'Hello Boys' ad, but the level of complaints was far lower – fifty-three in a year. On the one hand, there is the message reinforced endlessly by women's magazines that insist on women's sexual autonomy. 'Post-girl power' feminism considers objections to such imagery 'old hat'. Yet the radical potential is softened by the direct reference to heterosexual coitus, and especially the source of pleasure, the penis. More subtly, in 2002 Australian billboard ads for bras were captioned 'My mother always said I was a handful', and 'Get lost boys'. The woman advertising director claimed they are evidence for a new 'girlosophy', in which 'ballsy' images of women sell products to women by using the traditional images they, not just men, want to see (*Sydney Morning Herald*, April 2002). Yet the message about a new sexual aggression for women is modified by the traditionally available body language of the models.

Advertising sex has created a new context for the consumption of erotic imagery in public, beyond the censure both of political correctness and of more traditional objections to 'public sex'. Its ubiquity and content suggest that in late modernity two boundaries have shifted and perhaps dissolved. The first is that between private and public consumption of sexual imagery. By the nineteenth and for most of the twentieth century, public display, whether in text or image, of sex intended to titillate was unacceptable outside of the marginalized contexts of pornography. Advertising sex indicates the severe weakening of this margin. The second is that which identified sexual imagery of women with passive exploitation. Feminist sexual politics has for decades fought to establish this 'fun' as insidious and as perpetuating exploitative sexual politics. The concept of political correctness grew out of these campaigns. Now imagery that either directly or indirectly represents 'free-wheeling heterosexuality' is not just officially condoned; any objection to it is discouraged. Complaints are rarely taken seriously, and criticism is met with the claim that the material is 'tongue in cheek', ironic or camp. The term political correctness remains; its meaning appears reversed.

I make no value statement about whether or not these images should appear in the public space. The issue is to understand what is being conveyed by their presence and content. It would be premature to interpret the widespread phenomenon of advertising sex as evidence of emancipation from past pruderies, or for the effectiveness of postmodern 'ballsy feminism'. Nor can this be taken as evidence of the uncoupling of concerns about sex and pleasure from those of social order. A useful way of approaching the task of interpretation is to look at the distinction between form and content. The form distinguishes advertising sex as novel and as apparently indicating a shift towards greater acceptability of erotic experiences. The message appears to be that sexuality is an assumed source of pleasure and there is nothing morally objectionable in acknowledging the fact. More, these images serve to encourage active involvement in this celebration of sex in public spaces.

However, an examination of the content suggests an alternative, even opposite, interpretation. For what constitutes acceptable sex in this context is limited to heteronormative assumptions that are not gender neutral. Instead, it uses traditional features of male-orientated pornographic imagery. The widened appeal to include the recognition of women's active sexuality cannot be understood as a weakening of male-defined sexuality in either sex. Rather, a new form of packaging has been used to soften connections with older dichotomies of private sex/good, public sex/bad. The key to these 'new clothes' is the connection with humour and the 'naughty but nice' association that feeds laughter that often accompanies public sexual references. Packaged thus, advertising sex is sanitized from old ideas that freewheeling sex can 'deprave and corrupt' or, at least, offend. The use of these messages by the advertising industry suggests there has been a shift in both popular mores and understanding, since huge sums of money rest on their 'getting it right'. The second aspect of the sexual landscape, in which sexual desire is more directly associated with humour and fun, fuels this assumption, as it more directly associates the relaxation of sexual mores with the potential consumer.

Entertainment sex

The second key feature of the sexual landscape of late modernity is what I call entertainment sex. This format presents the same basic message about sex and pleasure – namely, that it is a source of not only physical pleasure but also light-hearted fun. Entertainment sex is, like advertising sex, to be found firmly located in the public sphere in both its production and its consumption. However, it demands a different category because it does not deal with fantasy or private imaginations but in the public performance of sexuality, sexual titillation and pleasure. The appeal to the consumer in this mode is the appeal to the hedonistic individual who is seeking amusement first and sexual gratification second. Historically in Western culture sex has always had the capacity to fascinate, attract and horrify in equal parts. Equally, the association between sex and humour has a long history; see, for example, the medieval romps in Chaucer and later Shakespeare or the Restoration comedies of Congreve and Sheridan. With modernity, sex became a much more serious business, in which displays of 'what people did sexually' was limited to the domain of science and medical expertise. In late modernity there appears a new mode of presentation of 'what people do sexually', one that involves amateurs, not experts, and whose rationale is the assumed entertainment value of sex. As with advertising sex, entertainment sex appears in specific formats bounded by appearance and forms of presentation. The most common are: the chat show format; 'reality television', especially *Temptation Island* and *Big Brother*; 'sexumentaries' – presented in documentary form but under this guise offering a wide-ranging diet of sexual perversity; and 'sex holidays', which are to be distinguished from 'sex tourism'.

In the UK in 1996 a game show called *Love in the Afternoon* was briefly transmitted (Channel 4, 5 p.m.). Voluptuous pink cherubs with prominent buttocks provided a background for the young women presenters seated on red lip-shaped couches. To encouraging whoops from the studio audience, it offered the erogenous potentials of kissing non-genital body parts (with practical demonstration), eating aphrodisiac foods (ditto), and interviewing self-proclaimed successful and prolific lovers. The transmission time raised questions over who was considered to be the viewing audience. At 5 p.m. all other channels were broadcasting young children's programmes. Perhaps the aim was to revitalize the weary parent over the fish fingers. This curious example soon quietly disappeared, but it was outlived by a series of programmes more typically located in late-night viewing slots: *The Good Sex Guide, The Girlie Show, Euro-trash, Carnal Knowledge, God's Gift* are the most well known in the UK context. All of these were transmitted during the late 1990s. In Australia a talk show titled *Sex with Sophie Lee* (media sex symbol) was launched in 1992. Originally intended to take a serious approach to sex in the post-AIDS era, this high-rating show rapidly developed into what was described as a 'nudge, nudge, wink, wink' format that began to play to the ratings rather than to inform with serious comment. In 1999 UK's Channel 5, whose output was described by their director of programmes, Dawn Airey, as 'films, fucking and football' (*The Guardian*: 8 June 1999), transmitted a game show called *Naked Jungle* as part of a naturism week. The presenter, naked except for a pith helmet, guided male and female contestants through a series of puzzles in a jungle environment. The tasks included tests such as the Pool of Death and Waterfall of Venus. Thirteen complaints from viewers who criticized the show on the grounds of taste and decency were dismissed by the ITC (the watchdog committee in the UK for commercial television). The programme gave a huge ratings boost to Channel 5 despite its late night slot. In the same year in the UK, *X-Certificate*, transmitted at 11 p.m. on a weeknight, devoted itself to 'porn videos' and their performers. Porn stars were interviewed and extracts from their movies shown. A panel of experts (two men and a woman) reviewed new releases of X-rated videos, evaluating them for erotic and entertainment potential. The format, which in set design and editorial approach was modelled on 'serious art programmes', suggests that what had formerly clearly been seen as the 'secret and sad' consumption of what are still called 'dirty movies' has moved from the margins to the centre of legitimate choice.

The satellite transmission of American chat shows, most notably *Jerry Springer* and *Rikki Lake*, presents an inexorable diet of sexual 'diversity', encouraging participants to seek temporary notoriety by parading their sexual proclivities for vicarious consumption by the worldwide audience. It is this distance between content and con- ⁄ sumption that operates as a boundary of acceptability. This is the sexuality of 'the other', not of 'us'. In these formats, entertainment sex draws on the fascination of the unknown as well as that of watching people performing or talking about performing sexual intimacy. This aspect of entertainment sex is developed on a higher level in the hugely popular transglobal *Temptation Island* and *Big Brother*. These so-called reality television formats command huge viewing audiences across national and cultural boundaries. The appeal of both lies in their use of the cameras as the viewers' eyes – dissolving completely, in the case of *Big Brother*, the boundary between the private and the public. But the role of sex in this form of entertainment is central to both. The rationale of *Temptation Island* is that of sexual promiscuity and infidelity, offering these otherwise socially condemned practices as a form of entertainment for the viewer. *Big Brother*'s 'contestants' are encouraged to engage in sexual 'horse-play', and whole programmes are devoted to *Big Brother Uncut*. These weekly outcuts of the regular transmissions are trailed sensationally with glimpses of naughty sex romps that are indistinguishable from cheap pornographic films shown on X-rated channels. Fans of America's *Big Brother* have seen some of the contestants naked on the show's official website. The early morning nude web cast marked the last day that CBS ran online footage without censoring it. The feed showed housemates Mike, Krista, Monica, Herdy and Sherlyn naked in the hot tub and licking whipped cream off each other's bodies. When she got out of the hot tub, Krista also flashed at the cameras. In Australia in June 2002 the second *Big Brother* finally broke the boundaries as two contestants were filmed allegedly having sex after the house was supplied with alcohol (*Sydney Morning Herald*, 16 June 2002). 'Reality television' by definition invites the inclusion of sex for entertainment, since its whole reason for being is its claim to offer insights into 'real people doing real things'. As with advertising sex, this format effectively dissolves the distinction between private and public sex. But unlike the former, and because it involves 'real people', this format dissolves another taboo of modernity, at least by implication – sex without commitment, transitory, anonymous and promiscuous.

This aspect of entertainment sex is more explicit in 'sex holidays'. In the UK and Europe, Club 18–30 has been highly successful in marketing cheap package holidays to young people (despite the company name, the *average* age of clients is twenty-one years). The catchwords for these holidays are 'sun, sea and sex', and their all-inclusive format in purpose-built compounds openly encourages sexual adventurism in its young clients. In 1994 the company's advertising billboards displayed the single word SEX in luminous pink letters several feet high. Much smaller letters below completed the sales slogan – 'sea and sand'. This campaign attracted sufficient negative public attention to warrant the Advertising Standards Authority request that the bill-boards be withdrawn. The reason for this, in the words of the press officer, was that the advertisements 'encouraged sexual promiscuity'. In 1995, the ASA banned Club 18–30's new 'Beaver Espana' poster campaign featuring slogans such as 'Wake up at the crack of Dawn . . . or Lisa or Julie or Karen' and 'Something deep inside her said she'd come again.' Despite these bans the message remained as enticing as ever. The company went from taking 20,000 passengers at the beginning of the 1990s to over 100,000 holidaymakers by the millennium. In May 2002 the trend continued.

> A cinema advert featuring dogs having sex . . . for Club 18–30 holi-days shows a mongrel apparently watching holidaymakers in bed. It then trots through a Spanish village engaging poodles, sheepdogs and Afghan hounds in a variety of 'human-style' sexual activities. The advertisement was given a certificate 18 by the British Board of Film Classification. A spokesman for Club 18–30 Holidays said: 'We're not aiming at the kind of people who go to Crufts [a famous dog show in the UK]. Some of the audience will think it's undignified but I don't think our audience will – I think they'll find it funny.' (*Daily Telegraph*, May 2002)

An interesting postscript is the presentation of the world's most coveted creativity award to Club 18–30 holidays in 2002 for its con-tinuing blend of sun, sea, sand and sexual entertainment.

A more sophisticated version of entertainment sex is provided by the late twentieth-century Jamaican and Brazilian resorts directed towards affluent North American and European clients. Like Club 18-30, Hedonism resorts are self-contained compounds. The selling point, like the image they wish to convey, is more upmarket – this is hedonism, not 'bonking'. But though the packaging is more ornate, the contents are the same. Holidaymakers are dared to come with an open mind and invited to join the clothes-free areas and the nude late-night jacuzzi sexual playgrounds. To quote from the official website of Hedonism III in Jamaica, 'Hedo is a physical place (affection included) for some people, but you only go where you are invited, just like the real world. People do jiggle each other's tits. They cup balls and give massages, but it's among friends – and you know who you can do this with if you have good socialization skills. This touching is for fun (read: cheap thrills) and doesn't last long enough to result in orgasm.' And from the same site, in answer to a question from a prospective client about appropriate dress on Pajama and Toga nights: 'For PJ night: from naked to doggie collars to severe bondage stuff to cutesy-wootsy to boxer shorts to full flannels with slippers and stuffed animal. Toga night can be judged by the number of breasts on display. A good Toga night shows at least nine breasts (some women wear a one-hooter halter)' (www.hedonism.org).

There is a disturbing colonial and racist aspect in their location in third-world countries. Jamaica was the first and now has three Hedonism resorts, where 90 per cent of the clients are white American and all the staff are black Jamaican. The sex-seeking tourists are considered fair game for the locals, who supply, for the price of a good time and free drinks and gifts, the kudos of a young black escort. Their peers refer to these young men locally as 'rent-a-rasta' (personal communication). The age cohort is different: the average age is between thirty and forty-five years, and women outnumber men by around four to one. Brazil's first Hedonism resort, in Rio de Janeiro, opened in 2001. In its pre-opening publicity, a spokesman for Hedonism Brazil identified outdoor sex as a key theme in the club. Three weekend parties were planned – the first naked, the second a 'Vice Versa' party and the third billed as 'Screws and Bolts': 'It's going to be a contest between couples who haven't necessarily met before – with very few clothes involved. Male guests will be given a screwdriver kind of costume and the women will get token bolts. The winners will be the couple who properly fit the right screw to the right bolt.'

In the postmodern world, sex is both the choice and the domain of the self-constructing and hedonistic individual. It has become the prime signifier of the well-rounded and successful individual male and, especially, female (see, for example, *Sex in the City*). In fictional narratives and 'factional' accounts of modern life, sex and its pleasures are presented as obligatory achievements in a variety of mainstream social settings (see, for example, *Vice: The Sex Trade*, *Sex and Shopping* and *Love in the 21st Century* – all transmitted in the UK in 1999). As Britain's *The Observer* commented, 'it has been estimated that in two weeks of British terrestrial television last year, 357 people were "sex participants". . . . Another 222 people were indulging in a week of satellite television' (*The Observer*, 18 July 1999). In popular entertainment, especially on television, sex is presented as disengaged from relationships and even emotion. In this 'free-floating' mode of expression, sex has become a commodity to be sold and consumed as a marker of self-expression. Three years later, *The Observer* commented: 'Television's obsession with very specific aspects of sex – explicit rather than erotic; action preferred to anticipation; seedy rather than cerebral – conveys the illusion that we are all objectified now, somebody else's sex toy, valued only for our sexual prowess; intercourse is the twenty-first century's gladiator sport' (Yvonne Roberts, 2 May 2002).

In these aspects of the sexual landscape, desire for sex is ever-present, of no more moral consequence than the desire for food. Like food, this product is prepared and presented in an ever-expanding variety. Just as in a supermarket aisle, the obligation to experience the variety is conveyed by the range of choice. The *act* of consumption is more important than its *content*. It is through this choice, at the same time rich and empty, that we are invited to express and illustrate our individuality. It is in this climate of choice that conventional morality is silenced. Vacation sex provides a context in which sex as a leisure pursuit has no more moral content than windsurfing or scuba diving. Similarly, advertising sex invites vicarious consumption of an anonymous erotic experience beyond the boundaries of formalized 'relationships' or emotional attachment. As if to underline the more 'enlightened' view, traditional gendered expectations of sexual desire are often reversed, as women more than men are celebrated as sexual hunters. Both advertising and entertainment sex suggest that the 'coupling' of sex and morality has been dissolved in the public space. However, the existence of these new contexts may depend on constant surveillance of their content, as new contexts inevitably mean new boundaries.

Beyond the boundaries: unauthorized sex

By examining examples of sex and desire in the public space that are censored, we can gain some insights into how and why these boundaries persist. There appear to be two main grounds for objections, expressed either through formal censorship by statutory bodies (advertising standards authorities or censorship boards), through representations from interest groups, or through the media. The most frequent objections made to both related to public nudity. While nudity and sexual desire are frequently linked, in the sexual ideology of the Christian West there are contexts in which nudity is disconnected from sex and desire. No anxieties, formal or informal, are expressed about nudity in naturism, in medical examinations, or in artistic modelling. The practice of 'streaking' will result in a charge of public disorder but not pornography. Yet the connection between nudity and sexual stimulation remains a central feature of 'authorized sex' in its various forms. It seems that some displays of naked flesh are transgressive, and again we see that it is the context, not the content, that is critical. In 1997 in Australia, a billboard advertising flavoured milk (trade name 'Dare') featured bare-bottomed rugby players enjoying a romp in the park (caption: 'You can do anything on a Dare). First the bare bottoms were covered with black strips, and then the poster was removed altogether by the Queensland Department of Main Roads (*Brisbane Courier Mail*, 6 June 1997). In May 2001 the US Postal Service banned as 'lewd and filthy matter' a postcard promoting a film featuring a group of men parading naked through a street in Wales (www.indexonline.org/indexindex/misc/20010809_unitedstates. shtml).

In 1998 police tried to order the UK's Birmingham University to censor a library book of photographs by Robert Mapplethorpe. A student preparing a thesis on fine art versus pornography photographed pages from the book and the chemist who developed the film called the police. The Crown Prosecution Service advised police that two images in the book were likely to 'deprave and corrupt' under the terms of the Obscene Publications Act. The case didn't get to court, but Dr Peter Knight, vice-chancellor of Birmingham University, was formally cautioned. In another similar example, only this time made more urgent by the involvement of children, an exhibition of photographs of an artist's children in various stages of being undressed also drew the attention of the police (www. indexonline.org, 20 March 2001). In all these cases the images were those of naked men, an unexpected finding if the grounds for objection was the 'objectification of women'. The display of women's bodies is subject to more narrow and detailed control. In 1999, for example, new censorship laws in Australia banned the display of 'breast nudity'. The Office of Film and Literature Classification (OFLC) is now empowered to make rulings on how much covered breast can be shown in newsagents. Apparently, small semi-covered breasts are less socially disruptive than large semi-covered breasts. In a related but more extreme example, the same ruling allows the naked display of women's genitalia providing the inner labia do not protrude. In a February 2001 edition of the *Australian Women's Forum* editors were not allowed to include, in an educational story about women having vaginal plastic surgery, pictures of the normal appearance of women's genitals. The OFLC would allow only 'limited genital detail' to be shown. This was even more irrational given the reason for the story in the first place. Erotic and pornographic literature is bound by the same controls, and the models' inner labial lips were airbrushed out, if prominent. The story by the *Australian Women's Forum* was about the negative impact this has had on women who, on seeing these images, thought that they were abnormal. This led to a marked increase in visits to plastic surgeons for what was called 'landscaping of the genitals' (Yolanda Corduff, *Eros Journal*, www.eros.org.au).

Earlier in 1993, the programme *Sex/Life*, transmitted in Australia, sought to take a responsible and non-sensational approach to human sexuality. The programme featured 'real people' speaking of their sexuality on screen. A leading sponsor, the maker of the largest-selling family car in Australia, withdrew its advertising contract because it wanted its cars to be associated with 'wholesome products'. In this context, real people having real sex were not considered 'wholesome'. Wholesome sex, it appears, has very narrow parameters. It certainly does not include masturbation, especially when it is suggested that women pleasure themselves in this way. In October 2000 Cameron Diaz appeared in an advertisement fully clothed but with her hands down the front of her knickers. The caption read 'Cameron 'the pleasure's all mine' Diaz'. Following three complaints from the public, the UK's ASA ordered the ad to be withdrawn. It was, they said, likely to cause 'serious and widespread offence' (news.bbc.co.uk/1/hi/entertainment/966981.stm). Two years later in Australia, the *Sydney Morning Herald* refused to run an advertising campaign to promote newly built apartments for young singles. The ad featured a woman in a sleek black dress with her hand resting on her thigh and with the tagline 'Home alone'. The grounds for the objection was the suggestion of solitary pleasure for the woman masturbating at home (www.bandt.com.au/news/f2/oc0036f2.asp). This censorious attitude to the representation of some aspects of sexuality is further suggested by the banning of two out of three Gossard lingerie advertisements in 2000. The campaign, entitled 'Gossard: Find Your G-Spot', drew on the 'new laddish' approach to young women's sexuality approvingly promoted and condoned in the globally transmitted *Sex in the City*. It featured three bedroom scenarios involving a woman alone and naked, surrounded by discarded lingerie. The approved caption read 'Moan, moan, moan'. The banned captions read 'If he is late, you can start without him' and 'Bring him to his knees.' The UK ASA banned the latter two ads following forty complaints from the public and ruled that 'allusion to masturbation and oral sex made the posters unacceptable in the public space' (news.bbc.co.uk/1/hi/uk/1258961.stm). Especially in the case of masturbation, this is something that has traditionally been associated with male sexuality. Similarly, with oral sex it is usually inferred that women are the givers, not the takers. It is of interest that the advertising industry used women in these contexts and that it was these sexual references that attracted official censure.

Perhaps some nudity is problematic because the interpretation of the images and the possible responses are not so easily manipulated and therefore controlled. This is especially the case where images might be 'interpreted' in ways that are beyond the acceptable boundaries of heterosexual stimulation. In 1999 a Calvin Klein advertisement published in the *New York Times* depicting young boys and young girls wearing only CK underwear drew an immediate response. Within twenty-four hours of their release, Calvin Klein withdrew the ads in response to 'public outcry'. 'The comments and reactions we received today raised issues we had not fully considered', Klein explained in a hastily called press conference. 'As a result we have decided to discontinue the campaign immediately' (Yolanda Corduff, *Australian Penthouse*, July 1999). Despite the images being of the type one would see in any family photo album – two five-year-olds bouncing on the couch – the main complaint was that these images were too provocative. It was suggested that the genitals of the young boys were too prominent in one shot and that in another the position of one boy's fingers suggested that his small penis was exposed. These objections can be understood in the current climate of fear and hatred about paedophiles. But identifying the source of distorted and compulsive desires in this way arguably encourages rather than prevents the further sexualization of children.

We are familiar with the use of 'f**k' to prevent the eyes from being corrupted by the word 'fuck'. In 1997 French Connection UK launched a campaign that resulted in a huge rise in international sales and profits. French Connection became FCUK – an inspired piece of advertising imagination. However, it also attracted complaints and official scrutiny by advertising standards authorities in the UK and the US. By 2002 the company had gone too far, the British ASA decided. Their latest campaign was headed by the words FCUKINKYBUGGER. The ASA banned this ad and required that the company submit all future ads for inspection. In a similar but less extreme vein in 2001 the UK Department of Transport decided that the word SEX was deemed too offensive to be displayed in cars in public and could not be used on a numberplate (www.ananova.com, 11 July 2001).

I think that these new boundaries have more to do with controlling the subject of these desires, rather than their object – the observer, not the observed. In 2002 the International Skating Union decided that sexually explicit poses by dancers would be penalized by point deductions. Singled out for special attention were 'upside down splits and spread-eagles while leaning backwards low on the ice' (ABC Online 8 Feb 2002). Who and what is being managed here?

Why is this female display censorable when Gossard bra ads are not? Perhaps unauthorized fantasy is that which is experienced in private beyond the manufacture and control of the dominant ideological 'factory'. This aspect of unauthorized sex is more revealing. It is not the body of the observed, or the observer of these banned images, that is the 'object of power'. It is the imagination, the capacity to inhabit an erotic world not derived from the physical. In Australia, for example, 8 per cent of the voting population have been found to be on adult video mailing lists. There are 12 million visits to sex workers per year and 1.4 million phone calls to sex lines every month ('Between the Sheets: Sex Facts from the Suburb', www.eros.com.au). In late 1999 an Act of the Australian Parliament (Consumers Protection and Standards Bill 1999) required that all potential users of sex lines register for a personal PIN, describing exactly what services they were interested in.

It is this element of fantasy, not unconscious bodily desire, which is perhaps at the core of fears about social disruption – that amateur eroticism will prevail outside the frameworks of the permitted and forbidden.

Conclusion

A defining feature of the first years of the twenty-first century is the high profile given to sex and sexual pleasure in a wide range of contexts, disengaged from the fixed categories of modernity. In late modernity the security offered by these categories has been removed. What is defined and experienced as acceptable and unacceptable presentations of sex is highly contingent. Old grounds for condemnation have been fragmented. For example, feminist arguments that explicit sexual material exploited women for male sexual needs have been modified by 'girlosophy' that promotes, encourages and celebrates not just female sexual autonomy but female sexual predation.

Behind all of this lies the phenomenon of commodification: this is nothing new in capitalist theory, but its form in late modernity is distinctive. In modernity it was material goods that were produced and marketed for their use value. In late modernity it is self-identity that is both produced and marketed. But this is not done directly. In late capitalism, the key to self-identity is choice. Sex sells, it has been said, and now it is sex itself that is being sold. Traditionally unauthorized sex has always been sold by the sex industry. The sale of 'authorized sex' in advertising is done indirectly – the sale by, not of, sex. Here the connection between sexual desire and sexual gratification is necessarily indirect. In entertainment sex, the physicality of authorized sex is more evident. This has moved the locus for consumption of sexual pleasure from the private to the public sphere. But, as with advertising sex, the end result is not sexual release. Entertainment sex, we are told, is just for a laugh. This claim for the humorous content of both phenomena creates a brief but recognizable vacuum. Much of the apparent moral neutrality of commodified sex lies in its being divided off from intimate pleasures and desires. This actively promoted ethos of 'fun' applies a veneer over the more serious (and persistent) vestiges of patriarchal sexual scripts. In the sexual landscape of the new millennium moral misgivings traditionally associated with a 'free market' in sexual pleasure appear to have been neutralized. The mixed fear and fascination that characterizes much Western sexual culture perhaps is the key to the success of commodified sexual imagery and the reason for its widespread and accepted use. What constitutes 'the sexual' is presented in pre-packaged form – with the meanings ready made for consumption. Just as supermarkets entice with 'ready-made' meanings and promises of sensual experiences, sexual pleasure and erotic titillation are presented in forms that are easy to process and unthreatening. The availability of sexual pleasure on the 'supermarket shelves' does not signal 'free choice' – to consume or not to consume. The process of 'choice' is actively manipulated. Old products are presented as new, useless ones as essential. Any vestige of use value in a product is dissolved in an illusory presentation that combines novelty with the promise of a thoroughly individual experience. These fictions are an integral part of what Bauman calls 'market dependency', in which 'new commodities create their own necessities.'

My two examples from the sexual landscape of the new millennium have been presented to support a popular contention that sex no longer has the ability to shock. Everyone does it, everyone enjoys it and everyone understands the boundaries that separate the OK from the not OK. But is this really so? Is it that simple? Have the centuries-long anxieties about the consequences of uncontrolled sexual pleasure been overcome in such a short time? We have seen how the face of 'anything goes' is modified by the identification of boundaries between authorized and unauthorized sex. In a cultural climate that claims to embrace sexual diversity, a claim underpinned in most Western contexts by some (albeit minimal) positive legislation for sex rights, two forms of sexual pleasure appear to remain outlawed. Within the hypersexualized context of late modernity it is not, then, all sex that is acceptable, nor all sources of pleasure. The high profile given to sexual pleasure on the landscape of the new millennium masks some more traditional concerns about how, where and with whom it is permissible to explore sexual pleasure. Most strikingly, entertainment and advertising sex and their unauthorized forms suggest the impact of certain aspects of sexual pleasure and desire on social and public order. In order to trace the threads of this complex situation, the following chapters will take a journey into the past, and into very different cultural contexts, to explore some of the roots of these issues.

1

Sex, Pleasure and Self-Control in Classical Antiquity

It seemed to me that by starting from the modern era and proceeding back through Christianity to antiquity, one would not be able to avoid raising a question that was at the same time very simple and very general. [Why] is sexual conduct, why are the pleasures and activities that attach to it, an object of moral solicitude? (Foucault 1987: 10)

Introduction

The reason for choosing classical antiquity is that ideas about sex held in this period could also provide some insights into the predominance of certain ideas about sex and pleasure in Western sexual culture. Additionally, commonly held ideas about Greek life, supported by evidence from art works of the period, suggest a celebration of the body and its naked beauty, especially that of young men. This reverence for natural beauty in both humans and their surroundings has been a lasting influence throughout Western history. Today we can easily find well-known examples, for example, of Michelangelo's David – created in the neo-classical style of the Renaissance. It is this continuity of the influence of Greek culture over millennia that invites an exploration of a reverence for sensual pleasure and of different attitudes to cross-generational as well as homoerotic sexual attraction. Classical Greece was characterized by a production of great literature, art, philosophy, drama and art in the years between 479 and 323 BC, with the death of Alexander the Great.

During these years sensual pleasure and the manner in which it was sought lay at the centre of what it was to be a balanced and stable human, in harmony with self, the gods and nature. However, pleasure and its pursuit were not to be undertaken in an uncontrolled and unregulated fashion. How pleasure was experienced was, as is the case throughout our history, defined in terms of morals and ethics. The basis for moral and ethical pleasures lay in the extent to which the individual could, through the experience, demonstrate self-control. Thus it was the manner in which pleasure was taken that was the crucial distinction, not the source from which it was derived. This was the first reason for pleasure being a central positive element in classical Greek culture. The second lay in the view that balance and harmony were essential for bodily health. In ancient medical practice, physical health was the sign of moral and ethical health, and pleasurable feelings an indication of this balance. In terms both of the individual and of the social order, the management of pleasure was considered of primary importance. Pleasure was seen as a positive sensation, but one that must be undertaken in a particular way in order to avoid negative consequences. The origin of these ideas lay in two pre-Platonic traditions: the didactic tradition and that of ancient medicine.

The didactic tradition made use of literature, especially poetry, to provide ethical and moral maxims for the proper living of daily life. Hesiod, the first of these poets, who lived around 800 BC, cautioned: '"wickedness lives near at hand, and the path to it is smooth, but excellence dwells far away up a rough steep path, and the gods make man sweat before he achieves [it]' (*The Works and the Days*, 287–92, quoted in Gosling and Taylor 1982: 13). Avoiding temptations and their consequences was essential for individual and social stability. Gosling and Taylor argue that, in these and other didactic texts, 'pleasure is treated with, to say the least, some reserve; the three maxims which mention it directly run "control pleasure", "avoid pleasure which brings distress", and "pleasures are mortal, but virtues are immortal"' (ibid.). The management of pleasure was thus a key element in the moral and ethical education of the ancients. Complete mastery was beyond human achievement, for only the gods were perfect. It was in attempting the control that one showed one's ethical health and balance. The means by which this was attained was a recurrent topic of the works of Plato, two of which will be discussed below.

The second tradition that addressed the 'problem of pleasure' was that of ancient medicine. Since the late fifth and the fourth century, the Hippocratic school of medicine taught that the body was an organism whose health was defined by the correct balance of its constitutive elements. In the context of medical practice and writing of this period, and for many centuries to follow, this balance was synonymous with health. A healthy body was one that experienced feelings of pleasure, not discomfort or pain. Imbalance produced by a deficiency or an excess in any one element that made up the human body was the cause of disease. In the course of normal life, temporary states of imbalance were unavoidable. But just as this was natural and expected, so was the ability of the body to redress this balance. And the feelings of discomfort, pain and pleasure were the primary sensations associated with this process of balance and imbalance. A deficiency caused feelings of desire, and pleasure was the sensation that accompanied the satisfaction of the desire. For example, thirst is a deficiency of bodily fluid, yet it is experienced as a desire for water. From a physiological point of view, if desire was the sign of the onset of imbalance, pleasure was the indication of its attainment. This simple explanation of the source and experience of pleasure hides a more complex process in which the management of pleasure has a moral as well as physical imperative. I will be discussing the regimen of ancient medicine and its emphasis on self-control and self-management to illustrate this second tradition of thought about pleasure and its social as well as individual significance.

The teachings of ethical literature and those of the early physicians did not condemn the pursuit of pleasure for its own sake. There was no assumption, in other words, that pleasure was morally wrong. Despite this lack of overt value judgements, there are three early ideas that were later to become more familiar warnings about the consequences of sexual pleasure. First, both traditions identified pleasure with bodily needs and desires. This suggested that desire and pleasure might be difficult to control by the conscious will. Second, both traditions placed an obligation on the individual to monitor their desires and control excessive needs and wants. This was considered essential for bodily health on the one hand, and for social order on the other. Finally, there is evidence of mixed feelings about desires and pleasures. On the one hand, these are associated with the human condition, and are therefore to be accepted as natural. On the other, this association means that they cannot be escaped or avoided. These pre-classical teachings and beliefs about pleasure, its management and its social as well as individual significance provided the foundation for the views expressed by Plato some four centuries later.

Plato on pleasure, desire and its social significance

The texts *Symposium* and *Phaedrus* are two key works in the transition years of Plato's contribution to Western thought. Born in 427

BC, the great philosopher was in his sixties when he wrote these and other 'dialogues' (accounts of conversations) which became central to what was to become the discipline of Platonic thought. Both texts explore the issues of desire and pleasure and their management. Both deal with the topic of the soul, of eros, and of pleasure. The symposia were gatherings of high-status male citizens chosen for their social skills, storytelling, intellectual rigour, entertainment value and humour. They were characterized by extravagant indulgences in sensual pleasures as much as by their levels of conversation. Women were present but only as musicians or dancers, while boys of the slave caste chosen for their physical beauty served the guests. In addition to the enjoyment of such immediate pleasures as food, wine, music and erotic titilation, much importance in these gatherings was attached to conversation and debate.

Plato's *Symposium* is the account of such a gathering, devoted to a discussion of love. However, it was love of a specific type, which alerts us to the very different cultural construction of desire, pleasure and the expression of sexuality. The love with which the dialogue is concerned, and which is accepted as a matter of course by all the speakers including Socrates, is homosexual love; it is assumed without argument that this alone is capable of satisfying a man's highest and noblest aspirations. '[The] love of a man and woman, when it is mentioned at all, is spoken of as altogether inferior, a purely physical impulse whose sole object is the procreation of children' (Plato 1951: 12). The first speaker is Phaedrus, who is uncritical in his praise of love. Given its status, as the oldest of gods, love lies at the very heart of humanity, representing all of its finer attributes. Being a lover adds to one's moral standing and ethical strength, he argues. The temptation to act 'dishonourably', to flout the social mores and standards, is resisted more easily by the lover, who fears that his beloved, and others, will see him as weak. This contribution is challenged by the second speaker, Pausanius, who reminds his listeners of the dangers that are hidden by love's attractions. For, as Pausanius reminds his listeners, there are two Aphrodites: 'One is the elder and the daughter of Uranus and had no mother; her we call Heavenly Aphrodite. The other is younger, the child of Zeus and Dione, and is called Common Aphrodite' (Plato 1951: 45). Humans must be wary when praising love unconditionally; they need to be aware which sort of love is receiving such praise and approval.

These two Aphrodites differ in their origins. One is born of humans, the other of the gods. The emotions to which both give rise – the love and desire felt in their presence – differ accordingly and are differently valued. The love associated with Common Aphrodite (born of woman) is the lesser of the two. It is an ignoble and even animal drive experienced by men, whether directed towards men or women. Its expression is limited to physical pleasure. There is no spiritual elevation to be experienced with this common love. Being physical in origin and in direction, this inferior emotion is deemed less susceptible to control or to will. It is random in its direction and mode of experience. In modern terms, this kind of love might be associated with 'promiscuous sex'. The second form is the opposite, in both origin and experience. This form of love and desire emanates from a divine source. Note that Heavenly Aphrodite has no mother, but only a father – a god. [Heavenly Aphrodite, born from the sea into which the dismembered Uranus had been thrown, 'has no female strain in her, but springs entirely from the male.] [She] is older and consequently free from wantonness' (Plato 1951: 46–7). The love that emanates from this source is expressed in a very different manner. First, having no earthly basis, this desire is free from any taint of the 'female strain', which would confine its expression to physical lust. Rather, this desire and its expression elevates the spiritual over the carnal. In contrast to the first form of love, this desire is predictable, not wanton. This morally superior form of love finds its expression in the love of boys by older and socially superior men.

According to Plato, there is a rational purpose in the existence of these two very different kinds of love and desire. [They offer a choice by which high-born male citizens can express their moral superiority, or find themselves wanting and thus correct their weakness. For they offer the opportunity for both lover and their youthful beloved to demonstrate their ability to control the short-lived and ultimately 'bad' desires. If a man or boy gives in to the temptations of Common Aphrodite he shows himself to be a 'common or vulgar lover', promiscuous and inconstant, 'a lover of the body rather than the soul'. If he resists this temptation, he shows himself to be a worthy man. Better still, if he follows the path laid down by Heavenly Aphrodite he shows himself to be an altogether morally superior individual who can exercise the required self-control and moderation of expression.]

Plato thus made a normative distinction between physical love (equated with bodily desire) and spiritual love (equated with moral excellence). But since the human race depends on the common sort of love, some logical place must be found for the desire between men and women, while retaining the moral superiority of love between men. Socrates, who uses an argument he attributes to a woman called

Diotima, solves this problem in his speech. Sexual desire of a man for a woman, or the other way round, is really an expression of the wish for immortality gained through procreation. This definition retains the physicality while moving the motivation to a higher plane beyond a transitory gratification of urges. It is also a more rational and therefore justifiable desire, which aims at a long-term outcome rather than a short-term sensual experience. Secondly, Diotima argues, attaching a high value to physical beauty presented a moral challenge. The love of beauty of the body is replaced, in an enlightened man, by love of a 'virtuous soul', a love of moral beauty against which physical beauty 'is a poor thing by comparison'. This is the goal to which all men should aspire – a goal to which desire is properly directed. This 'absolute beauty . . . pure and unalloyed' is superior in every sense to that 'tainted by human flesh and colour and a mass of perishable rubbish' (Plato 1951: 95).

In this discussion of physical beauty and sexual attraction, sex, as we understand it today, is absent. There is no mention of physical acts that are, or are not, considered moral or socially permissible. For example, the issue of pleasure is one that is largely removed from its physical experience. This understanding is now alien to contemporary sexual orthodoxy. What remains familiar is the moral distinction made between short- and long-term pleasures. Then and now, the temptation to indulge in fleeting and uncommitted sexual pleasures is recognized and condemned. Intense human effort is needed to rise above mere physical desires and their ultimately disappointing experience. The truly sensual experience is one that takes time and effort, and is a victory of the mind over the body.

Plato's *Phaedrus*: lust, desire and 'the charioteer'

Phaedrus is the second work of Plato that devotes detailed attention to the experience and expression of desire. Written some years later, estimated between 372 and 368 BC (Plato 1951: 7), this is the most explicit recognition of the social and individual dangers of sexual desire. It also offers a blueprint for the means by which to contain this risk. This text, and the use of the metaphor of the charioteer, develops the themes suggested in *Symposium*, especially those about the difference between lust and self-control, and the struggle to maintain mastery over desire. Here, Plato argues that all who experience it have a choice in how they respond to this desire. 'There are two sorts of ruling or guiding principle that we follow: one is an innate desire for pleasure, the other an acquired judgement that aims at what is best' (ibid.: 38). 'Irrational desire' is defined by response to physical beauty. Surrender to this temptation marks the lover as a selfish and destructive individual, both of himself and of his 'beloved'. The beloved is portrayed as a prisoner trapped by the desire of his older lover, and as one whose character, physical health and status as a citizen will ultimately be destroyed. Irrational desire is the response to superficial physical beauty. It results in the loss of control of self and indifference to the needs of others. The answer is not celibacy or retreat from temptation. Desire is the natural response to physical beauty, and if ignored it will result in madness. Salvation lies in the fact that there is also a natural ability to control excessive desire and thus avoid its negative consequences.

This ability Plato illustrates in his story of the charioteer and his two horses, who together represent the human soul. The soul has three parts, one that tends to good, one that tends to wilfulness, and the third (the charioteer) that can apply reason to action. When confronted by physical beauty or sexual attraction, it is the charioteer who, despite his capacity for reason, is the first to experience 'the sensation of warmth . . . and the pricking of desire'. Yet the sight of the beloved inspires a reaction in the other two parts of the soul, represented by two horses. The good steed is white 'with black eyes, a lover of glory but with temperance and modesty . . . needs no whip, being driven by the word of command alone.' The bad steed 'is crooked in frame, a massive jumble of a creature, with thick short neck, snub nose, black skin, grey eyes, hot-blooded, consorting with wantonness and vainglory.' The charioteer is reminded of the true purpose of beauty by the sight of his beloved close at hand. This gives the driver the strength to rein in and control the steeds: 'the one willing and unresisting, but the wanton sore against his will. . . . For a while they struggle, . . . but at last, finding no end to their evil plight, they yield and agree to do his bidding' (Plato 1951: 254a, 104).

This story provides the resolution to the tension between the two forms of desire discussed in *Symposium*. It also emphasizes the capacity of the individual to control their own physical urges by will and reason. Humans are thus not at the mercy of their desires. Desires can be controlled. In addition, success in these efforts is rewarded in their material lives. For those who tame the wanton steed (and their physical urges), 'their days on earth will be blessed with happiness and concord; for . . . they have won self-mastery and inward peace' (Plato 1951: 256b).

Gender and masculinity in classical antiquity

[Everything that made Greece great, everything that created for Greeks a
civilisation which will be admired as long as the world exists, has its roots
in the unexampled ethical evaluation of the masculine character in public
and private life. (Licht 1994: 440)]

In *Symposium* and *Phaedrus*, the love and desire, unless otherwise
qualified, is that between adult male citizens and young men. The
young men in question might be lower class or slaves, but most often,
especially in these formal accounts, the young boys were, like the
men, high born and future citizens. This socially sanctioned love
between boys and men is perhaps the most striking difference
between this distant epoch and our own. In classical Greece, civil or
moral laws did not see intergenerational sex as criminally abusive.
Instead, the practice of loving boys was the means by which balanced
citizens were made. This love had a significance that reached far
beyond any more modern notion of 'sexual pleasure'. 'The crucial
point seems to be not sexual behaviour in itself but rather some
notion of preserving the political order' (Winkler 1990: 193). The
manner in which men, both young and mature, deploy the desires of
their bodies and minds had profound consequences for the political
health of the nation and of its culture. While the art forms of antiquity emphasized physical beauty and sensuality, the sexual – in the
sense of physical gratification – was secondary. Control of sexual
desire (among other desires for pleasure) was seen as a sign of political as well as social competency, but only in relation to those who
occupied positions of power and leadership. The mastery exercised
over sexual desire was only one aspect of the attainment of 'correct
maleness', an outcome that demanded self-surveillance as well as self-
control. The sensual, even sexual, pleasure acknowledged in Plato's
works is only one aspect of a complex ideological structure that legitimated and reproduced the male-defined social order.]
  There was another critical difference from contemporary understandings in this story of sex and gender in classical antiquity. [Since
modernity, it has been understood that gender was fixed in the
anatomical differences that designated a body either male or female.
In classical antiquity, and as we shall see for many centuries to follow,
no such clear distinction was believed to exist. Gender was fixed
neither in physical sex nor in appearance. Indeed, as Winkler argues,
'there is no word for (anatomical) sex in Greek' (Winkler 1990:
182n.). Nevertheless, this was a society in which proper masculine

behaviour was very important. The achievement of correct masculinity was made much more difficult by the view that male and
female were located on a continuum that could be traversed (ibid.:
182). 'Male' and 'female' tendencies were equally present in men, and
it was incumbent on the individual man to work to attain the state
of proper masculinity. Failure to do so would allow the feminine in
him to emerge, and he risked becoming the condemned figure of the
kinaidos, a figure of shame – just as, centuries later, the 'sodomite'
was to become – but who had a wider social significance. He was no
accident of nature, nor was his condition a disease. The *kinaidos* was
the outcome of an excess of femaleness – of a step too far along the
continuum. 'The signs of the *kinaidos* are an unsteady eye and knock
knees; he inclines his head to the right; he gestures with his palms up
and his wrists loose; and he has two styles of walking – either
wagging his hips or keeping them under control' (Aristotle, *Physiog-
nomics*, quoted in Winkler 1990: 200). This pitiful figure represented
the fate of all men who allow desire for easy pleasure to deflect them
from a life of personal challenge.

The maintenance of correct manliness also shaped the construction of female sexual desire. The feature that distinguished masculinity from femininity was the capacity for self-control, especially
in relation to sexual desire. As Dover points out, 'the element
common to all that was said about women by the Greeks is the
woman's inability to resist fear, desire or impulse' (Dover 1974: 100).
Woman was considered to have no 'charioteer' to control her desires.
Hesiod wrote in the seventh century BC that 'woman derives ten-times
more enjoyment from intercourse as a man' (quoted in Walcot 1984:
40; see also Dover 1974: 101). Three hundred years later, in the classical period, the threat posed by this superior but undisciplined sexuality of women was modified. Though the capacity for pleasure
might be greater than that of men, the source of this pleasure was
very different. The reason for women's superior enjoyment of sex lay
in their natural disposition to sexual passivity. As we have seen, masculinity and femininity were not directly linked with physical sex or
even direction of desire. Proper masculinity was defined by active sexuality – the penetrator, not the penetrated. Women could not pene-
trate, and therefore were 'naturally' sexually passive – that is, they
received the phallus. In keeping with the belief in the natural harmony
and balance of appetite and bodily needs, evidence of sexual pleasure in women was evidence of the 'rightness' of sexual penetration
or, to put it in a modern sense, heterosexual coitus. The evidence of
this pleasure signified the harmony of a naturally established sexual
as well as social order. 'The positive pleasure women take in passiv-

ity . . . signified to Greek men that women are naturally constituted in such a way that they actually desire to lose the battle of the sexes' (Halperin 1990: 271).

There were three models of womanhood and of sexuality in this period. The *hetaerae* were high-class concubines who were valued not just for their beauty and sexual expertise but also for their intelligence and education. Prostitution was legal in Athens providing the woman or man who practised it was not a full citizen. *Hetaerae* were usually of slave caste or not of Athenian parentage, and therefore not eligible for citizenship. Despite this, and unlike the lower-class prostitutes, *hetaerae* enjoyed considerable social freedom as well as social status. Although their primary role was the provision of sexual services and entertainment for men, many were to be found in sacred sites. The most well known of these was the temple of Aphrodite at Corinth, 'on a terrace walled by mighty blocks of stone . . . visible from afar by seafarers approaching either from east or west . . . a thousand temple girls welcomed a stranger' (Licht [1931] 1994: 341). These women were also praised and immortalized in tragedy and comedy, and the admiration in which they were held suggests a modification of the belief that sex with women was considered erotically inferior to that with young men. In this sexual and social order, there was a clear place for the desire for women, whether for pleasure or for procreation. Moreover, properly undertaken, there was no tension between a masculine man desiring both men and women. 'People did not have the notion of two distinct appetites . . . The enjoyment of boys and women did not constitute two classificatory categories . . . a man who preferred *paedika* [young boys] did not see himself as being "different" from those who pursued women' (Foucault 1987: 190).

At the other end of the spectrum was the figure of the *oikonomos* – the married woman – who had been brought up in a secluded female sphere and married at the age of fourteen or fifteen to a chosen spouse at least double her age. The life of the married woman differed in most respects from that of the *concubine* (Blundell 1995: 120ff). To begin with, she was the legal property of her husband, both sexually and socially. There was no place for married women to exercise the sexual freedom allowed to their husbands. The laws relating to adultery were far more stringent than those relating to rape. Athenian law allowed an aggrieved husband to kill a man who dishonoured him by sexual involvement with a woman under his jurisdiction. Nevertheless, the severity of punishment for adultery indicated doubts about the ability of the *oikonomos* to adhere to the motivations of the 'good woman' who merely seeks to procreate. The view that all women lacked self-control and were inherently irrational was reflected in the construction of their gender and sexual characteristics. Woman 'is at the centre of what is secure, nurturing, life-giving; but in her passionate and emotional nature and the violence of her sexual instincts . . . she is regarded as irrational, unstable, dangerous. Hence she is seen as integral to the civic structure on the one hand, but also regarded as a threat to that structure on the other') (Cohen 1991: 113).

This anxiety about the specific nature of women's sexuality is most clearly indicated in the case of the third category of ideal femininity – the *parthenos*. These were young but physically mature unmarried girls, who were outside the rigid sexual control of wifehood, and whose status precluded them from being courtesans. The mixed feelings about the sexuality of women and the social threat this posed are reflected in the fascination in which these young women were held in both myth and reality. 'What was provocative about Greek attitudes to the *parthenos* is [that] she was thought to harbour a curious and ominous ambiguity. . . . The *parthenos* and the married woman she became were believed capable of reverting to her unsocialised origins causing men to revert with her, and therefore destroying the whole social order' (Reeder 1995: 14). Not only were they physically the epitome of female beauty, they were also considered at the peak of their intelligence, wit and physical strength (Lefkowitz 1986: 32). In mythical accounts, they are represented as possessing exceptional courage and daring, leading often to self-sacrifice for a noble cause. On the other hand, these qualities render them dangerous to mankind, since, as women, they lack rational minds and self-control. The well-known myth of Pandora, whose wilfulness leads her to open the box and release the destructive aspects of human life, is a good example of the mixed fear and fascination engendered by this aspect of womanhood. Pandora epitomizes the outward beauty yet inner treachery of all women – a representation that has persisted over the centuries and across cultural and historical change.

Physicians of late antiquity and the management of self

As might be expected, the beliefs and practices of ancient physicians differed from the scientific approach of medical practice in modernity. In examining some of the features of ancient medicine, we can, however, see some distant precursors of modern-day holistic medicine, in which the whole self, not just the physical body, is the focus of attention. The aim of ancient medical knowledge and practice was the perfectibility of the whole self, mind, body and soul. Physical health was necessary before this perfection could be attained. The body was an active element in this harmony and balance rather than a passive shell. This placed sensuality at the centre of the regimes for holistic health. The second feature of ancient medicine that has some echoes with contemporary practice is the focus on the maintenance of health as much as, if not more than, the treatment of disease. Ancient medicine was an art, rather than a science, and practitioners shared much with their counterparts in the philosophic traditions (Edelstein 1952: 300).

Before the fifth century BC, it was believed that health and disease were under the control of Apollo and his son Asclepios (Marketos 1997: 205–8). The view that gods were responsible for illness meant that any attempt at prevention was futile. The distinctive feature of Greek medicine in the classical era was that it rejected this belief. This challenge came from the 'father of medicine' Hippocrates, who, in the fifth and fourth century BC, 'did with medical thought what Socrates did with thought in general – he brought it down from heaven to earth. His watchword was "Back to Nature"' (Galen, quoted in Brock 1928: x). The argument of both held that the forces of nature were equal to those of the gods. This new focus on prevention and cure through human knowledge of natural forces distanced human endeavour from the control of the gods. However, medical practice did not disengage itself totally from divine influence; the oath of Hippocrates, for example, began with the words 'I swear by Apollo and his son Asclepios'. Rather, the focus on earthly forces in disease and health gave a new significance to the natural harmony of the body. Just as Greek philosophical traditions assumed the innate good of the soul and sought ways through which this goodness would prevail, Greek medical traditions assumed that the body would naturally tend towards balance rather than imbalance.

This emphasis on the maintenance of the harmonious whole fostered the development of methods by which to maintain the balance. Erixymachus, a physician and son of a physician, was a key speaker at Plato's symposium. In his speech he associates love with the proper care of the body and the soul. This applied especially to the organs of reproduction. *Bodily* balance was to be sought between the opposite elements of its constitution: heat, cold, wet and dry. Love offered the means to attain *spiritual* balance between the mortal and immortal aspects of humanity. The experience of love thus linked the material body with the spiritual self, and this link was reflected in strategies for management of both. The desiring body, by this reasoning, was not a threat to social order, but lay at the centre of a harmony essential to the health of the individual and society. This positive valuation attached great status not just to health but also to those who were the practitioners of the art of its maintenance.

The rules for this self-management were contained within a regimen (derived from the Latin *regere* – to rule). Maintenance of health through these regimens was as important for moral integrity as it was for physical health. The body was not seen as a separate entity to the soul, as would become the case under Christianity, where the body was associated with earthly life and the soul with the life hereafter. In this period, both the body and the soul had a material reality and earthly significance. The reality of the soul was evident in the capacity for emotion, thought and reason, for which philosophy was the source of spiritual health and illness. The regimen provided by the physicians represented the means by which bodily health and balanced physical development were ensured. The wide-ranging scope of the regimen covered exercises and detailed advice about what food to eat and in what seasons of the year this must be done. It also gave advice on excretion and on the importance of, and methods successfully to achieve, a good night's sleep. All these aspects of the body were considered important to maintain health.

Though written by physicians, these rules placed the responsibility for healthy behaviour on the individual. The distinctive feature of the regimen is the vigilance required in its proper adherence (Edelstein 1952: 308). This vigilance meant that awareness of sensual experience was part of daily life. However, despite these advantages, physicians cautioned against the dangers of excessive concerns about health. Foucault offers the example of Herodicus the trainer, whose life was entirely taken up in the effort to avoid breaking the least rule of the regimen he had imposed upon himself. As a consequence, he was viewed as 'living the life of a dying man' (Foucault 1987: 104). In the classical Greek view, loss of self-control was akin to the state of approaching death. The key problem in maintaining a healthy body lay in the balance between the inherent human tendencies of sensual excess and the proper adherence to the strict rules of the regimen. This danger was avoided not so much in the adherence to the rules, but in the manner in which this was done. Excessive following of the rules was as dangerous to the mastery of self as excessive indulgence outside the rules. This amounted to the recognition of what we now call 'addictive behaviour', where the means for self-mastery would be subverted into slavery of self. This can be seen clearly in the restrictions recommended for sexual expression.

Greek physicians in the fourth and fifth centuries BC did not see the control of sexual desire as in need of special attention. The underlying assumption was that sexual desires – the works of Aphrodite – were natural and therefore intrinsically good if managed properly. But that sexual desire and pleasure required some management was evident in the specific role of the *aphrodisia*, the works and acts of Aphrodite, in the management of the healthy body. Reproduction as an elemental factor of existence, along with food and shelter, made logical nonsense of any physical 'wrong' of sex. But, at the same time, these original characteristics were shared with all animals that, incapable of rational activity, were at the mercy of the drives that would ensure their survival. Thus while the overall connection with nature was positively valued, it was also reason for caution. For, like the animals with which they shared these characteristics, humans could be driven by, rather than control, these sources of pleasure. The key to retaining control and therefore healthy balance was the imposition of reason over blind desire. This entailed a conscious struggle against the tendency of all humans to excessive pleasures. 'The relationship to desires and pleasures is conceived of as a pugnacious one: a man must take the position and role of the adversary with respect to them' (Foucault 1990: 67). However, there was no moral virtue associated with total abstinence. Rather, it was associated with training the body to contain desire, thereby attaining the moral virtue of *enkrateia* (continence). Thus training, or *askesis*, fostered self-control, and 'proper' pleasures could be experienced by men and by women. Ancient physicians recognized the capacity of women for sexual pleasure, orgasm and even seminal emission. All were believed to be required for conception.

Despite this recognition, women were not considered capable of effectively attaining *enkrateia*. The desires of married women were expected always to be subservient to and dependent on those of their husbands. *Hetaerae* may have been more sexually autonomous, but were nevertheless considered to be less well developed sensually, and therefore the demands of the regimen on their will-power were less severe. But this was a comment more about their moral integrity than their sexuality. 'The one who rules – i.e. the man – possesses moral goodness in its full and perfect form', whereas the ruled, including women, 'need only have the moral goodness required of them' (Aristotle, *De generatione animalium*, quoted in Foucault 1987: 84).

In addition to the spiritual development gained from correctly controlled sexuality, classical medicine recognized the advantages of sex for a healthy body. Sexual activity aids sleep, encourages strong masculine growth, 'predisposes the soul to tranquillity' and 'dampens immoderate ardour' (Foucault 1990: 118). Heterosexual coitus was valued for its moisture-giving qualities, for the release of tension, for relaxation, and for the experience of moderate (and procreative) pleasures. However, too much or too little sex would compromise the health of the whole body. As men and women could equally experience desire and the pleasure in its relief, they could both be adversely affected by extremes in either direction. Sexual frustration could lead to unpleasant physical consequences, including muscular spasms, fits, temporary paralysis, and even unconsciousness. Women denied the health-giving qualities of coitus risked developing the dangerous condition of hysteria (disease of the womb). Deprived of its moisture and of the necessary release of tensions, the womb would be found 'roaming around the body like a wild animal' (quoted in Rousselle 1988: 69). This terrible affliction could occur equally in virgins and in sexually active women. In both, the body was suffering from an imbalance due to a lack of sexual pleasure, and in both the cure was sexual intercourse.

The view of the ancient physicians on sexual abstinence at any stage of life echoed some of the themes that were evident in the later practice of sexual abstinence by early Christians, as we shall see in the next chapter. The crucial difference between the two lay in the fact that if sexual abstinence was practised it was through rational choice, not demanded as a duty. In classical Greece, sexual desire and pleasure were not, in themselves, sinful. However, the ancient physicians did emphasize their power to influence the whole body for good or ill. Sexual pleasures must be taken in moderation and with a rational mind informed by the expert advice of the physicians. In effect, this aspect of the regimen might be thought of as a cross between a science of sex and an erotic art. The founding ideas of Hippocratic medicine provided a rationale for the management of sexual pleasure in both men and women. The terms under which this was to be achieved differed for both, but in both the key lay in the achievement of a harmony and balance between desires and the mode of their experience. It is important to remember that it was not what was done in response to desire or for pleasure, but how it was done. Women's sensuality was acknowledged, though it was considered more problematic, not to be left to women themselves (due to their emotional and physical lability) but to others. The socially adjusted man's sensuality was not a threat to be avoided, but simply a key aspect of existence to be managed. Dominion was the essential element, not denial.

Conclusion

> At first glance many aspects of Athenian life might appear to justify the belief, favoured by some popular writers in our own day, that the Greeks lived in a rosy haze of uninhibited sexuality, untroubled by the fear, guilt and shame which later cultures were to invent. (Dover 1974: 205)

Vase painters of the late archaic and early classical periods depicted a wide variety of practices involving couplings between men, women, men and women, women and mythical satyrs, men and voracious maenads, and even animals and women (Dover 1978; Reeder 1995; Johns 1982). Sexual pleasure, as a gift from the gods, values delights of the flesh, but 'the uses of pleasure' were subject to stringent social and moral restrictions. The conception of the soul and its relationship with the physical body is crucial in the shaping of ideas about sexual desire and pleasure in this period. The soul represents the presence of the gods in their creation while the body is the frail carrier. Yet, this conception cannot be interpreted as being 'anti-body', as will be evident in early Christianity. The body is the creation of the gods as well, and (again, at its best) the object of the overriding cultural characteristic – the love of beauty. It is through the body that pleasures are experienced – even if, as we have seen in *Symposium*, these bodily pleasures are considered inferior to pleasures of the soul. In the ethics of classical antiquity, this separation of the body and soul made possible the dominion of the latter over the former. The conception of the soul in *Phaedrus* illustrates some of the obstacles faced in this struggle. One horse represented impulsive irrational desires that deflected the trajectory of the chariot and its occupant away from enlightenment and truth. The other represented human amenability to reason and its expression in moderation. In this story, the frailty of humanity, represented by desire for physical pleasures, is acknowledged but not damned. The qualities of the compliant steed and the mastery of the driver illustrate the possibility of balancing reason and control, while retaining the capacity for desire and pleasure. The message from both *Phaedrus* and *Symposium* is that seeking pleasure is not, in itself, a cause for moral censure. It is the manner in which the pleasure is experienced that is the issue of concern. The obligation of the ethical system of classical antiquity to engage in the struggle between the 'good' and 'bad' self does not deprive the individual of autonomy. Rather, it ensures the freedom necessary for effective self-mastery: 'to be free in relation to pleasures was to be free of their authority; it was not to be their slave' (Foucault 1987: 79).

The second distinctive feature of this era, and the one that is most confronting, is the positive moral evaluation of the love of boys by older men. An important aspect of this cultural practice was the extent to which this can be understood as a sexual relationship in modern terms. For important (and erotic) though these relationships were, they did not demand sexual gratification. The significance of the love of boys was primarily pedagogic in the broadest terms. The education involved was intellectual, moral and social. Though this was a culture dominated by masculine needs and identities, there was nothing automatic in the acquisition of the defining characteristics of the masculine man. Men had to learn to be masculine. They were not born that way. The love of boys and its role in the shaping of correct masculinity of both adult and youth in these relationships was thus essential to the social and political superiority of men in classical antiquity. It was in the relationship between boys and men, one that had explicit sexual content but did not have gratification as its primary aim, that the distinctions between masculinity and femininity were established and maintained. The key factor that separated the masculine from the feminine was self-mastery – the ability to drive rather than be driven. The responsibility for maintaining this distinction lay with the male citizens, both as youths and as men. The advantage offered by the love of boys by men was that they offered the opportunity to demonstrate the superiority of the higher form of love that controlled, rather than was controlled by, the body and its desires.

This theme of the desiring body and its control is equally evident in the works of the ancient physicians and in the regimen by which physical health was accomplished and maintained. The art of management of the physical self drew on and was related to the management of the soul, and there was a close relationship between the two traditions. The regimen contained within the dietetic discourses was explicitly related to the training of the body and particularly to containing its tendency to excess. While directive in their content, the emphasis was on the positive advantages of moderate desires. Yet the importance of the regimen went beyond the successful direction of the self – for the moderate individual was a microcosm of the whole polity. 'Moderation, understood as an aspect of dominion over self . . . was a virtue that qualified a man to exercise his mastery over others. The most kingly man was king of himself' (Foucault 1987: 81).

In the traditions of both philosophy and ancient medicine there was a strong pedagogic theme. The management of self required the superior perceptions and attributes of the thinking elite in the former, and the specialist knowledge and authority of physicians in the latter. The task of both sets of 'experts' was not to restrict or punish but to offer guidance and prescriptions for the individual attainment of the harmonious body and soul. In seeking the balance between desire and excess necessary for a healthy body, pleasurable sensations were identified and controlled. This strategy had implications for the management of sexual as well as other desires. It marked the distinction between the ethics of self and the Christian practices of sexual asceticism – the latter view holding that sexual desire expressed in lust was, in essence, evil and uncontrollable.

The centrality of pleasure in classical Greek culture, coupled with the centrality of the ethics of self-management, provides a clear understanding of the connection between pleasure, desire and the social order. Despite the male-centred frames of reference, and strategies for management, it is difficult not to admire the complexity of a culture that managed to maintain a positive love of sensuality and bodily pleasure while conserving a balance between the positive and negative implications that it had for social and political order. Nevertheless, there is evidence that this was seen as an eternal struggle that demanded continuous engagement both at a personal and a societal level. It is this recognition of the lack of resolution of human frailties that was to be reflected in the next great era of concerns with sex and pleasure in a very different system of beliefs – Christianity.

FURTHER READING

Licht, H. ([1931] 1994) *Sexual Life in Ancient Greece*. London: Constable.
Lefkowitz, M., and Fant, M. (1992) *Women's Life in Greece and Rome: A Source Book in Translation*. London: Duckworth.
Halperin, D. (1990) *One Hundred Years of Homosexuality and Other Essays on Greek Love*. London: Routledge.
Dover, K. J. (1974) *Greek Popular Morality in the Time of Plato and Aristotle*. Oxford: Blackwell.

2

Sinful Sex: Early Christianity and the Problem of Desire

Introduction

The world in which Christianity was born did not provide a comfortable setting for a new religion. It was a world dominated by the Roman Empire, deeply stratified, deeply unequal and characterized increasingly by social unrest. The response to this was to intensify repression of the majority and violently constrain any dissidence. A monotheistic faith that preached equality under an all-powerful God whose son had lived among men was a dangerous threat to an already insecure political and social power structure. The new faith grew slowly and often secretly in the first years after Christ's death, fed by the teaching and writings of the Apostles and then their successors, the Church Fathers. Interpretation of Christ's words was from the first influenced by the philosophical traditions in which these men were educated – Judaism, Gnosticism, Manicheism and Stoicism, as well as those of the philosophers of classical antiquity. It took more than four hundred years for Christianity to make the transition from a radical sect to the dominant religious faith, supported by the still reigning Roman Empire. But, from its earliest beginnings, the creators of the new faith sought to establish a way of living on earth that was as important as the search for immortal perfection. The foundation for these new rules of life was sought in existing texts and traditions of thought, but these were to establish very different ways of thinking about the body, the soul and, especially, sex and pleasure.

The opening chapters of the Old Testament, the book of Genesis, 1–3, were the source of the Christian association between sex and sin. In these key verses, the disobedience of the first humans to the will of God gave rise to a new representation of the shameful and disruptive body. Yet once banished from Paradise, these first sinners are commanded to 'be fruitful and multiply and replenish the earth' (Genesis 9: 1). This contradiction between sex as the 'original sin' and a command to procreate was, nearly five centuries later, to be resolved by the most influential scholastic figure in early Christianity – St Augustine. His reconciliation of sinful with procreative sex formed the basis of teachings on sexual matters, in which the problems of sexual desire and the unruliness of the sexual body were perpetuated. The disobedience of Adam and Eve allowed the body to triumph over the will, according to this interpretation.

Thus, from its earliest thinking, Christianity formulated a separation of body and soul. This was the first consequence of the original sin of disobedience that left the body and soul in permanent conflict. The second was that the desire for pleasure had been indelibly engraved upon the body. If spiritual perfection were to be attained, then these tendencies of the flesh must be eradicated. At its most extreme, this expressed itself in the mortification of the flesh – through sensual deprivation, self-mutilation or voluntary martyrdom. The body was, in the new interpretation of the fall from grace, antagonistic to spiritual development rather than just presenting a surmountable obstacle. This negative view of the body in the new faith was underlined by the virgin birth, the crucifixion of Christ and his ultimate triumph over the mortal body in the resurrection. Christian teaching thus saw the body as a literal and metaphorical battleground in which the inescapable fight between good and evil raged. This demanded of early Christians, as well as their teachers, extreme vigilance over the body and its sensuality in both its outward and inward manifestations. Conceived in its mildest form as a 'weakness' and in its most extreme as 'active evil', this characteristic expressed itself in the unruliness of all bodily appetites. But it was in sexual desire that the negative and disruptive qualities were most manifest.

But the attitude of the early Christians to the body went beyond the philosophical to the practical and visible. From the beginnings of their public statements of faith, followers of the new religion distinguished themselves by their apparent indifference to bodily pain and, indeed, to all the needs of the body. To some extent, this was aided, in the early years after Christ's death and apparent resurrection, by the certainty that the second coming was imminent. The belief that Christ would soon return to collect his followers did not encourage much attachment to the material world. At a more immediate level, the denial of bodily indulgences by early Christians distinguished

them from the followers of pagan faiths, whose lifestyles were characterized by luxury, self-indulgence and cruelty. The rejection of the
sexually desiring body predated the emergence of the Christian practice (see, for example, Pagels 1988; Veyne 1987). Before the birth
of Christ, sexual abstinence had long been associated with religion
and with spiritual purity. 'In many pagan cults, rules of sexual purity
governed entry into the temple and sometimes participation in
worship . . . In the late second century BC the rules for a public cult
in Pergamum demanded a day's interval after sex with one's wife, but
two days' interval after sex with someone else's. . . . Some cults were
only served by virgin priests or by women who were not sexually
active' (Fox 1986: 347; Foucault 1987: 39). In the world beyond the
temples, the rejection of ostentatious luxury in place of more moderate lifestyles was becoming fashionable. The positive value of
chastity was increased by family customs of the late Roman Empire,
which demanded that women were virgins at their marriage. This was
ensured by the betrothal, if not marriage, of young women immediately after puberty. In the first two centuries AD both these more
worldly factors were reflected in an 'increasingly stern and reductive
assessment of sex' (Ranke-Heinemann 1991: 11). The philosophical
and practical underpinning of the rejection of the body was
powerfully supported in the doctrines of Stoicism and Gnosticism
(Murnstein 1974: 86).

The body and its enemies in the first centuries
of Christianity

Stoicism (301 BC to AD 263) was the leading Hellenic influence on
the development of later Christian attitudes to sex and pleasure
(Brundage 1987: 18). It was 'in the air the intellectual converts to
Christianity breathed' (Noonan 1986: 46). Stoic teachings stretched
back into antiquity, and it was only in the last stages that they influenced the content of the early Christian doctrine. Stoicism offered a
system of beliefs and practice that taught indifference to any sensual
input – whether experienced as pain or as pleasure. Both were
considered to be irrational aspects of human life. In this respect it
mirrored views of Aristotle and Plato – that an ethical life was a life
governed by reason. However, there were crucial distinctions.
Whereas Platonic philosophy valued pleasure as an integral element
in the natural balance of existence, for Stoicism pleasure was the
opposite. All passions, especially those that entailed uses of the body,
were antithetical to a proper and moral life. Passions must therefore

be confronted and annihilated. Sexual pleasure, more than any other bodily sensation, posed a direct and irreversible threat to reason. However, with an effort of will (an application of the intellect), bodily sensations of desire could be translated into 'the intellectualised love which the Stoics esteemed' (Brundage 1987: 21). This rational management of the senses provided a strong foundation for the control of sexual desire and of fidelity in marriage. Seneca (4 BC to AD 65), a Roman Stoic philosopher and dramatist, wrote: 'All love of another's wife is shameful; so, too, too much love of your own. A wise man ought to love his wife with judgement, not affection. Let him control his impulses and not be born headlong into copulation. Nothing is fouler than to love one's wife like an adulteress' (quoted in Noonan 1986: 47). Desire for sex and the pleasure from its satisfaction were seen as distractions from the higher achievements of life. While necessary for human survival, sex should be given no more significance than the need to eat and sleep. All of these indications of bodily needs were seen as spiritual weaknesses. 'Hunger, dumb fear of extinction, the sensations necessarily associated with sexual desire: these were unavoidable, muted creaking of the biological self' (Brown 1988: 129).

The Gnostic movement, drawn from a more wide-ranging amalgamation of Eastern and Western philosophy, supplied a more uncompromising basis for the early Christian renunciation of the body. For Gnostics, 'the body was a disposable tunic, prison or tomb' (Chorlton 1987: 51). Yet, since the breath of God created them, there was a potential in all humans to rise above their flawed state and become more like their creator. But the body was an obstacle to this salvation, one that could be overcome only by self-denial and fasting. For Gnostics, the body was an active enemy to be confronted and overcome. 'The human body is said to be something that is beastly, that will perish like the bodies of beasts, and that can never beget anything different from what beasts beget, since it itself is produced through sexual intercourse, just as the bodies of beasts are produced' (Seneca, quoted in Williams 1996: 123). This could be achieved only by ignoring any appetites or desires from whatever source. But it was desire for sexual pleasure that was the most easily stimulated. The consumption of food, particularly of meat and wine, inflamed desire, and led to unnecessary sexual intercourse. To desire was thus to 'err in ignorance like beasts' (ibid.: 122). The association of sexual desire and intercourse with bestiality was a recurrent theme in Gnostic writings over the centuries of its greatest influence. These views were reflected in the distinction between pure and defiled marriage. A defiled marriage was one in which sexual intercourse takes place. A pure union demanded sexual abstinence as a necessary route to spiritual perfection – the means by which the body can be controlled and transformed.

While it exerted a powerful influence over the development of Western Christianity's view of the body, Gnostic rejection of the material world and of the body conflicted with one fundamental aspect of the new faith. Material life – with all its pleasure and pain – had, through the example of Christ, been given a divine significance and purpose. For early Christians, earthly existence offered the opportunity to emulate the ways of Jesus until his return. This was to become an irreconcilable tension between the new faith and its influential predecessor. By the fourth century AD, significantly when Christianity was becoming more integrated into social and political life, the beliefs of Gnosticism were declared heresy, and the following of its beliefs and lifestyle was banned. 'By an edict issued by Constantine [the first Christian emperor of the Roman Empire] before his own reception into the Church, all their "houses of prayer" were confiscated for the benefit of the Catholic Church, their meeting even in private forbidden, and their books seized and burned' (Legge 1915: 359). The faithful apparently hid the key texts in a pot in the desert at Nag Hammadi, near Cairo, where they were to remain undiscovered until a peasant farmer found them accidentally in 1945.

Rejection of the body was illustrated dramatically in voluntary martyrdom, a widespread practice of the early Christians in the first two centuries AD. The Greco-Roman Empire valued the public spectacle of human sacrifice above all other popular entertainments, and the huge gladiatorial shows, sometimes with audiences of 150,000, provided much needed showcases for the political power of the emperors (Bottomley 1979: 5–14). Devout believers, fuelled by their conviction in the second coming, viewed the body as a temporary cell, useful only as the means by which to demonstrate both their faith and the power of their God. They saw it as their duty to make public as well as private their contempt for the flesh. Even before the great persecutions of the third century, Christians were often to be seen alongside criminals and slaves in the great gladiatorial arenas of the Roman Empire. These martyrs were a great source of wonder and fascination, since they appeared to be impervious to fear and pain, even when enduring the most extreme physical torture. The public nature of martyrdom as well as its extremes of bodily torture offered early Christians the forum within which to demonstrate their certainty of a life hereafter. The powerful message of the resurrection of Christ was that the body offered Christians a pathway to redemption. 'For since by man came death, by man came also the resurrection of the dead. For as in Adam all die, even so in Christ shall all be made alive' (1 Corinthians 15: 21–2).

But there was to be one other source that was drawn on to confirm the negative significance of the body and its uncontrollability. Early Christian scholars returned to the Judaic text of Genesis, chapters 1–3, and the story of the first humans and their fall from Paradise. It is of interest that it was to the words of the Judaic prophets to whom the Church Fathers turned to formulate and establish the Christian orthodoxy about temptations of the flesh, and especially the view that sex was the original sin. The story of the fall from grace and expulsion from the Garden of Eden became the centrepiece for Christian ideas about the body as the source of all evil, encompassed in the idea of the sins of the flesh.

Sex, the Bible and the first Church Fathers

The iniquity of our heels which compasses us about . . . of that heel which was bitten by the serpent and causes us to go on limping (St Ambrose, Bishop of Milan, quoted in Williams 1927: 303)

The first chapters of the Old Testament, Genesis 1–3, are now popularly accepted as those that established the Christian connection between sex and sin. Yet the story of the fall of the first humans from Paradise was written many centuries before Christianity began. The story of Adam and Eve and their wilfulness that resulted in expulsion from the Garden of Eden was the amalgamation of three historically unconnected stories, the first having its origins between 1000 and 900 BC. The second and third elements were added over the space of four centuries (Pagels 1988: xxiv; Goergen 1974: 14ff). Genesis is the first of five key texts – the Pentateuch – that formed the foundation of the Judaic faith. The Old Testament gave priority to the stability of marriage and the question of divorce and remarriage, rather than the management of sexual behaviour. The dominant Judaic view of sex was that it was a natural (and therefore intrinsically good) aspect of all living things. In the Judaic faith, and frequently in the Old Testament, these approving attitudes can be found towards sexual love at the centre of a binding faithful relationship between two people. The Song of Songs is an example of this attitude: there is no suggestion of any sinfulness in sexual desire (Goergen 1974: 16–22). Sexual love was not an obstacle to spiritual purity: as a

creation of God, sexual pleasure, experienced in the right circumstances, was a way of worshipping the creator (Bottomley 1979: 30).

> How fair and how pleasant art thou, Oh love, for delights!
> This thy stature is like to a palm tree,
> and thy breasts to clusters of grapes.
> I said, I will go up to the palm tree,
> I will take hold of the boughs thereof:
> now also thy breasts shall be as clusters of the vine, and the smell of
>   thy nose like apples;
> And the roof of thy mouth like the best wine for my beloved,
> that goeth down sweetly,
> causing the lips of those who are asleep to speak.
> I am my beloved's, and his desire is toward me.
> Come, my beloved, let us go forth into the field . . .
> let us see if the vine flourish, whether the tender grape appear, and the
>   pomegranates bud forth:
> there will I give thee my loves. (The Song of Solomon 7: 6–12)

In the New Testament, the first books of which were begun several
decades after the death of Christ, these sex-positive views were
reversed. The words of Jesus offer no explanation for this. Christ
made mention of the story in Genesis 1–3 only once. In responding
to a question about the acceptability of divorce (of considerable
importance in the Greco-Roman world), he quoted the following Old
Testament words: 'Therefore shall a man leave his father and mother,
and shall cleave unto his wife: and they shall be one flesh' (Genesis
2: 24). He then commented, 'What therefore God hath joined
together, let not man put asunder' (Mark 10: 9). His most direct
references to sexual activity, reflecting his education in the Judaic
faith, related to adultery, not fornication. There was no evidence of
his rejection of those who had been weak in the face of temptation.
Look, for example, at Mary Magdalene, the 'fallen woman' whom
he embraced rather than rejected.

Revisited by the first scholars of the Church, Genesis was argued
to illustrate the Garden of Eden as a paradise created by God for
man. It was a world free from death and pain and in which harmony
between all elements, animate and inanimate, prevailed. The temptation of Eve by the Serpent to 'eat the forbidden fruit' and the subsequent banishment from Paradise sentenced the first humans to live
as mortal man, subject to hunger, cold, pain and, ultimately, death.
A wide body of scholarship in theological history now offers insights
into the interpretations of this story, and especially of the connection
between sex and the original sin (e.g. Pagels 1988; Clark 1986; Payer

1994; Bottomley 1979; Brown 1988; Ranke-Heinemann 1991; Brundage 1987; Williams 1927; Goergen 1974; Fox 1986; Hunter 1992; Williams 1996).

[But the common feature of the earliest reinterpretations was the belief in the fall as the source of the original sinfulness of the body (Williams 1927: 148).] From the first writings of the Apostles in the New Testament, proof of this was to be found in the experience of sexual desire, a sensation that occurred independently of the will. The Apostle Paul made this very clear in a cry of anguish: 'But I see another law in my members, warring against the law of my mind, and bringing me into captivity to the law of sin which is in my members. Oh wretched man that I am! Who shall deliver me from the body of this death?' (Epistle to the Romans 7: 23–4). [The original sin was engraved in 'the flesh', its presence demonstrated in the lust for sensual pleasure and the weakness of the will to resist this temptation. In the view of St Paul, sexual desire was one of many forms of sensuality that were associated with this construction of the body as 'weak flesh'. 'Now the works of the flesh are manifest, which are these; adultery, fornication, uncleanness, lasciviousness, idolatry, witchcraft, hatred, variance, emulations, wrath, strife, seditions, heresies, envyings, murders, drunkenness, revellings and such like' (Epistle to the Galatians 5: 19–21). But later Paul identifies the special dangers and power of the desire for sexual pleasure, expressed in the notion of 'fornication'. Fornication referred specifically to the use of sex for pleasure. In his epistle to the Corinthians he warns: 'Now the body is not for fornication, but for the Lord; and the Lord for the body' (1 Corinthians 6: 13), and later: 'Flee fornication. Every sin that a man doeth is without the body; but he that committeth fornication sinneth against his own body' (ibid.: 18).

However, for Paul and for later more moderate commentators, there was the possibility that the body could also be the instrument of redemption if these desires could be controlled (see Hunter 1992; Bottomley 1979; Williams 1927). In demonstrating victory over the flesh, humankind could aspire again to follow God's original intention for its use. Paul lived a life of celibacy, but he also acknowledged that many could not manage this level of self-control. [Marriage offered an acceptable way to avoid sinful use of the body if each partner was responsible for the other's management of desire: 'The wife hath not power of her own body, but the husband: and likewise also the husband hath not power of his own body, but the wife' (1 Corinthians 7: 4). This 'sexual contract' was devised to moderate sexual pleasure through mutually agreed, though limited, periods of abstention] (Hunter 1992: 4). If complete celibacy was neither practical nor attainable, this contract provided an acceptable alternative. But it remained inferior, in the Apostle Paul's eyes, as a road to true piety and purity. He therefore advised early Christian communities to practise sexual abstinence in marriage. In this way they could experience the flesh and spirit as one and avoid the constant challenge of managing the unruly flesh.

By the end of the second century, the faithful began to realize that their expectation that Christ would soon return was mistaken. This intensified the problem of the sexual body for those who sought redemption for the original sin. The resulting anxiety is illustrated by the preoccupation of the early Christian ideologues with chastity and virginity. Despite Paul's more rational instructions about how to manage sexual desire, early Church writers, especially Clement of Alexandria (150–230 AD) and Tertullian of Carthage (155–225 AD), made clear that the most righteous path was that of sexual chastity, even if intercourse was necessary for procreation. 'Our ideal is not to experience desire at all . . . We should do nothing from desire. . . . A man who marries for the sake of begetting children must practice continence so that it is not desire which he feels for his wife. [But] that he beget children with a chaste and controlled will' (Clement, quoted in Pagels 1988: 27). In order to reduce the possibility of sex for pleasure, Clement acknowledged that there were times of day when sex was most pleasurable. These, of course, were forbidden. 'Clement excludes not only such counter-productive practices as oral and anal intercourse but also intercourse with a menstruating, barren, pregnant or menopausal wife, and, for that matter with one's wife "in the morning", "in the daytime" or "after dinner"' (ibid.).

Tertullian of Carthage was a follower of Stoicism who converted to Christianity in middle age. He was considered the greatest early theologian until Augustine. His attitude to the body reflected his schooling in Roman rather than Greek philosophy. Tertullian's key contribution in relation to ideas about the body and desire was grounded in the view that the soul and the body were one entity (Williams 1927: 235). In the creation of the first humans, God fashioned the body and then brought it alive with his breath. This breath represents the soul – the divine in the human, which persists after the death of the physical body. This understanding reflected the Platonic argument that the soul has two parts – the rational and the irrational. But Tertullian departed from Plato's conclusions about the manageability of the body by the mind. He maintained that irrationality of the soul (its susceptibility to temptation) was not the original intention of God. This fault was brought to life by the serpent in the

Garden of Eden. Leading Christian scholars of the third and fourth centuries devoted many tracts to arguing that sex did not exist in the Garden of Eden. In the view of Gregory of Nyssa (*d.* 386) and John Chrysostom (347–407), the pleasure associated with sexual inter-course had no connections with God's original pattern. Gregory, for example, argued that man was originally made in the image of God, that is, without passion: 'The passions do not belong to man's true nature, they were at first peculiar to animals: the carnivorous animals subsist through rage, the weak ones through fear, and the species are maintained through the longing for pleasure' (quoted in Ranke-Heinemann 1991: 54).

A similar approach to the inherently sinful body can be seen in the works of Jerome (340–420) and Ambrose (340–397). These two Latin Fathers of the Church were responsible for providing a moral script for living for the first converts. St Ambrose, the Bishop of Milan for the last twenty years of his life, devoted himself to a practical rather than philosophic approach, providing clear instructions as to proper behaviour. He was an especial enthusiast for virginity, writing several treatises on the topic in the 370s. St Jerome was an equally central theologian who translated the Old Testament from the origi-nal Hebrew in order to revisit and revise the true meanings to be found there. Together they formulated a powerful argument for the outright rejection of sexual activity of any sort. So persuasive was Ambrose that mothers were said to keep their daughters away from his influence in order that they be prevented from becoming brides of Christ. Jerome and Ambrose argued that the physical dimension was distinct from and inferior to the spiritual. More than this, one had to be denied in order to experience the other. The spiritual realm could be accessed only if one rejected and withdrew from the world of physical sensations. Spiritual and physical were therefore opposites, not coexistent, as was the case in classical Athens. All sensations – whether smell, hunger, thirst, desire for sex or sleep – were inherently corruptive, since they distracted the faithful from the spiritual realm. Though both men and women experienced these, it was women who were the more susceptible and who therefore represented a great threat to men. Hence the intense focus on the importance of virginity among women. Women's sexuality was deemed such a danger to the attainment of spiritual perfection that they must, if they were to join men in following Christ, give up all aspects of femaleness, and become like men (Salisbury 1986: 280–1).

Jerome and Ambrose supported these arguments, Salisbury argues, by their claim that God never meant humans to experience sexual pleasure or, indeed, to have sex. At the same time, both were fully aware of the pleasures of sex and of the enticing charms of women. This was not contradictory. For both men, all pleasures of the flesh were an obstacle to spiritual perfection. All sensual experiences, even a good meal, acted to inflame the body's desire for the greatest of all pleasures, sex (Salisbury 1986: 282–3). This inherent danger within the sensual body was a direct consequence of the actions of Adam and Eve. For Ambrose and Jerome, sex was the original sin, the weakness of the flesh that separated Adam and Eve from eternal life. The proof of the indelibility of desire was the difficulty experienced in giving up sex. The necessity for vigilance kept in focus the reality of the desires of the body, made more intense by extremes of bodily deprivation that resulted in sexual fantasies and disturbing visions. In the extremes of chastity and fasting, and with no companions but the scorpions and wild beasts, Jerome recalled, 'I often found myself amid bevies of girls . . . My face was pale and my frame chilled from fasting, yet my mind was burning with desire and the fire of lust kept bubbling up before me when my flesh was as good as dead' (quoted in ibid.: 284).

In the first three centuries the adoption of sexually ascetic practices offered a common ground on which new and very different converts could unite (Brown 1988: 60). At its most successful, sexual asceticism offered a pathway back to the certainties of asexual paradise, on earth. Young women who had embraced the life of chastity were commonly taken into Christian households of clerics and deacons 'with whom they were said to be sleeping chastely in the same bed' (Fox 1986: 369). The presence of chaste women in the household was believed to act as protection against danger and disaster. But given the propensities of the flesh, even accidental physical contact was sufficient to inflame the senses. 'The citation that "all flesh is grass" was interpreted as meaning that men and women, as indelibly sexual beings, were permanently liable to spontaneous combustion' (Brown, in Veyne 1987: 298). The mortification of the body demanded that the individual deny themselves all but the bare necessities for life and reject indulgences of any kind. It offered the means by which to practise 'spiritual martyrdom', in which faith was demonstrated not by death but by the living rejection of the world and its bodily and psychological comforts. In the first century or so after Jesus's death, this form of self-denial was practised in the centre of society, not in isolation from it. By the mid-third century the faithful of either sex took themselves into the deserts of what we now know as the Middle East, especially Syria, where they initiated the practice of desert asceticism (Lecky 1880: 102n.). The originators of this practice were a source of much admiration. So popular did they become that thousands of individuals, both men and women, took to the desert to follow the example of these first saints of the desert (ibid.: 105). This was not surprising given the dramatic contents of their exploits. 'Macarius of Alexandria is said during an entire week to have never lain down, or eaten anything but a few uncooked herbs on Sunday. Of another famous saint, named John, it is asserted that for three whole years he stood in prayer, leaning upon a rock; that during all that time he never sat or lay down, and that his only nourishment was the Sacrament, brought to him on Sundays (ibid.: 109). Many of these followers congregated in communities that were the forerunners of monasteries. Although both men and women involved themselves in these practices, it was rarely together. Physical proximity to women was considered too perilous. With many of the hermits it was a rule never to look upon the face of any woman, and the number of years they had escaped this contamination was commonly stated as proof of their excellence. Given the extremes of deprivation, it was not surprising that these devout individuals experienced hallucinations. 'Sometimes, in the very ecstasy of his devotion . . . , he seemed to see around him the fair groups of dancing girls, on whose warm undulating limbs and wanton smiles his youthful eyes had too fondly dwelt' (ibid.: 117). Thus, even within these communities of the devout, the dangers of women's sexual attractions were never forgotten. 'A dying celibate priest, parted from his wife for 40 years, and reunited with her on his death bed, repelled her last embrace with the words "Get thee away, woman: a little fire is yet left, away with the straw"' (*The Dialogues of St Gregory*, quoted in Murnstein 1974: 93). Even after death, the body remained a spiritual threat. 'One Church edict directed that a male corpse was not to be buried next to a female one until the latter was safely decomposed' (ibid.).

Radical asceticism offered the possibility of the return to a 'sexless paradise' – to the pre-fall state of Adam and Eve and to a world freed from the tyranny of the flesh. The conversion of Emperor Constantine to Christianity in the early fourth century led to the incorporation of Christian teachings into civil life. Subsequently, over the succeeding century and a half, the Church and the clergy became established in the privileged ranks both materially and socially. The alliance of Church and state had the effect of relaxing the extremes of radical asceticism, especially in relation to the demands of complete sexual celibacy (Brown, in Veyne 1987: 138). It was in this context that the problems with continuing to demand an ideal of celibacy in a fast growing mass religion became more urgent. It was time for a more moderate and practical solution to be found, one that would still retain the central importance of the sinfulness of sex.

Augustine, sex and the compromise

> For what food is unto the conservation of the man, this sexual intercourse is unto the conservation of the race: and both are not without carnal delight: which yet being modified, and by restraint of temperance reduced unto the use after nature, cannot be lust. (Augustine of Hippo, *The Good of Marriage*, 16.18)

The incorporation of Christianity into the wider social context offered grounds for a review and modification of the severe approach to the body and to sexuality. The key figure in this revision, Augustine of Hippo, was to provide a compromise that would become the orthodoxy of Western Christianity's doctrine on sex and marriage for the next 1500 years. His intellectual interest in the role of sex in a devout Christian life may have been intensified by his personal emotional and sexual history. Born in the late fourth century of a Christian mother and a pagan father, Augustine converted from his Manichean background to Christianity in his late twenties. Manes taught that both sexual desire and reproduction were the source of evil and corruption and were to be avoided by all believers. As a result, this sect was outlawed as heretical during the fourth century (Noonan 1986: 115ff). Augustine's conversion to Christianity demanded that he abandon a passionate twelve-year relationship with the mother of his only son. This caused him great emotional pain. He wrote at the time: 'the woman with whom I was in the habit of sleeping was torn from my side on the grounds of being an impediment to my marriage, and my heart, which clung to her, was wounded and broken and dripping with blood' (Augustine, quoted in Ranke-Heinemann 1991: 79). Later, his arranged marriage was delayed and, despite his broken heart, Augustine again gave in to his desires. 'I could not bear the delay. So since I was not so much a lover of marriages as a slave to lust, I found another woman for myself' (ibid.: 78). The extent to which this personal history impacted upon his sexual doctrines can only be surmised. But as an intellectual of high political standing in Rome, he was in a strong position to confront the doctrine that sex was anathema to spiritual salvation. The anti-body stance was too close to the Manichean teaching that Augustine had rejected in his youth. His mature intellectual interest lay in the doctrine of the original sin, and of the place of sex and desire in God's plan.

Augustine argued that the sensual body was created by God to strengthen the relationships between his human creations. Sex and desire was part of this plan to bond people together, and this divine intention gave a new legitimacy to a Christian sexual marriage. In his text *The Good of Marriage* (401 AD), he argued that the creation of two sexes was proof that God intended there to be sexual intercourse. This was not just for reproduction but also to establish a foundation for human sociality. In God's intended Paradise, Adam and Eve and their descendants were to live among the other animals and creations, free from any anxiety or stress, and experiencing extremes of neither pleasure nor pain. Their bodies, like those of all other animals, were organisms created for a purpose. Given the command from the creator to 'go forth and multiply', one of these purposes was pro-creation. Although Augustine spent much time struggling with the question of how God intended procreation to occur (including the postulation that this was not carnal but spiritual), he concluded in his later work *De Genesis* that:

> Adam and Eve would have reproduced in Eden even if they had remained sinless. Although they had animal bodies, they did not feel the appetite of carnal pleasure. They could command the organs of reproduction in the same way as they commanded other bodily parts, such as their feet. They would have conceived offspring without experiencing bodily passion, and Eve would have given birth without pain.
> (Clark 1986: 371)

Given that Eden was without sin, this planned, procreative act was also without sin. But the harmony in Paradise was destroyed by the wilfulness of Adam and Eve, who placed their wishes above God's. For Augustine, this was the first sin, not of the body but of the will. It was a sin of disobedience that resulted in the loss of control over feelings and passions and especially of the experiences of pain and pleasure. This was the first ingenious distinction Augustine made to retain the need to control sex while at the same time avoiding the necessity for total chastity. Disobeying the will of God, in Augustine's view, meant that *all* human activity suffered from lack of order and harmony. Just as Adam and Eve had disobeyed their creator, the eternal punishment was that the body would henceforth disobey the will of the mind. Men and women would suffer emotional turmoils and dilemmas that God never intended for them. Sexual passion and lust were, like the loss of immortality, punishment for the disobedience of Adam and Eve. But the loss of control was experienced also in relation to other aspects of bodily functions. Women would experience severe pain in childbirth and men could not control their erections. This bleak prospect was softened by the ability for humankind to *choose* self-control over their desires. The key to his plan to reverse the original sin was sexual continence, not sexual abstinence – more demanding and less easy to attain.

Marriage offered the best conditions for demonstrating sexual continence, so long as it was undertaken following strict rules. Sexual activity must follow not spontaneous desire but a rational plan. Sex in marriage must therefore be under the direction of the will and of reason. For Augustine, God's will in relation to sex was clear – it was created for the purpose of procreation within marriage. Only in this way could humankind demonstrate some control over the disobedient body. Only in this way was it possible to avoid the spiritually destructive consequences of 'concupiscence'. 'Concupiscence insinuates itself where it is not needed, and by its troublesome and even wicked desires it agitates even the hearts of the faithful and the saints' (Augustine, *Letter to Atticus*, quoted in Hunter 1992: 125). Sexual desire was just as sinful as the act that followed, because to lust or desire is to have already given in to the will of the body. Marriage offered the opportunity to reverse this relationship, and provided the only context within which reason could be exercised over passion. This potential, however, was not unproblematic. It required that, above all, sexual desire must be subjected always to reason and to will. But this was no easy task, even for the devout married Christian. For not only must 'he' avoid temptation from outside the marriage, he must also be vigilant about how sex is undertaken in marriage. 'He will have to struggle to avoid using even his wife intemperately, since he will have to abstain for a time from sexual relations with her consent, in order to be free for prayer, and then return to them so that Satan will not tempt them because of their lack of control' (ibid.: 126). The correct use of sexuality was one in which passion was consciously excluded, whether by directing it towards procreation or by using it to 'dampen down' the ever-present lustful desires.

Augustine's revision of the doctrine of sex as the original sin remained the orthodox position of the Roman Church on sex and marriage for the succeeding 1500 years. It retained the notion of the corruptible body and of its inherent lustful tendencies. It also offered a framework within which to intensify condemnation of sex for pleasure. However, it provided a more balanced ideal towards which to strive, a foundation for an orderly sex life in which lapses of desire could take place in a 'mutually deliberate union unhurried by the hungers of lust' (Augustine, quoted in Clark 1997: 79). Augustine's tracts on the themes of desire and its management bring together the multitude of threads which emanated from pagan philosophy and its dualism, from the anti-body stances of the Gnostics, Stoics and Manichees, and from the hands of a religion which over four centuries had become a major political force in the Western world of the fifth century. His works also represent the triumph of Western interpretations of sex as sin over the more moderate Eastern traditions, reflecting as they did still the influences of Greek philosophy (see Williams 1927: 165ff). This ascendance of West over East was given impetus by the conversion of the fourth-century Emperor Constantine, as well as attesting to the intellectual power of Augustine and his forbear Tertullian. 'Fifteen hundred years later', Elizabeth Clark reminds us, 'Augustine's views are still the basis for Catholic doctrines on "the goods of marriage"' (Clark 1997). Yet, despite the detail in which Augustine presented his recipe of rational desires, there was little confidence in the effectiveness of this strategy. With the establishment of Christianity as the religion of the West, and with the increasing masses of uneducated followers, clerical anxiety about the possibility of 'harnessing desire' (Payer 1994) increased, as we shall see in the following chapter.

Conclusion

From its very beginnings, Christianity has considered an orderly sex life to be a clear second best to no sex life at all. (Fox 1986: 355)

Even in this brief history, it is immediately obvious how important controlling sex and pleasure was for the new religion of Christianity. The reason for this is not obvious. There was no evidence in his teachings that sex and pleasure were of especial concern to Jesus. Nor were there any similar ideas to be found in the Judaic teachings of the Old Testament. It was in the century that followed the deaths of the Apostles that sex and sexual pleasure became the centre of anxieties about the attainment of spiritual purity. The key influences appear to be the philosophies of Stoicism and Gnosticism, ways of thinking that were prominent in the education of the first theologians. The common view of both was that the body was inherently corrupt and there was no connection between the carnal (bad) and the spiritual (good). These convictions directed the interpretation of the Old Testament. The opening chapters of Genesis, with its account of the untroubled world of Paradise and of the weakness of its first human inhabitants, provided early Christian writers with the means by which to formulate the connection between sex and sin, and to establish more firmly the idea of the corrupt body. But before the close of the first century AD, attention began to shift towards examining the nature of the 'prison', and especially to the distinctions between the carnal and the spiritual that were clearly seen in the works of Ambrose and Jerome. All sensations of the body, whether sexual or from hunger or thirst, were considered a threat to spiritual growth. Augustine's great contribution to the sexual culture then and now was to reconfigure this moral landscape, and to clarify the distinction between good and bad sex. In doing so, he established a new and more refined framework for the management of sexual behaviour. The acceptance of marital reproductive sex directed towards reasoned outcomes retained the category of sinful sex – now undertaken for selfish pleasures and to satisfy carnal desires. The compromise integrated sex into the Christian script for existence, but did so in a manner that introduced the concept of accountability in sexual behaviour – of a sort of moral scoresheet that for the first time in the new faith placed responsibility on the individual for demonstrating the manageability of the flesh. Formerly, the view that all flesh was grass removed any responsibility for sexual misbehaviour. But with the refinement of the understanding of the role of the body in sinful behaviour, following Augustine's clever readjustment of the world of Paradise, the body was no longer a tainted shell but an active battleground on which the war against lust was to be waged.

The compromise solved one problem while introducing another in the history of sex and pleasure. For the genie had not been permanently shut in the bottle of abstinence. Every act of desire or of sex demanded that the individuals involved subjected their actions to scrutiny and to active management. And, of course, the success rate was from the outset severely compromised, by Augustine's own admission. The growth of Christianity over the five centuries covered in this discussion is evident in the increasing organization of the lives of its followers, in the emerging structures of administration, the synods. By the beginning of the fourth century the regulation of five million Christians' sex lives was already well established. At the Elvira synod, thirty-four of the eighty-one rulings were directed at marriage and sexuality (Brown 1988: 206). The lesson of the first four centuries, and personified in the sexual nature of the original sin, was the inevitable presence of sexual desire. Efforts to eradicate or control this human quality served only to underline its tenacity. The choice was stark: either chaste exile from the world and its temptations or the subjection of the senses to constant vigilance and scrutiny within the narrow confines of matrimony. But such management could not be left to the individual. The contest was too unequal. What Augustine prescribed was a script for life management of lustful desires. The centrepiece for this was the distinction between marital and carnal lust – the one harnessed and directed by the choice to follow God's will, the other surrendering to the powers of desire and lust. The consequence of this division between good and bad sex was to make necessary new mechanisms for ensuring that these distinctions were understood and practised. This, in turn, required Christians who chose marriage over monastic celibacy to expose their private expressions of sexuality to the scrutiny of the Church. The formulation of sex or, more accurately, lust, as sin, alongside Augustine's insistence on the duty of marital sex, thus required the intensification and refinement of the scrutiny of sexual desire and pleasure.

The influence of early Christianity on Western sexual culture was significant and powerful. It might be concluded, after further reading, that Christianity and sexual culture were integrally related in their development. The still familiar connection between sexual and moral behaviour testifies to a strong ethical link between the new faith and ideas about sex and pleasure. However, it would be too easy to 'blame' Christianity for its condemnation of sex and pleasure. The development of such negative ideas did not occur in an ideological vacuum. They carried within their formulation the influences of pre-Christian beliefs as well as the repressive social and political structures with which the new faith had to contend for the first 400 years of its existence. The greater significance of these ancient ideas and struggles for contemporary studies lies in their offering some insights into the origins of ideas that remain familiar today.

It is not remarkable that the issue of sex and pleasure was one of interest and concern. We have already seen, in classical antiquity, that these aspects of human behaviour were considered to be in need of some control and management. There were three features of Christian ideas and teachings that were different from any that had gone before. First, the connection between the body and sexual desire was firmly established in the notion of 'the flesh'. The flesh was not considered to be subservient, but rather a threat, to the will and to reason. The second feature was the association between the sexual body and eternal punishment. The interpretation of Genesis by the early Fathers of the Church laid the blame for the expulsion from the Garden of Eden on the act of sex. As a consequence, sex was constructed as the most threatening aspect of humanity – one that had mortal as well as eternal consequences. The fight against the lustful flesh had been lost in the Garden of Eden, and, for the pre-Augustinian theologians, there was no regaining the original sexless purity. Sex was thus constructed as fearful and to be avoided at all costs. The third feature came with Augustine's review of this early orthodoxy. He reformulated the concept and significance of the original sin. Through his work and argument, the social significance of sex was also reformulated. The task was not now to avoid *all* sex and desire, but to impose strict controls on the *manner* in which desires were expressed, even experienced. The moral danger was not all sex but lustful and pleasurable sex, undertaken without a purpose beyond gratification. Augustine's modification of the idea of sex as the original sin did not modify the anxieties that were increasingly surrounding sex and its expression. What he offered was a model of marital reproductive sex, purposeful and controlled. This provided a blueprint for the faithful to follow in their individual lives. But, as importantly, it established the means for managing sexual behaviour on a wider social scale. The integration of acceptable sex into the now powerful religion of Christianity placed sex and pleasure at the centre of what it was to be a good Christian. Vigilance and anxiety over sexual pleasure did not wane, but was to continue in one of two great themes of the medieval period in discourses of sexual pleasure. But the first four centuries had been decisive in establishing the Church as the mediator in the struggles of the flesh. It was instrumental in establishing sex as sinful – thus providing the logic for anxieties about, and the negative constructions of, sexual desire and pleasure for all succeeding centuries. For it was against the doctrine of the Church Fathers, inscribed in canon law, that lawful natural and pious sex was to be defined and maintained. And the key element in this task was that sex and desire became the moral problem for Christianity in the Middle Ages. It is to this extensive historical era that the next chapter will turn.

FURTHER READING

Salisbury, J. (1986) The Latin doctors of the Church on sexuality. *Journal of Medieval History*, 12, 279–89.

Brown, P. (1988) *Body and Society: Men, Women and Sexual Renunciation in Early Christianity*. New York: Columbia University Press.

Pagels, E. (1988) *Adam, Eve and the Serpent*. London: Weidenfeld & Nicolson.

Clark, E., ed. (1997) *St. Augustine on Marriage and Sexuality*. Washington, DC: Catholic University of America Press.

3

Guilty Sex, Courtly Love and the Unruly Body: Medieval Themes and Practices

Introduction

> That medieval society was more concerned with sexual behaviour than many other societies has been in part, at least, because the Western church monitored the intimate details of its members' sexual activities with horrified fascination. (Brundage 1984: 81)

The period known as the Middle Ages spanned nearly a thousand years of Western European history. From the collapse of the Roman Empire, which was in long decline from the third to sixth centuries AD, this epoch extended to the fifteenth century. This was a period that would appear to be very remote from our own, both in time and in culture. Indeed in common speech the term 'medieval' is sometimes used as an adjective to describe the 'older than old'. There are two reasons for choosing this topic for discussion. The first has to do with historical progression. As we have seen in the last chapter, early Christianity identified sexual desire and its associated pleasures with sin and damnation. For three hundred years after the death of Christ, the early Church Fathers grappled with the problem of the need to condemn pleasure while maintaining the reproductive role of sex. Augustine's solution to this was to condone marital sex, directed by the mind, not the desires of the body. But this was only the beginning of the problem. By 470 AD the Roman Empire had dissolved and was replaced by what was then called 'Christendom'. In the Middle Ages the concept of 'Europe' did not exist. Christendom was a civilization, just as were Greece and Rome. Its boundaries shifted over the centuries, but the term Christendom referred to the one aspect common to all – the Christian faith. Theologians possessed primary social and political authority. Thus, Christianity ruled political and social life just as it did the spiritual life of its followers.

It is for this reason that we are taking our first slice of medieval history. Church historians have shown that, from Augustine onwards, the Church Fathers began to develop rules and guidance to help the increasing numbers of priests and monks who had to exercise localized authority. These documents were called 'the penitentials'. Written between the sixth and eleventh centuries, these texts covered all aspects of the lives and behaviour of the Christian devout. But since books were largely the privilege of the educated priests (few others could either read or had access to printed texts), these medieval guidebooks were a symbol of the Church's authority as well as offering the means by which behaviour could be monitored. Though dealing with all aspects of social life, the greater number of rules and punishments concerned sexual behaviour. We will be looking at the work of scholars of these texts to gain some detailed understanding of their role in the construction of both the meaning and the practice of sexuality in this era.

The second reason for attempting to make sense of such a wide span of history is to offer some contrasting influences to the blanket condemnation by the Church of sexual desire and pleasure. I have chosen two traditions of thought that are quite different. The first is the medieval tradition of courtly love, and I will be illustrating some of the counter-presentations of sex through the medium of the *fabliaux* or bawdy tales. The second school of thought consists of the writings about sex and pleasure in the literature of medieval medicine. In these secular discourses, the topics of sexuality and desire receive very different treatment that of the Christian doctrine. The wide popular circulation and influence of these alternative presentations of sex and desire – one for entertainment, the other for the treatment of disease – suggest that the topic of sex in people's daily lives did not provoke fear and trembling, nor was the concept of sex effectively outlawed. The final short example will look briefly at medieval church architecture and especially at the gargoyles that characterize this period of church decoration.

'Never on Sunday': sex, the Church and the penitentials

For clear and certain prohibitions on coital experimentation we must turn to the penitential literature of the seventh and eighth centuries. (Brundage 1984: 82)

Ideas about sex and desire in the Middle Ages are, despite the inter-vening centuries, not unfamiliar to our modern ears. This is not to argue, of course, that there are no differences, just that there are some recognizable ideas that are more familiar to us now than, for example, St Simeon standing on one leg for three years in the Syrian desert. The first of these would be the assumption that sex should only occur within marriage. The second familiar idea is that enjoy-ing sex too much, and having a lot of it in different ways, is morally wrong – indeed, promiscuous sex remains condemned today. The third, perhaps less familiar but still not unknown, is the association between sex and physical defilement and impurity. Sex was to be had for a higher purpose, and only in this purposeful rational manner could the perils of the flesh be avoided. This provided a rationale for the active promotion of heterosexual coitus, by identifying this expression of desire as the only mode that was acceptable in the eyes of God.

The legacy of Augustine's resolution of the problem of the flesh was the need to scrutinize people's sexual behaviour. This was the logic of the view that, left to its own devices, the lustful flesh would prevail and fornication – a deadly sin – would triumph. The only way to avoid this outcome was to monitor closely the direction of sexual desire towards a single purpose – that of procreation with the minimum of pleasure. In the early centuries of the faith, there were no rules by which to judge whether or not what people did sexually was sinful or righteous. Passing references were made to unnatural practices, but this tended to operate as a 'blanket term' applied without distinction to all expressions of sexuality.

The confession of sin was a central element in the Christian faith from the earliest writings of the Church Fathers and Apostles. Matthew wrote of the keys to the kingdom of heaven that were avail-able only to those who admitted their sins. From these words came the concept of the 'power of the keys' – the power to absolve con-fessed sins and allow the penitent to become purified. This power was originally held by all the faithful, and thus the very earliest confes-sions were held in front of the whole congregation. The penitents marked their status by the 'wearing of sackcloth and ashes, engaging in fasts, and uttering groans, prayers and outcries to God' (McNeill and Gamer 1990: 6). In addition to being visibly identified, sinners were excluded from the congregation until they had served their penance. They were denied the pleasures of secular life through fasting, and were forbidden to marry or to have sex if married. They were also liable to be subjected to public whippings or other humil-iations (Brundage 1987: 153ff). Not surprisingly, therefore, most people left this ordeal as late as possible before their death, thus maximizing the possibility of their entry to the kingdom of heaven.

Such public confessions and punishments were replaced, in the fifth century, by what were called 'auricular confessions', that is, those into the ear of the priest. The public display of sins and the involvement of the congregation was superseded by a 'private and secret rite involving confession to and absolution by a priestly confessor, entailing acts of penance which were mainly or wholly private' (McNeill and Gamer 1990: 6). The Church still did not require this as a regular feature of worship. Compulsory confessions were instigated at the Council of Trent in 1215. But the advent of private confessions, combined with the widely circulated and extensive books of rules for confessions and penances, increased the intensity of the examination of individual behaviour. Confessions now entailed an increasingly finely tuned system for the 'treatment of the soul', in which wrongdoings were uncovered through direct questioning and the punishment was finely graded according to their severity.

It was in the monasteries of northern England and Ireland that this practice of private penance first emerged, initially involving monks and abbots within their monasteries. Payer argues that 'the earliest penitential we possess is the Penitential of Vinnian, which was written before the Irish missionary Columbanus wrote his penitential (circa 591 AD) and it was through the Penitential of Columbanus that these manuals were introduced to continental Europe' (Payer 1984: 9). Even in their earliest forms, the penitentials provided the basis from which the Church sought to impose its will on a widely differentiated flock that had not been versed in Christian morality. Thus it was that, in the early Middle Ages, private penance, conducted under the guidance of the penitentials, became the key moral instrument of the Church, and through this of society. The penitentials were central in establishing this framework. Between the sixth and ninth centuries, two features remain constant in the lists of sins: those acts defined as wrong, and the ordering of wrongness from worst to least. Through detailed questioning about the sexual uses of the body, sources of sexual pleasure were identified before being condemned and punished as sins. Thus, the penitentials not only listed sins; by naming them they also brought them into existence.

The purpose of the penitentials was twofold. First they were to establish, by direct questioning, any lapses in self-control in thought or deed, or any failure to observe the discipline of worship. Second, for each transgression listed, they gave a penance, a punishment appropriate to the sin. Penances could range from the very trivial – not eating meat that day – to the fairly catastrophic – living on bread and water for a month. Questions asked by priests at confession covered such diverse elements as gluttony, slaying of men, lying, spiritual laxity, use of magic, and misuse of animals. Sins were graded in relation to originally eight and later seven principal vices: gluttony, lust, avarice, anger, despondency, moroseness, vainglory and pride. While they were not concerned solely with sexual behaviour, 'sexual offences constituted the largest single category of behaviour that the penitential treated' (Brundage 1987: 153). The detailed questions relating to how, with whom and how often one had sex underlined the importance of establishing the difference between acceptable and forbidden sex. All the texts studied in detail by Payer concern themselves consistently with fornication, 'homosexuality', bestiality, masturbation and 'pollution' ('wet dreams'). Other sexual transgressions mentioned in some, though not all, refer to adultery, periods of sexual abstinence, proper positions for intercourse, incest and the use of aphrodisiacs or potions to prevent or terminate pregnancy. Later texts appear to be more comprehensive (Payer 1984: appendix A–B, 124–6). Not only were various sexual acts forbidden, the only remaining legitimate source of sexual pleasure was subject to severe monitoring and rationing. Sex between man and wife was restricted to only one position, to certain times of day, to certain days of the week and, when in relation to the menstrual cycle, to pregnancy and to entry into the church. The penitentials thus served two purposes. They provided grounds for the establishment of forbidden sexual acts on the one hand, while on the other they offered guidance as to the only acceptable way to have sex in the eyes of God. This ensured that the Church never averted its gaze from the marital bed.

The focus on sexual positions reflected the concern about the consequences of experiencing excessive sexual pleasure. For thousands of years it had been known that certain positions gave more pleasure than others. The only one acceptable to Augustine and subsequently to the Roman Church was that which gave the least pleasure for the woman – the one we now know as 'the missionary' position. Even if sex was restricted to only one position, there was still a danger that the couple might fall into the sin of fornication (sex for pleasure). However carefully and rationally undertaken, sex without pleasure could not be guaranteed. Periods of abstinence provided at least a partial safeguard against this risk. One way of convincing the reluctant parishioner to view sex with alarm and not anticipation was to emphasize its harmful effects on the health. According to the penitentials, both men and women had to wash after sex and before entering the church. Sex with a woman who had just delivered a baby was forbidden until she had been cleansed in a special service. The need for women to be ritually purified after birth in a special ceremony has been commercially replaced by the secular celebration of 'Mother's Day'. The original Christian justification for purification was not a cleansing of the birthing blood but a 'cleansing' of the sin of sexual pleasure. Medical science in this period held that both men and women needed to climax and ejaculate for conception to take place. The pleasure associated with a successfully procreative sex act was increased with the birth of a female child. This belief, Brundage suggests, reflected and nurtured the view that women's sexuality was by nature more impure than that of men (Brundage 1987: 157).

The possibility of having sex for pleasure was further discouraged by severe restrictions on frequency and opportunity. Sex on Sundays was forbidden, since the resultant pollution would make it impossible to enter the church and partake of the sacrament in communion. Thursdays and Fridays were likewise sex-free days, being devoted to pre-communion fasting and self-denial. The early Christian calendar had not one but three Lenten periods. The first precluded sex for between forty-seven and sixty-two days. The second period covered the weeks before Christmas, for a period of at least thirty-five days. The third period related to the feast of Pentecost (fifty days after Easter), which again required sexual abstinence for forty to sixty days. The total period of Lenten sexual abstinence extended from between eleven and thirteen weeks of the year. Sex was also forbidden on the numerous 'feast days' of the Church calendar, and on the days before communion on each of these (Brundage 1987: 158). The church calendar was thus also a sex calendar, underlining the integral relationship between sexual and religious life.

But the penitentials probably unwittingly contributed much more to Western sexual culture. By their intense and detailed focus on the sexual uses of the body these texts constructed an erotic map of the body in which pleasures were named and catalogued. They served clearly to distinguish and confirm the difference between moral and immoral sexual activity. The association they established between certain uses of the body, sin and punishment laid the foundations for feelings of shame, guilt and fear about certain parts of the body and about certain acts. The penitentials and their usage over six centuries firmly created a language of forbidden parts and acts, whose impact has long outlived these ancient books and their readers. At the time they were produced there were no terms to identify the practices marked as forbidden. 'An English-language writer discussing sex in the penitentials will find himself in the curious position of employing a vocabulary which has virtually no counterpart in the works being analysed. There are no Latin words corresponding to our fornication, homosexuality, lesbianism, masturbation, aphrodisiac, impotence' (Payer 1984: 141). The additional detailed work of Brundage (1987), Ranke-Heinemann (1991) and Noonan (1986) on the penitentials illustrates the degree to which this period was one in which there was the first classification of sexual acts, many centuries before the first 'scientists of sex'. But a further contribution was made in this process. For, in identifying certain acts as more or less sinful, there was created a ranking of sexual acts and pleasures that outlawed all but limited heterosexual coitus. The restrictions served not just to distinguish between heterosexual sex (acceptable) and any other source of sexual pleasure (unacceptable). They also distinguished between sexual positions taken by the man and woman. 'The female-superior position was thought to be peculiarly lustful and an obstacle to conception' (Ranke-Heinemann 1991: 150). The woman being entered from behind (*coitus a retro*) was forbidden both as giving excessive pleasure and also as more 'bestial' (Brundage 1984: 82).

The sexual position that was subject to the most scrutiny and uniformly severe penances was 'fornication as the sodomites did', or 'sinning with a man as with a woman' (Columbanus, quoted in Payer 1984: 42). But this could not be interpreted as a judgement against homosexuality. Neither the term nor the concept existed at this time. What was being judged here was the degree to which an expression of sexual desire deviated from the only permitted form of sex. As Payer points out, 'the term sodomy and sodomites is probably their way of referring to those who practice anal intercourse' (ibid.: 40). In this, as in all other sexual acts referred to in the penitentials, the identification of the sinful act came before its being given a name. The act of anal sex was identified as sinful as early as the seventh-century Irish penitential of Cummean. In this case, it was in a banned list that included oral, anal and inter-femoral sex as well as mutual masturbation. Masturbation was identified as another sexual sin, often in the same ruling as bestiality. However, surprisingly, neither was viewed as a serious sexual sin, especially if the sinner was not a clergyman. But, with the intensification of scrutiny, there were finer distinctions made between the meanings attached to sexual acts. For example, in the questions asked about marital sex, the penitentials distinguished between *coitus a tergo* (anal penetration) and *coitus a retro* (vaginal penetration from behind) (Brundage 1984: 82). The former was penalized because it was unnatural and the latter because it was both more pleasurable and thought less likely to lead to conception. Similarly, sexual acts between men were classified in severity according to the age and rank of the man concerned. Thus, acts between priests and laymen were punished more harshly than those between priests, and acts between boys and adult men attracted the most severe penance. Payer argues that this detailed attention illustrates the particular concern about sex between men and that between men and boys. While not the cause of as much concern, same-sex practices between women were recognized as early as the seventh-century Canons of Theodore: 'If a woman commits fornication with a woman, she shall do penance for three years' (Canons of Theodore; quoted in Payer 1984: 43), while 'several penitential censures of lesbian relations make reference to the use of . . . instruments' (ibid.). Such women received more severe penance than men, especially if the act was autoerotic or 'coitus alone with herself' (ibid.: n. 173) and involved the use of phallic substitutes (ibid.: 46; McNeill and Gamer 1990: 185).

A surprising inclusion in the serious sin category to modern eyes was the sin of 'wet dreams' (Payer 1984: 49). This involuntary emission of semen was viewed as being as blameworthy as a voluntary sexual act. Spontaneous male ejaculation at night offered proof of the possession of the body by uncontrollable desires for sexual pleasure. Even if the man was deeply asleep, he was still held morally responsible for his body and its behaviour. Although the penance was not so severe as for acts that involved will and choice, the identification of nocturnal emissions as sinful intensified not just the obligation of self-control, but also anxiety about the lustful flesh. 'The absence of will or of consciously entertained thought seems not to imply total lack of sinfulness or guilt' (ibid.: 52). However, the worst of all sins was 'depositing semen in the mouth', or 'satisfying their desires with their lips'. Oral sex attracted penances usually from three to seven years, but sometimes for life (McNeill and Gamer 1990: 186; Bailey 1955: 102).

For four centuries, these texts defined, labelled and controlled human sexual desire and its expression. However, the explicit detail required for the clear identification of sexual sins was eventually to have the opposite effect than that originally intended. 'The early writers regarded themselves as preparing booklets for the physicians of the soul; while later ones began to be concerned that the specific descriptions of sexual activity might well encourage the penitents to discover activities they had not known before' (Bullough 1982: 60). By the eleventh century the use of the penitentials to control sexual activity had been replaced by the *summae confessorum*. Following the Council of Trent, in 1215 regular confession became obligatory, and was aimed less at punishment than at correction and education. With this shift to a gentler and less punitive approach, the references to sexual acts became less explicit. Rather than being lists of sins and fixed punishments, the *summae* operated more as manuals for the forgiveness of sins. 'No-one forgets that the confessor is a punisher and corrector of vice . . . but the emphasis is on persuasion, friendly and gentle, with only the more prudent use of sanctions to discourage sin' (Tentler 1977: 96). By the central Middle Ages, these changes led to an intensification of penitents' feelings of shame and individual responsibility for their acts. If this were achieved, the act of confession would become a penance in itself in the short term. At the same time the *summae* encouraged the development of an internal mechanism in which the sinner would begin to operate their own systems of self-control and punishment.

A further indication of the development of internal mechanisms of shame to control sexual behaviour can be found in another element of the Church's authority in medieval society. The medieval churches of Western Europe are recognizable even to the layperson's eye by their particular form of architecture. Though the niceties of column shape may escape those of us who lack an artistic education, what is hard to avoid is the startling figures carved in stone, sometimes inside but usually outside the church. These figures, known as gargoyles, were originally included to drain water from the great ramparts and buttresses of the buildings. In this respect, they have a long history, going back more than 5000 years. However, in the medieval period, the figures used to perform this function became increasingly exaggerated and frightening in appearance. Some were distorted human figures; some were hybrid monsters. Though many of these carvings depicted distortions of nature and of animals, there was one variation that is distinctive – carvings that are distinguished by their depiction of sexual organs of both men and women, or both together. While they were originally explained as remnants of pagan fertility symbols, more recent scholarship has argued that the origins of these extraordinary effigies can be established accurately from the thirteenth century (Weir and Jerman 1986). The authors undertook a study of hundreds of medieval churches across Europe and in Ireland. Spanning three centuries, the essence of these carvings was the flagrant sexual exhibitionism of both men and women, but particularly women. The figures were deformed and grotesque, the genitals of the male and sometimes of the female figures enlarged. They were depicted engaged in either genital or anal display or in sexual intercourse. In many carvings, these genital displays were incorporated with masturbatory or other forms of autoeroticism (ibid.: 80ff). Especially in the case of displaying women, the figures of animals, serpents and swine were included. The singularity of these displays, and (some forms of) the sex itself, is emphasized by the introduction of serpents, toads and dogs. These creatures are commonly depicted attacking the genitals of the figures – devouring women's breasts, entering their ears, biting off men's testicles (ibid.: 89–90).

Taken at face value, these carvings would appear to be inexplicable in the context of the prevailing teachings of the medieval Church. It is not possible, the authors argue, to sustain the previous argument that these carvings had found their way accidentally into the medieval buildings. Far from being at odds with the Church's project to outlaw sexual pleasure, such carvings were an important element in this strategy. Positioned at the entrance of great or small churches, or adorning central supports or lintels inside the buildings, the figures were intended to terrify rather than titillate. The ugliness of the anal and genital displays remains both shocking and fascinating, intended no doubt then to serve as a powerful visual reminder of sexual sin and its consequences. The prevalence of the female figure in these stone texts is striking. Women appear in a number of forms and activities. A common figure is that of the mermaid. The medieval mermaid was not the harmless fantasy figure of modernity. Known in French as *la luxure* or *la concupiscence*, she was a hybrid monster whose name emphasized the connection between sin, lust and pleasure. The imagery of lust indicates its primary position in the catalogue of medieval sins. The visual impact of the gargoyles enhanced the effectiveness of the message for an impressionable and illiterate population, and their impact remains profoundly visual, and is intended to be. Their physical ugliness, their associations with animals and the explicitness of the genital displays leave no doubt as to the associations intended between a free sexual licence over one's body and the sub-human consequences. From a twenty-first-century perspective, there is a clear reminder of contemporary pornography. Arguably it would not stretch historiography too far to suggest that across the centuries the message remains the same. These were the images of socially unacceptable manifestations of sexuality, presented in such a manner as to be visually arresting, on the one hand, and, on the other, to underline the moral distinctions between acceptable and unacceptable sexualities.

The rise and decline of the penitentials mark the Middle Ages as a key watershed in the negative valuation of the desiring body. These extraordinary documents provided a blueprint for attitudes to expressions of sexual pleasure for the following millennium. They also serve to illustrate the degree to which the control of sexual desire and pleasure figured centrally in the social world in which they emerged, while their succeeding incorporation into ecclesiastical law testifies to the continuing need for vigilance over persistently unruly and disorderly desires. Yet, while the Church had developed more sophisticated tools to monitor the sex lives of its parishioners, its authority did not extend to all spheres of medieval life. In the next two sections, we will look at two examples of this: the first from medieval literature and the second from medieval medical texts.

Stories about sex, 1: courtly love and little fables

When dealing with a period so remote from the present, there is a danger that one can choose historical evidence and interpret it out of the historical context. If future historians sought to understand twentieth-century sexuality from the literature of the period, the picture they might construct would differ depending on what texts were chosen. An accurate historical reconstruction would also depend on the ability to get inside the heads of the authors and understand their motives in writing. Was it social commentary? Was it social satire? Was it to promote a particular moral project or movement? Medieval historians have engaged in such a debate about the literature of the period, especially that relating to sexual behaviour. The first example is the phenomenon of courtly love or *fin'amors*, meaning 'a perfectionist non-consummated love' (Utley 1972: 317). This new model for romantic relationships between men and women of the nobility appeared first in eleventh-century France. Before this period, relationships between men and women were not expected to entail passionate attachment. Marriages were unions of practicality rather than emotional attachment. Courtly love was to provide the foundations for the romantic love that we still associate with the most socially acceptable sexual relationships. It was considered suitable only for the nobility, and its exponents were, if not of noble families, certainly schooled in the art of chivalry. The poems and songs of the troubadours provided fictional accounts of courtly love for the entertainment of the feudal nobility across Europe.

The originator of this tradition was William II, Duke of Aquitaine, in 1071. It was to spread throughout France and England with the ascension of his daughter Eleanor, first to the throne of France, then to that of England in 1122. Eleanor and her daughter Marie, Countess of Troyes, established a Court of Love in Poitiers and commissioned the court chaplain, Andreas Cappelanus, to write a rulebook for courtly love. This text, known in English as *The Art of Courtly Love*, but originally written in Latin, comprises three books: the first two lay down the rules of love and the third appears to satirize the practice and especially to denigrate women as deceitful and sexually rapacious.

Courtly love was a pastime suited to the nobility, who alone were considered capable of the finer forms of behaviour and the levels of self-control. The peasantry were considered much closer to animals, so this stylized romanticism would be wasted on them. 'If you should, by some chance, fall in love with some of their women, be careful to puff them up with lots of praise and then, when you find a convenient place, do not hesitate to take what you seek and embrace them by force' (Cappelanus, quoted in Utley 1972: 150). There were two other key features. First, this form of love was initiated by men who, though the active partner, were bound by the rules of courtly love to concede most of the power to the adored woman. Second, this was not an emotion considered proper for marriage, or between married couples. Marriages were for practicalities, whether economic or social. The Church, of course, viewed as sinful any sexual passion in marriage. Courtly love was an emotion suitable only for single men and women or a single man and a married woman. Though women were still considered the property of their husbands, they were not transgressing this ownership relation by allowing themselves to be adored. It was the man, not the woman, who was the active initiator. Any active sexuality on behalf of the married woman would have been severely punished.

Though associated with passion and devotion, courtly love was not, primarily, physical in its expression for either sex. It was, especially, not carnal, in the sense that it was directed towards sexual consummation. It was elevated above these by its distinguishing and even ritualistic features. Foremost among these was that the love and the beloved were not married to each other. Second, these relationships were secretive and often conducted at a physical distance. Physical longing was a central feature, as was the pain associated with doubts about the lover's self-worth. Courtly love, in its idealized form, was a selfless emotion; service to the beloved was a reward in itself. Courtly love was characterized by service, separation, suffering and at least partial chastity. Though the poetry and song associated with this tradition was often highly erotic and even sexually explicit, physical consummation of the passion was considered unworthy. It was a 'love which yearned for, and at times was rewarded by the solace of every delight of the beloved except physical possession of her by intercourse' (Denomy 1946: 142). This 'pure love' was distinguished from 'common love' by its spirituality as much as its open eroticism. In a climate that either banned sexual love as sinful or devalued its uncontrolled physical expressions, courtly love offered an alternative outlet for sensual pleasures. However, this is a form of sexual expression that was written by and for men, reiterating their supremacy in the works of love. Indeed, the distinctive feature of pure love – its controlled eroticism – is equated with masculinity, with heterosexuality and with a further construction of 'nature'. 'Just as the masculine member of the family is considered the nobler, of more worth than the feminine, so true love is nobler, of more worth than false [spontaneous sexual intercourse] love' (ibid.: 28–30). It is men, not women, who are considered capable of the spiritual virtue and self-control necessary for the proper expression of pure love. Women who are too willing to 'grant a request' are to be avoided, since such women are unable to contain their lust, a sign of 'over voluptuousness', which is a 'stranger in the Court of love'. Such women are dangerous because they devalue their lover's 'property' – their adoration and attention; they 'pretend to be a lady while acting like a strumpet' (Cappelanus, *De amore*, quoted in ibid.: 145–6).

But even if the gender norms were not disrupted, the eroticism openly challenged the teaching of the Church about the sinfulness and dangers of carnal desires. 'She seems so svelte and plump and sleek under her linen chemise, that when I see her, by my faith, I do so much better my pleasure when I have her naked beneath the figured veil' (Denomy 1946: 156, n. 19). In this tradition, desire and its expression in erotic pleasure was distinguished morally from spontaneous lust and its expression in coitus. The exclusion of the act of intercourse adds to rather than detracts from the erotic appeal. For the lover seeks to experience every intimacy: 'to assist his lady to undress . . . to be present when she undresses, to feel her arms about his neck; to look at her fair body as she lies abed . . . He asks that he might lie beside her . . . a kiss, an embrace, to lie in her arms, . . . to fondle and kiss her and to draw her bare svelte body to him' (ibid.: 171). To the extent that courtly love encouraged and celebrated carnal sensuality and sexual pleasure, it stood in opposition to the Church's teaching and thus to the mainstay of medieval sexual morality. Yet, there was spirituality at the centre of this tradition that equally devalued the unmediated expression of sexual desire and experience of bodily pleasures. Instead, it encouraged social acceptance of romantic passion between men and women, as well as acknowledging its erotic content. In this respect, this social movement of the high Middle Ages offered an alternative discourse to the single and negative voice of the Church. Yet both offered, from different moral positions, instruction in the art of love. The distinction made repeatedly between the animal lusts and noble courtly practices reinforced the rigid social structures, while at the same time restating more deeply embedded anxieties about the consequences of unbridled bodily pleasures, more closely associated with women's sexuality.

The second example of 'sexual stories' also offered a challenge to the sexually oppressive demands of the Church, but in its content could not have been more different from courtly love traditions. The *fabliaux*, meaning 'little fables', were a popular literary form that first appeared in thirteenth-century France. They were the beginning of a humorous literary tradition that became popular all over Europe. While consciously 'manipulating and violating the taboos' of Christian orthodoxy, their reception suggested that the audience 'did not take very seriously the medieval Christian ascetic injunction against sexual pleasure' (Muscatine 1986: 109). Whereas courtly love promoted and encouraged a spiritual expression of desire, the *fabliaux* celebrated the most boisterously physical and crude expressions of desire. Sex and excretion figured centrally in satires and parodies of human failings, especially sexual weaknesses. These sexual adventures were hugely popular in their written and spoken forms, and 'hawked all over medieval Europe' (Rougemont 1956: 185). Well-known writers of these tracts include Dante, Chaucer and Boccaccio. The characters of these tales did not offer examples of moral excellence, self-control and sacrifice. Instead they were variously sexually voracious and unfaithful young women, stupid older husbands and foolish younger lovers. Clergy and nobility were often targets of ridicule, but these were texts enjoyed by all strata of society, even those who were their targets. The *fabliaux* celebrated 'medieval culture unembarrassed in the midst of its everyday pleasures and transgressions' (Muscatine 1986: 2). In a social setting where the majority were illiterate, such texts contained complex messages. On the one hand they were irreverent dirty jokes; on the other they served as cautionary tales about the dangers of social transgressions, sexual and otherwise. The *fabliaux* offered vivid pictures of 'lusty monks, jealous maniacally overprotective husbands, oversexed, clever wives, eager lovers, frequent adultery, and a marked disinterest in the legal or moral implications of their acts. We also see copulation in the most bizarre fashions, under the most dangerous and ludicrous circumstances' (Berger 1988: 173).

Though *fabliaux* would appear to come from the opposite of the courtly love tradition, Berger argued that both the audience and the writers of these verses would be familiar with the ideals of courtly love. Indeed, in his view, the content of these bawdy verses drew directly on the concepts of courtly love for their meaning and humour (Berger 1988: 163). The idealization of women, a centrepiece in courtly love, is inverted in the *fabliaux*. Women are highly sexed, articulate, clever individuals who are almost always in the ascendance over men as they pursue their erotic adventures (ibid.: 165). Yet there were limitations to this positive construction of women's sexuality. Though the lustful woman was a key theme, she was thus characterized to provide the context for men's sexual performance. The recognition of active and autonomous sexuality of women supported rather than challenged the prevailing masculine bias. The sex that was represented was always heterosexual. The singling out of same-sex desire for condemnation that was a feature of the penitentials was duplicated in the *fabliaux*. The mere mention of the possibility of a man having sex with another man was a common vehicle for extreme humiliation of the characters of the stories.

One way of interpreting the *fabliaux* is as extended 'dirty jokes'. Their humour depended on the subversion of the expected, like all jokes, but the vehicle for this inversion was explicit sexuality and scatology. Their universal appeal was ensured by the delivery as performance, though, of course, they appeared in print as well. In this respect, they breached the social barriers of literacy and of class behind which courtly love flourished. Their performers, likewise, spanned the social spectrum, from poets to itinerant jugglers (Muscatine 1986: 7). They were much in demand, being a popular source of after-dinner entertainment for the rich as well as for the rural peasant. But, although they encapsulated social stability and operated within shared meanings, these tales also bore witness to the shifting social stratification of the fourteenth century, in which the rise of the money economy offered new opportunities for social mobility. They offered, says Muscatine, 'social snapshots of the classes, of the changing social order, of the rising bourgeoisie and of the emergence of the rich peasants: and generally of the ambivalence that inevitably accompanies social stratification' (ibid.: 70).

But at the same time as they satirized social and particularly sexual mores, these tales could be argued to be essential elements in the maintenance of social order. To begin with, they reinforced the hierarchy of the social structure. Thus, noble men, or celibate monks, tended to be the victims of jokes, while young peasant women frequently figured as objects of lust. All male figures appeared at the mercy of women, whose duplicity was outweighed only by their voracious sexuality. As entertainment, the *fabliaux* appeared in a time of social change, to reinforce, through popular appeal to such shared norms, a social world both familiar and changing. In humorous form, these tales matched the Church in their preoccupation with sex and with the modes of its experience, and, as such, might, despite their open irreverence, have operated more to stabilize than to rupture the prevailing social structure. It may be this factor that contributed to the apparent tolerance of their content by the establishment. Perhaps they provided a sort of 'moral holiday' from the stringent attentions of the Church – offering a beleaguered sexual population a break, while reinforcing the parameters of their sexual lives.

Stories about sex 2: the sexual body in medieval medicine

The nature and purpose of sexuality, the appropriate circumstances for intercourse, the relationship between intercourse and reproduction, the practices of contraception and abortion, and the implications of virginity fell within the domain of the physician, natural philosopher, moralist and theologian. (Cadden 1986: 57)

Medieval medical practice was directly influenced by ancient astronomy and alchemy drawn from Arabic, Indian and Greco-Roman traditions. Medical tracts were held in the monasteries that rapidly expanded from the eleventh century in Europe. Many monasteries also served as hospices, the first hospitals. Those who practised the art were often clerics. The connections were also established and strengthened by the Church's view that disease was caused by sin. The onset of illness was often related to, for example, gluttony, fornication, envy or one of the other deadly sins. From AD 942 until the fourteenth century the Church forbade dissections. After this, the number was strictly limited – one cadaver of each sex per year. The practitioners of medicine were divided into physicians, surgeons, midwives and apothecaries. The services of physicians were for the most part restricted to the rich in urban settings. The midwife or apothecary served, where possible, the needs of the poor and rural sick. Epidemic and incurable disease was a feature of the later Middle Ages, ranging from measles and smallpox to the plague, and the usual fatal nature of these intensified anxiety about the causes and treatment of diseases in lay people and practitioners alike.

The mixture of ancient traditions in medieval medical knowledge can be seen in the approach to the prevention and treatment of disease. The first was Greco-Roman medical knowledge and writings. Though the originals were in Greek, medieval scholars and physicians, notably Constantinus Africanus (1027–1080), translated them into Latin for use in the first medical schools of Europe, established in Salerno, Italy, in 1100. The key ancient physicians were

Hippocrates (460–377 BC), Aristotle (384–322 BC), Soranus (98–138 AD) and, perhaps the most influential of all, Galen (129–201 AD). The texts of the last named were still translated and presented for medical training as late as 1833. The modern significance of these great thinkers and practitioners lies in their emphasis on observation of the body and its secretions in the maintenance of health as well as the treatment of disease. For this reason, they did not dissect human bodies, but derived any guidance about the internal organs of the body by the dissection (and sometimes vivisection) of animals. However, this information was considered secondary to that gained from direct observation of the living human body. The primary concern of the ancient tradition of medicine was founded in a holistic view that saw the spiritual and physical health of the body as integrally related. The body was not treated as a machine made up of distinct organs but as a conscious entity. Disease was viewed as the result of an imbalance in the four constitutive elements of the body – phlegm, yellow bile, black bile and pneuma. The imbalance was brought about by either excessive heat or excessive cold. 'Disease' could manifest itself in a spiritual as well as a physical sense. Treatment was aimed at restoring the balance between the physical elements on the one hand and the spiritual on the other.

The second source of knowledge was Arabic medical texts, which began in the seventh century AD and continued to expand until the thirteenth century. The original sources of this Eastern tradition were also the texts of Hippocrates, Aristotle and Galen, which were translated from Greek to Arabic by the earliest physicians. Though sharing the same source, Arabic medical knowledge and practice cultivated independent skills and insights that were drawn back in the later developing Renaissance medicine of the West after the fourteenth century. The great Arab physicians and surgeons were Al Razi (841–926), Zahrawi (930–1013) and Ibn-Sina (980–1037), known respectively in the West as Rhazes, Albucasis and Avicenna. The development of Arabic medicine and its practice in the Middle Ages was in advance of that of the Roman Empire and other parts of Europe. It was not until the Renaissance that Western medicine caught up with Eastern medical knowledge and practice.

It was the independent insights and teaching from Arab physicians and Indian alchemy that contributed to another discourse on sexuality in medieval medicine that increased its independence from the prevailing Christian orthodoxy. This discourse had two levels, one that was more directly derived from Arabic texts and the other that remained faithful to the more familiar pronouncements of the Greco-Roman tradition. In both there was a positive connection made between sexual pleasure and health for both men and women. The origins of both can be found in the Greco-Roman writing that emphasized the importance of sexual release for physical health. Similarly, Arab physicians and philosophers, for example, Avicenna, recommended potions and love-making techniques to maximize pleasure for both men and women. Medical literature from the classical period to the high Middle Ages consistently paid attention to sex and pleasure – sometimes in passing, sometimes with whole tracts devoted to the subject (Bassan 1962: 134). Two features characterized these writings, whether they derived from the classical Latin or Arabic sources. First, they 'established coitus as a valuable remedy for various afflictions' (ibid.: 134) for both men and women. Second, the Galenic theory that accorded both men and women the ability to produce and ejaculate 'seed' during coitus placed sexual pleasure firmly in the domain of medicine, in ways that differed radically from those of the Church and which at times brought it into conflict with prevailing sexual mores.

There were, however, limitations to the challenge posed by medieval medicine to the orthodoxy of the Church. Both the ancient sources and their medieval interpreters were concerned predominantly with coitus and saw it as the natural source of sexual pleasure. The primary focus of attention was the production of sperm – both male and female. We must remember, at this time, and for some centuries to come, there was no knowledge of the existence of two distinct and different sexual anatomies of male and female. Women had internal (and inferior) male sexual organs, and thus could and did ejaculate 'seed'. As one of the bodily fluids, sperm was considered to be a vital element in maintaining the balance of the life forces. Too much or too little of this fluid disturbed the vital balance between the humours of the body. Sexual continence thus had important implications for the maintenance of bodily health and for the diagnosis of disease. 'If the semen remained too long in its receptacles it not only became altered and gave rise to gonorrhoea, but sent off acrid vapours which . . . caused epilepsy, mania, melancholy and led to sexual irregularities' (Bassan 1962: 134). But too much sex also threatened health. A man who had had sex seventy times before matins, and expired as a consequence, was, on autopsy, found to have 'a brain the size of a pomegranate' (Jacquart and Thomasset 1988: 5–6).

The relationship between excessive sex or chastity and dramatic physical consequences was equally of concern to women (Cadden 1984: 149ff; Bullough 1973: 485ff). Prolonged retention of female spermatic fluid manifested itself in symptoms that ranged from the irritating to the catastrophic: 'For the medieval doctor, suffocation of the womb was without any possible doubt a disease caused by chastity' (Jacquart and Thomasset 1988: 174). Depending on the level of the woman's sexual desires, these consequences also ranged from the irritating to the life-threatening. In some celibate women, whose temperament rendered them less 'naturally' inclined to coitus, dizziness and fainting were signs of spermatic retention. Others suffered near fatal consequences as a result of abstinence: 'Some of the afflicted lie senseless and immobile, with a weak pulse, or no pulse at all. Others are conscious but exhibit a defect of the spirit and laboured breathing; still others suffer contractions of their thighs and arms' (Lemay 1981: 177). Treatment for these symptoms, first described by Galen in the second century, was masturbation, in emergencies to be undertaken by a midwife. 'Hysterical paralysis' brought on by sexual frustration should be treated by sex immediately if the sufferer is married and by marriage if she is single. But in the severest cases, where signs of life are absent, 'burial should be delayed for two days' (ibid.: 178), during which time the feet of the sufferer should be vigorously rubbed and powders administered to induce sneezing.

This preoccupation with the health-giving properties of ejaculation was complemented by the promotion of coitus as an erotic art in the Arabic medical and astrological tradition. While also concerned with the prevention of illnesses due to the retention of bodily fluids, the Arabic literature 'stressed the erotic character of the sexual act, and indeed often concentrated on telling lascivious tales and prescribing aphrodisiacs than on treating hygiene proper' (Lemay 1981: 166–7). It also laid great emphasis on women's sexual pleasure. Women's satisfaction was necessary, Avicenna wrote, to ensure the birth of a son and to prevent masturbation or an adulterous affair. Avicenna's *Canon of Medicine* (a text that remained the central medical text until the seventeenth century) represented the synthesis of Greco-Roman with the Persian and Indian traditions of philosophy and medicine. It provides a detailed description of foreplay and of methods to increase the size of the penis and prolong time before ejaculation, while describing in detail 'three stages' of women's orgasmic journey.

The works of such leading figures as Arnold of Villanova (1232–1312), William of Saliceto (1210–1270) and Peter of Spain (1205–1277) drew from Arabic works advice on details of foreplay, and of the correct methods for the arousal of women. They also pronounced on the most effective time and place for intercourse and suggested uses of potions and pessaries to enhance pleasure. But in their 'purely Western discussions of orgasm' they wrote of the natural interaction of the body parts and the importance of balance. In this way, Lemay argues, they shifted the emphasis away from the most creatively sensual sex and towards the most successful in ensuring health-giving ejaculations (Lemay 1981: 171–2).

This did not mean that men and women were considered equal, either politically or erotically. Misogyny was a key feature of medical just as it was of theological writings (Bullough 1973: 486). Peter of Spain, one of the most important physicians of the thirteenth century (and later to become Pope John XXI), established an ingenious matrix within which to establish, scientifically, the relative sensuality of men and women. In his view, women experienced more pleasure, while men experienced greater intensity. Thus while 'the question of female sperm provided the opportunity for affirming the benefits of shared pleasure' (Jacquart and Thomasset 1988: 133), it did so in ways which retained the ascendance of male over female sexuality. The discourse of pleasure in medical tracts also retained the restrictions on coital positions, and in this can be seen clear links with Christian mores. Any variation of the female below and man on top was considered 'shameful' (ibid.: 134). In these ways, the relaxed and positive attitude to sexual pleasure which constituted a pure *ars erotica* was adjusted by the Western medieval medical tradition to mark the boundaries of propriety in the Western discourse.

Throughout the writings of sexual medicine in the Middle Ages, the focus was heterosexual coitus. Though same-sex practices were acknowledged, very little was said on the subject – particularly relating to women. The less serious consideration of lesbianism by medical writers is in keeping with both juridical and social frameworks. The lack of opportunity the medieval world offered women for freedom of sexual choice meant that 'recourses to "practices against nature" will only be occasional and will put neither the future of the species nor civilisation in peril' (Jacquart and Thomasset 1988: 160). The views about male same-sex practices attracted more attention. There was disagreement about the 'causes' and the medical significance of male sexual intercourse. For the classical predecessors, 'the affliction comes from a corrupt and debased mind' (Lemay 1981: 179). For Avicenna it is caused by 'weak sexual potency in individuals with strong imaginations'; for other Arabic sources, it is an inborn condition (ibid.: 160–1). But while male homosexuality was clearly condemned in terms borrowed from clerical discourses, the physicians 'considered [homosexual desire] neither as an illness nor a disorder of temperament', but as a 'corruption' in the soul with no physical basis. Other aspects of sexual behaviour were considered to be more suitable topics for physicians' attention. The thirteenth-century work of William of Saliceto, *Summa conservationis* (on the diagnosis and treatment of sexual disorders), includes 'nine reasons for difficulty of erection, . . . a discussion of priapismus, or constant erection and excitation in male or female; and direction on how to treat a man who is weakened by excessive sexual activity' (Lemay 1981: 168). Other translations of the Arabic physicians deal with recipes that increase or decrease sexual desire, methods for narrowing of the vagina and of 'falsification of virginity' (Cadden 1984: 165), and of the best times of the day for pleasurable and successfully reproductive coitus.

The role played by medieval physicians in the construction of sexual pleasure was a complex one, in which the worlds of science and religion coexisted uneasily. While there is some reticence about allowing sexual desire free rein of expression, the view of the body as a system of balanced humours encouraged emphasis on the importance of sexual release. A healthy body required the maximization of pleasure for both men and women, though in limited and gendered forms. While often startlingly explicit (even in modern terms) in their descriptions of the sexual act and the means by which it should be undertaken, this was not 'pleasure for pleasure's sake', as the possibility of an *ars erotica* implies. Sex, like all other matters pertaining to bodily health, was a serious business, not one to be left to 'nature'. The emerging medical science, and the terms in which physicians sought to establish their craft, emphasized the *mechanics* of the body, not its sensual experience. The resulting texts, though modified by the influences of a deeply religious and still superstitious society, formed what was, arguably, the first 'science of sex'.

Conclusion

The Middle Ages spans nearly a thousand years of Western cultural history. Covering the period from the fifth to the fifteenth centuries, it was a complex era, variously associated with extremes of inhumanity and violence and a gentle reverence for visual beauty, both animate and inanimate. It was a social order whose rigid hierarchy allowed no acknowledgement of individual rights or expression and whose stability depended on unquestioning allegiance to duty. It was also to provide the context for a worship of beauty and of 'purity' not seen since the world of classical antiquity.

The moral theology of the age was 'plagued by an antithesis, as unrealistic as it was uncompromising, between irrational pleasure and rational control' (Tentler 1977: 165). This tension was made the more urgent in a context in which Christianity was morally synonymous with society; it was the Church that operated as the key mechanism for social control. Just as the emerging technology of medicine had begun to scrutinize, chart and pronounce on the health of the physical body, so the Church and its clergy operated as 'physicians of the soul'. For, as Joan Cadden points out, 'Human sexuality was both a medical and moral issue in the Middle Ages' (Cadden 1986: 157). Augustine's distinction between rational, orderly and procreative marital sex provided the foundation for categories of sexual sin formalized in the penitentials. While relatively short-lived, these documents were significant for two reasons. First, they described in detail a wide variety of sexual acts, listing these in order of sinfulness. In doing so, they laid down the boundaries that clearly demarcated 'acceptable' and 'unacceptable' uses of the sexual body. Homosexuality, masturbation, self-pollution and 'unnatural positions' (any other than the 'missionary') were identified repeatedly as the key sexual transgressions – parameters that persisted after the penitentials disappeared. Subsequent fears that description would encourage experimentation led to this detail being replaced by a 'catch-all' phrase of 'unnatural acts'. Second, while providing the means for control of sexual behaviour by an external authority, they fostered the development of internal feelings of guilt about uses of the body while encouraging self-surveillance over the use of the body in private.

The phenomenon of courtly love offered insights into an alternative discourse of desire and pleasure in the medieval period. Characterized by explicit yet stylized erotic expressions, courtly love gave a positive moral value to the link between romantic love and the idealization of femininity by active masculine desire. This was an art that was written by and for men. In acknowledging the erotic power of women it nevertheless objectified and rendered silent their sexual agency, while continuing to associate their sexuality with irrationality. These features were repeated in the less refined sexuality of the *fabliaux*. Sexual humour was based on humiliation, trickery and double meanings, while being infused and enlivened with gendered stereotypes. Behind the subversive settings the effectiveness of these depended on firmly embedded social structures and social roles.

For the medieval physicians, the starting point for a distinctive sexual discourse was the role of sexual release in the maintenance of bodily health. The importance of mutual satisfaction was established in Galen's belief that, at orgasm, both men and women produced sperm. This was necessary for conception, it was believed, thus providing the physiological justification for maximizing sexual pleasure during intercourse. The importance of avoiding either excessive loss or retention of sperm for either sex provided a scientific rationale for another means of controlling the experience of sexual pleasure. Though influenced by the Arabic valuation of erotic arts, medieval physicians modified the sensualism of these writings, incorporating the necessity of sexual pleasure into a more rational model that emphasized the physiology of pleasure. For these physicians, sexual pleasure was the means by which the essential balance of the sexual body could be maintained, establishing health, rather than erotic pleasure, as the primary motivation.

There is a kaleidoscopic feel to medieval sexuality, in which the 'pieces' variously overlap, collide with and influence each other over the centuries. But if there are two themes to sum up this complex era in the problematization of sexual pleasure they are the management of the earthly body and that of the immortal soul. Both entailed the management of sexuality and of sexual desires. Filtered always through the disruptive potentials of sexual desire, the more secular language of science offered the means by which to challenge the control of the Church over sexuality. But rather than relaxing the attention paid to sex and desire, these new approaches offered new grounds and strategies for the management of sexual pleasure in the social context.

FURTHER READING

Jacquart, D., and Thomasset, C. (1988) *Sexuality and Medicine in the Middle Ages*, trans. M. Adamson. Princeton, NJ: Princeton University Press.

Brundage, J. (1987) *Law, Sex and Christian Society in Medieval Europe*. Chicago: University of Chicago Press.

Payer, P. J. (1984) *Sex and the Penitentials: The Development of a Sexual Code, 550–1150*. Toronto and London: University of Toronto Press.

Bullough, V., and Brundage, J. (eds) (2000) *Handbook of Medieval Sexuality*. New York and London: Garland.

4

Sex, the Body and Desire in the Premodern Period

Introduction

This chapter will deal with the early modern period – indistinct in its boundaries, but which we will take to span the years 1450 to 1650. Encompassing but not being fully defined by the Reformation and the Renaissance, this was a period in which the major features of modernity were being forged. Alongside the 'rebirth' of classical ethics and ideals, there was a 'birth' of new social structures and, accompanying them, a new sense of self and others. Though still remote from familiar features of modernity, changes occurred during this period which were to set the stage for recognizably modern understandings and constructions of sexuality and sexual desire. First, a direct challenge was mounted to the authority of the Church of Rome, which had since the earliest days of Christianity preached an unchangeable relation between sex and sin. The challenge to medieval norms came from both secular and Christian humanism – the former expressed through the development of medical knowledge, the latter finding its voice in Puritan teachings and the Protestant faith.

Humanism was one of the key features of the early modern period. Though not an organized movement, humanism comprised a coherent set of beliefs for the successful challenge of the old monastic and medieval social structure. Its followers pursued and promoted their philosophy in both secular and religious spheres. Humanism followed the principles of classical philosophy that admired the strength of will and reason, which they saw as the defining feature of humanity. To this belief in human potential was added a veneration of the natural world and the role of humanity in taming its forces and tendencies. Secular humanism influenced the spheres of literature, painting and music, where its exponents sought to revive the morals and aesthetic principles of the classical world. If secular humanism meant the rediscovery of the classical world, and the rediscovery of 'man' as the master of all things, Christian humanism applied this humanist principle of rediscovery to the Scriptures. Leading exponents of humanist beliefs, such as Desiderius Erasmus of Rotterdam (1466–1536), returned to the original writings of the Church Fathers and the Apostles in the New Testament. By reverting to the source, humanist Christians hoped they would rediscover the simplicity and certainty of early Christian beliefs. Thus both secular and Christian humanism looked backward while facing forward. The past was consulted to lighten the way to new modes of thinking. The future offered the opportunity to use the wisdom of the past to formulate alternatives to present problems.

There were two features that distinguished humanism as 'premodern'. First, though its exponents were the elites of their spheres, education was an important part of their strategy for improving humankind. Only through education could the natural attributes of humanity be developed. This ambition was aided by technological developments in printing and reproduction of visual imagery. From the mid-fifteenth to the sixteenth century, due to the invention of the printing press (in 1452) and advances in types of paper and of ink, the production and circulation of texts and reproduced images were no longer the sole domain of the Church. Secularization of printing extended both the numbers of readers and the boundaries of permitted content. The second and recognizably modern consequence of humanism was the resurrection of the rights and duties of the individual. For centuries, and especially in the establishment of the control of the Church, the rights of the individual threatened the success of a single belief system and the harmony of the society of which it was the foundation. Humanism, with its resurrection of classical reverence for reason and self-control, rekindled the faith in the essential goodness of the individual. It emphasized the inherent dignity of humanity as the image of the divine. Any human failing and weakness could be reversed by individual effort and by education. But some have argued that humanist ideals were limited (Zweig 1979: 85). Humanism did not challenge the privilege of either class or gender (Jones 1988: 299).

The Renaissance is most commonly associated today with famous works of architecture, literature and music, but especially with artists and their work. The term Renaissance, adopted from the French equivalent of the Italian word *rinascita*, meaning literally 'rebirth', describes the radical and comprehensive changes that took place in European culture during the fifteenth and sixteenth centuries, bringing about the demise of the Middle Ages and embodying for the first time the values of the modern world. During the period between 1300 and 1650 artistic representations of the body lost their dark associations and began to illustrate joy and pleasure in the naked form, both male and female. Vivid examples of this are to be found in the work of Botticelli, Raphael, Michelangelo and Titian. Yet alongside this celebration there remained a fear and distrust of the body, especially in relation to epidemic disease. It was only half a century previously that the Black Death (bubonic plague) had eradicated more than a third of the population of Europe, and during the early modern period outbreaks of the plague were still common, alongside other communicable diseases. Paradoxically, in a period characterized by its challenge to the superstitions and irrationalities of the past, it was in the latter half of the Renaissance that the first officially sanctioned persecutions of witches occurred. Interest in the occult, magic and astrology was widespread, and many intellectuals felt a profound pessimism about the evils and corruptions of society. Renaissance anatomists under the direct influence of natural philosophy and of humanism developed a new science of the body. This was based on the exploration and observation of an actual body, as the ban against dissection of human bodies was lifted. Natural philosophy, as it applied to medicine and science, insisted that empirical truths must not only be able to be observed, but must be reproducible.

In some senses, to use the term 'early modern' in relation to this period is misleading. The majority of populations lived in rural, not urban, settings. The gaps between the rich and poor widened over the period as the traditional rights and privileges associated with common land and the feudal order began to be eroded. Infant and maternal mortality was high, and life expectancy, particularly in urban areas, rarely exceeded forty years. Incurable epidemic disease added to the insecurity of existence as smallpox, typhus, and tuberculosis were periodically joined by outbreaks of bubonic plague. Only a small percentage of the population, mainly male, could read or write by the mid-seventeenth century, and the firm hand of the autocratic monarchical state on the one hand and the established Church on the other continued to guide the social and political structure. The 'modern' element lay in the conviction of the creative thinkers, in the spheres of art, philosophy, religion, medicine and science, that humanity was not the victim but master of its fate. It lay also in the view that nature was a tool to be tamed, not a force to be feared.

The early modern epoch is a significant period in the story of sexuality and desire. But its influence was complex, being both backward and forward facing. It was a world in which human capacity to reason and reshape the world coexisted with a deeply embedded belief in magic and witchcraft and in the influence of the stars on human destiny. It was a world in which the optimism of neo-Platonism was matched by a deep pessimism, what was then called 'melancholy' – a sense of being at the mercy of the mysterious body and its unpredictable workings. This chapter will attempt to sift through these paradoxes and complexities. It will draw out the indicators of 'modern sexuality' and identify the emergence of new boundaries and rules for its containment.

Renaissance, the civilized body and the civilized self

The Renaissance celebrated the sensual and the sensitive as the core of humanity. It was this sensuality that fed the creativity as well as enriched the experience of life. This was reflected in works of art, paintings and sculptures. The 14-foot high marble statue of David by Michelangelo Buonarotti (1475–1564) typified the celebration of the naked human form in classical tradition. In portraits, individuals revelled in their humanity (Plumb 1964: 266) – opulently dressed, self-content and self-satisfied, and certainly not wracked with guilt. The body expressed the divine and spiritual – a view not confined to the arts but evident in changes to social mores that modified customs, penetrated politics and confronted the prudery of the Church. The period was characterized by the celebration of all sensuous pleasures, food, wine, elaborate clothing, living arrangements and, of course, those of the flesh. But the style in which this was done was not the raucous bawdy of the Middle Ages. Renaissance scholars viewed the immediate past as barbarous and uncivilized. Renaissance sensuality drew on the traditions of the civilizations of ancient Greece and Rome. The model for 'Renaissance man' took active delight in beauty and sensual pleasure across a wide range of experiences. This included but did not necessarily make a special case for sexual pleasures.

In the plays of Shakespeare, for example, *Twelfth Night* (1601), *The Merry Wives of Windsor* (1602) and *As You Like It* (1599), homoerotic as well as heterosexual pleasures were celebrated and encouraged, while much was made of the unstable connections between sex, gender and desire. At a less elevated but equally popular level, the period produced visual and written erotic imagery to nourish and excite sexual fantasy. There was a great demand for sexually explicit images. Perhaps the most well known of artists who supplied this demand was the individual who may have been the first modern pornographer, Pietro Aretino (1492–1556). A self-educated illegitimate son of an artisan, he was also a writer, poet, playwright and political satirist, and became the favourite of princes, cardinals and even popes. He gloried in excesses of gluttony, drunkenness, sexual licentiousness and luxury. By his own admission, he 'mocked the universe' until, 'in his glorious sixties, he roared too vehemently at a bawdy joke, had apoplexy and died' (Plumb 1964: 267).

The period was 'early modern' in the sense that it was then that a wealthy merchant class emerged, in Italy first and then across Europe. Wealthy and ambitious, these 'novi homines were pushing their way into positions of social and economic power' (Baumer 1978: 104). This was a period that nurtured levels of creative human endeavour unprecedented since the dissolution of the classical world. It produced individuals whose names remain synonymous with creative genius: Shakespeare, Milton, Locke, Wren, Newton, Leonardo da Vinci, Raphael, Machiavelli, Michelangelo and Rabelais. Behind the splendid façade of the Renaissance lay the solid framework of humanism – a belief system that directly challenged the fatalism and pessimism of the medieval Church. For both humanists and natural philosophers, the forces of nature were ultimately subject to the control of the human intellect and the application of human knowledge. The conjunction of humanism and natural philosophy, aided by the geographical insulation of the northern provinces of Italy, fostered the emergence of what would become a Europe-wide intellectual movement.

There were two radical aspects of this new world vision. First, humans possessed a natural capacity to reason and to make informed choices about their earthly existence and destiny. This teaching directly confronted the power base of the Church, whose ability to control its followers depended on the maintenance of distrust of the world around them for which faith alone offered a refuge. Second, in order to reason and choose, people must be educated to develop not just individual skills but also insights into the social consequences of their actions. In the sometimes unpredictable and chaotic world of the early modern period, humanism reversed the notion of the individual's subjection to the divine and unknowable will of their creator. This they replaced with the doctrine of a freedom of will and a capacity 'to achieve dignity and virtue amidst the perils of human existence in the teeth of economic and political vicissitudes' (Baumer 1978: 105–6).

While encouraging the flowering of individual will, this new framework for social order also emphasized the importance of acknowledging the rights and importance of others. There was a strong pedagogic strand to humanism, expressed both through the institutions of formal education and in countless volumes of courtesy books and books of manners. Norbert Elias illustrates the emergence of *civilité* in the early modern period as a new rationale for acceptable social behaviour (Elias 1982). He dates the emergence of this basis for social order during the fifteenth century and identifies Erasmus as being one of its major exponents. While sharing the humanist ideals which fed the artistic and scientific advances of the Italian Renaissance, Erasmus represented the more sober, Northern European interpretation of humanism. His model for the advancement of humankind was not that of classical civilizations; rather, he advocated a more recognizably modern approach – that of education. His still familiar maxim, that 'men are not born but made', expressed his devotion to the importance of the provision of education, in purpose-built institutions – schools and universities.

From the early sixteenth century, the changing model for social order reflected alterations in social structure. Rising densities of populations and shifting power relations in the elite weakened and made less effective, Elias argues, the old methods of social control represented by *courtoisie* (Elias 1982: 79). A new 'way of seeing' self and others emerged, and in its first stages was presented as formal social education. The reference point for this was the sense of one's 'visibility' to others, and the ability to see oneself through the eyes of others. With the expansion of written texts, and a growing audience of newly emerging gentry, there was in this period a new genre of courtesy books or books of manners which distinguished themselves in a number of ways from their predecessors. First, they were more detailed – increasingly addressing all aspects of daily life. Second, the focus of the direction and rules was not the soul or the spirit, but the body. 'The soul was disciplined by controlling the body' (Duby 1988: 174). Third, these pedagogic tracts were directed towards children at least as much as adults. As rules for behaviour became more and more refined in their focus, appropriate behaviour for children was differentiated from that expected of adults. The aim was to educate the senses through the body and its functions, as well as its public performance, and 'readers were exhorted to abide by ever more imperative and intrusive rules' (ibid.: 182). Finally, and most importantly for establishing shame and embarrassment as principal dynamics in the control of the social body, different normative definitions of public and private spaces became evident.

Elias makes clear that the focus on the education of a modern social self was the body in its entirety – its outward appearance through dress, its placement in social situations and its deportment in the activities necessary for its health, rest, nourishment, ablution and, especially, bodily excretion. Distinctions were made also between the *spaces* in which the display and functions of the body were appropriately undertaken. The bedroom, for example, was before this period a public space, rather like a sitting room in modern households. Inhabitants of the bed were not necessarily confined to sexual partners, especially in inns, but also in private houses. Before these early modern changes, it would not be uncommon to be expected, in either context, to share one's bed with a stranger of either sex. The rescrutinizing of this social contract signalled a new relationship between the body and social order. It also signified a shift in the dominant authority over the body, from the Church to secular educators. A new sanction accompanied this shift, where rituals of public humiliation and penance were exchanged for the internalized emotion of shame. It was the knowledge of the existence of rules shared by all which engendered these emotions.

The effectiveness of these rules for uses of the body depended on the new awareness of self. *Civilité* gave rise to 'a new stage of courtesy and its representation [in which] one is to some extent obliged to observe, to look about oneself and pay attention to people and their motives. In this, a new form of relationship of man to man, a new form of integration is announced' (Elias 1982: 63). People were bound to each other in society not by custom or duty but by their mutual expectations of certain modes of behaviour. If individuals were required by these new codes to observe others, they could not escape awareness of how they themselves were using their bodies. Self-surveillance was thus a crucial and new aspect of *civilité*. 'What was born in this period was not "selfhood" but the modern idea of corporeality' (Sawday 1997: 48).

Humanism, the body and society: the new anatomy

Dispel from your mind the thought that an understanding of the human body in every aspect of its structure can be given in words; the more thoroughly you describe the more you will confuse . . . I advise you not to trouble with words unless you are speaking to blind men. (Leonardo da Vinci)

The meanings of the terms anatomy and physiology are today taken for granted, and these scientific disciplines form the core component of the training of modern medical practitioners. But this is a relatively new approach to medical knowledge and practice. It was in the early modern period that anatomy and physiology became a modern science. For millennia before, medical knowledge was more like philosophy. Galen of Pergamum (129–201) was the foremost authority and had been for more than a thousand years. Galen was among the first to dissect animals and to make careful records of his observations of internal structures. However, his descriptions of the human body contained some remarkable errors, for they were based on dissections of pigs and monkeys rather than of humans. The beliefs of humanism and natural philosophy provided the impetus for crucial developments in medical science. Prohibitions against human dissections were lifting from the thirteenth century onwards, and the combination of these changes marked the 'beginning of [an] anatomical Renaissance' (Cunningham 1997: 3).

Humanism's revival of the traditions of ancient medicine provided one impetus for this development. But the beliefs of natural philosophy meant that the establishment of a visible science of the body also entailed a challenge to the long-standing fear of the body, alive or dead, which the Church nurtured. Humanism's most influential claim was that God had fashioned every part of the body with a specific and complementary function (Labisch 1992: 53). In this, natural philosophy directly challenged the idea of the body as flawed and possessed by evil after the fall, and did so in ways that invited a new understanding of divine purpose. The body was intended by God to be healthy and harmonious, and determining the purpose of its components was therefore God's will. This must be the foundation for a humanist medical science; by understanding the divine purpose of the body's complexities, physicians could map the mechanisms of harmony that in illness became disturbed. Direct observation would yield the true purpose, through seeing and therefore understanding. This search for a rational knowledge of the body lent a new legitimation to the dissection of human bodies. The objective was to establish the function of the bodily parts and their interconnection and through this to understand their dysfunction in illness. This secular understanding challenged the long-standing view that disease was a punishment for moral transgressions. Now understood as a receptacle, the body had no inherent moral characteristics – specifically not those of sin and corruption. Nor, following this new understanding, could the body be influenced by the mind. The medieval belief, for example, that a woman's fantasy or vision at the moment of conception could lead to the birth of a deformed foetus was rendered nonsensical in this new approach. The most famous figure in this movement was Andreas Vesalius (1514–1564), a Flemish physician who produced an accurate visual representation as well as a verbal description of observed bodily phenomena. He employed one of Titian's students to draw his findings in depictions as accurate as they were artistically beautiful. The drawings of his dissections were engraved on woodblocks and reproduced in his major work, *De humani corporis fabrica libri septem* (The Seven Books on the Structure of the Human Body), commonly known as the *Fabrica*, which was printed in 1543.

This new enthusiasm for anatomy and physiology was not restricted to practitioners of medicine. There was a general fascination with the body and its accurate representation. Leonardo da Vinci dissected thirty corpses and noted 'abnormal anatomy'; Michelangelo, too, performed a number of dissections. Earlier, in the thirteenth century, Frederick II ordered that the bodies of two executed criminals be delivered every two years to the medical schools, one of which was at Salerno, for an 'Anatomica Publica', which every physician was obliged to attend. These public dissections were held in a makeshift or purpose-built arena – the origin of the operating theatre – with an audience of students, physicians, priests and teachers. The results were reproduced in visual texts, often drawing on the iconography of classical artistic representations (Gilman 1989; Laqueur 1990). Through these channels, 'medicine started to break the chains of religion [and] started to create its own field of activity' (Labisch 1992: 89). Thousands of dissections were carried out in the medical schools and university precincts of Western Europe between the sixteenth and eighteenth centuries.

The view that observation yields full understanding offered a powerful argument against the idea of the flesh as essentially evil. Natural philosophy supported and nurtured the possibility and moral value of individual management and control of the body, as well as of its perfectibility. It disrupted the pattern of religious authority over the body and undermined the prevailing mysticism and fear surrounding its workings. From 'bedevilled flesh' to 'manageable machine', humanism and natural philosophy beliefs loosened the command of the Church over the social as well as the individual body. These advances in knowledge did not signal an end to authority over the body. The commitment of humanism and natural philosophy to enlightenment and education accorded new social prestige to expertise. The possession of privileged knowledge gave voice to a new moral authority, and new mouths through which it was articulated. Though old negative meanings had been successfully challenged, the body and its functions retained a social and political significance. 'The interests of the scientific community were not arbitrary: anatomists focused attention on those parts of the body that were to become politically significant' (Scheibinger 1987: 42). It was in this early modern period that attention turned again to the distinctions between male and female, this time relying on the science of anatomy and physiology to deliver incontrovertible truths.

It would be a mistake, however, to assume that humanism and natural philosophy were entirely successful in modernizing beliefs and behaviours in early modern Europe. Nor could it be claimed that these ideologies tamed the fears and insecurities that characterized medieval societies. First, the period was riven by violent and often deadly conflicts between the established Roman Church and the Protestant reformers of Christianity. The radical elements within humanism, in particular their direct challenge to the infallibility of the Roman Church, led some prominent humanists to be viewed as heretics. The calm and measured surface of Renaissance humanism contrasted with the nature of punishments, especially for heresy. Second, the condition of 'melancholy' was a widespread and even fashionable phenomenon of the period. The sufferers were thought to have brought this condition on themselves by allowing their reason to be overcome by passion and excess of indulgence. The resultant guilt caused them to withdraw further from the world. While it may have been experienced in physical terms, melancholy was indicative of moral dislocation from society. An increase in suicide in this period further supported prevailing concerns about the reality of this illness and its cure. Robert Burton's *The Anatomy of Melancholy* (1621) 'went through five editions before the author's death in 1640' (Delumeau 1990: 169). This hugely detailed work addressed all aspects of human life and their connections with the pandemic condition of melancholia. It also served as a 'self-help' manual, which detailed not only the causes of but also ways to avoid the condition.

But the clearest indication of the underlying insecurity of the period was the witch-hunts of early modern Europe. Persons who practised magic and claimed connections with the supernatural had a history as long as human society, and usually occupied a marginal position in social ranking. The persecution of heretics was not new. Periodic directives from papal authorities ordered the identification of heretical practices, and among these was the worship of the devil. But the witch-hunts of the early modern period had distinctive features. First, though there were some variations from country to country, witch-hunts occurred in cycles over a 300-year period – from the mid-fifteenth to the mid-eighteenth century. Second, though the underlying justification for these persecutions was religious heresy, as many secular as ecclesiastical authorities were involved. Finally, the punishments were especially and distinctively horrific and painful. The extremes of torture and the utter inescapability of the charge suggest a logic that goes beyond the simple need to remove destructive elements from society. The torture and often dismemberment of the body is indicative of a belief in diabolic possession, intensified by inherent tendencies of the uncontrollable flesh. Although children, men and animals were subjected to charges and punishment, women, both old and young, usually single or widowed, were by far the most often accused and put to death. The bull of Pope Innocent VIII (1484) specifically reminded its readers that women had always been susceptible to temptation, since the Garden of Eden, and that this weakness was frequently expressed through sexual depravity. The document gave official papal sanction to the publication *Malleus maleficarum* (1486) by two friars who were also professors of theology: Heinrich Kramer and James Sprenger.

This text contained detailed descriptions of what acts were considered to be proof of witchcraft. Apart from the first requirement, that the individual had denied the tenets of the Catholic faith, the questions related to acts and spells which weakened men and rendered them impotent or castrated, copulation with the devil, induced miscarriages or murdered children. Once an individual had been accused of witchcraft, the only outcome was torture and death. But it wasn't just the Church that was involved with the witch-hunts. Successive English monarchs passed statutes, beginning with Henry VIII in 1542 and ending with James I in 1602. The 1602 Act was not to be repealed until 1736, the last witch being executed in Scotland ten years earlier. That these statutes reflected a political advantage, perhaps diversionary, in these persecutions can be demonstrated in other European contexts. Maybe for different motives, both Church and state legitimated what was effectively the systematic terror, torture and murder of thousands of individuals, mainly women, in a climate of mass hysteria.

The most remarkable feature of the witch-hunts was that they coincided with the ascendance of humanism. The beliefs that underpinned the persecution of witches are, at first sight, directly opposed to those of humanism. Indeed, leading humanists, for example, Erasmus, spoke out against these activities, claiming that the accused were not dangerous heretics whose alliance with the devil gave them superhuman powers, but simply individuals who had knowledge of magic. Levack (1995) argues that this view represented the weakness of humanism's counter-claims to the witch-hunts. For, although they opposed the activities morally and logically, there remained a prevailing belief in magic and the existence of the devil that made effective argument against the persecution difficult. The reasons for the witch-hunts occurring at this time are argued by scholars to have multiple sources. First, they cite the changeable and unpredictable material conditions under which people lived. Endemic disease was rife. Famines were not uncommon. The shifts in the economic base from entrenched feudalism to early capitalism meant that poverty was an ever-present threat. Subtler but possibly more influential factors related to demographic trends. Numbers of unmarried women and widows expanded in the early modern period. Such women were not immediately subject to the control of husbands or fathers and as such were seen to be more susceptible to temptation, especially of the sexual kind. In the changing world, where old social structures were beginning to weaken, the 'loose woman' in all senses of the term posed a threat to an already unstable social order.

Religion and sexual behaviour

> Two crucial intellectual and political revolutions, humanism and the Reformation, contributed to a radical structuring of moral and public life. (Aughterson 1995: 9)

At the core of the Reformation was the challenge by Martin Luther (1483–1546) and John Calvin (1509–1564) to the idea of the infallibility of the Roman Church's leader and the essential role of priests as the gateway to salvation in the confessionals. From different directions, these great theologians and scholars passionately maintained that God and only God could pardon sins and grant salvation. The true Protestant was the one who heard and responded to their internal 'God' – their conscience. Two things followed. First, believers were directly responsible for their immortal soul, so attention could never be deflected from the task. Second, the body was (again) the enemy – as it had been in the first centuries of Christianity. The teaching of Martin Luther, and even more so of John Calvin, emphasized the view that the body was 'damned before it was born' by the original sin. As such, it was prone to all forms of sinfulness simply by virtue of being alive. This was to become the major point of battles between Christian humanists and the European Lutherans and English Puritans. Both preached fearsome warnings about the inherent wickedness of the body and mind. Like Augustine, Luther argued that Adam and Eve were in control of their sensual bodies before the fall, but, through their disobedience, their senses were debased and they lost their ability for self-control and reason. The ease with which sexual desire was experienced was proof of this. 'Should you pray till you can speak no more; should you sigh to the breaking of your loynes; should every word be a sigh and every sigh a tear; and every tear a drop of blood, you would never be able to recover that grace that you lost in Adam' (Christopher Love (1618–1651), quoted in Delumeau 1990: 501).

However, the new faith had a more positive view of the desire and pleasure experienced in the act of procreation. Luther taught that through sexual intercourse man became one with God (Turner 1987: 76). Marriage offered the possibility of a 'little paradise', a 'kind of heaven on earth' (quoted in ibid.: 75). Enjoyable sex was not sinful, but a way of celebrating the creation of God. Despite the approval of sexual love between man and woman, Protestant teaching enhanced and encouraged the superiority of the husband over his wife. 'He and he alone was commander of his wife, author of his children, priest, confessor and the pope' (King 1991: 38). Christian sexuality, properly and lovingly managed in marriage, under the tutelage of the father of the house, and performed at the proper times, was 'seasoned, natural and sanctified' (Turner 1987: 77). Marriage manuals commonly laid down 'rules of engagement' in marital pleasures. Sex could not be too frequent; excessive nudity should be avoided; couples should adopt only one position, with the woman below, the man on top. Ejaculation outside the vagina was sinful and any other expression of desire or source of pleasure was morally intolerable. Milton sums up the measured love and passion that was Protestant sexuality, in which humanist sentiments promoted the joys of marital sex while keeping alive the dangers of misdirected lust:

> Hail wedded love, mysterious law, true source
> In Paradise of all things common else.
> By thee adulterous lust was driv'n from men
> Among the bestial herds to range; by thee
> Founded in reason, loyal, just, and pure,
> Relations dear, and all the charities
> Of father, son and brother first were known.
> (*Paradise Lost* (1667), bk IV, 750–6)

The story of Adam and Eve was equally important in the Protestant sexual morality. Luther's insistence on the fact of sex in Paradise gave intercourse a divine significance. However, pleasure was not the purpose of sex but its accompaniment. Though sex offered a way to complete God's plan that his creations become 'one flesh', its pleasure must be under conscious control and with a specific purpose. The distinction between this and Augustine's recipe for reasoned sex was that Protestants claimed that pleasure in sex was part of God's purpose. These new claims provided the foundations for the paradigm of heterosexual marital coitus. Milton's description of love without passion typifies the distinction:

> Perpetual fountain of domestic sweets,
> Whose bed is undefiled and chaste pronounced . . .
> Here Love his golden shaft employs, here lights
> His constant lamp, and waves his purple wings,
> Reigns here and revels not in the bought smile
> Of harlots, loveless, joyless, unendeared,
> Casual fruition . . . (*Paradise Lost*, bk IV, 757–77)

Here Milton summarizes the key features of Puritan sex: marital, private, tempered, neither frivolous nor spontaneous. It is sex undertaken in the right manner, context and time and with the right motives. But Puritan writing was not blind to the dangers of sexual passion and uncontrolled desires. The Puritan Philip Stubbes (1555–*c*.1610) paints a picture of this danger and its social consequences in his *Anatomie of Abuses* (1583). For Stubbes the greatest of all sins was 'adultery and whoredom'. The Catholic confessionals and even the Church courts had long treated these crimes too leniently, and, he says, their penance is insufficient and ineffective: 'For what great thing is it to go one or three dayes in a white sheete before the congregation, and that sometimes not past an hour or two in one day, having their usual garment underneath as commonly they have?' (Stubbes 1877: 98). Confession and public penance was a veil behind which lust and desire continued to flourish unchallenged and uncontrolled. Stubbes's recommendation for punishment is that 'those who have committed the horrifying fact of whordome, adulterie, incest, or fornication' (ibid.: 99) should either be made to drink poison or be branded with a hot iron in a place visible to the public eye, so they can be distinguished from the virtuous.

Another feature of this period supports the growing social significance of marital sex, especially among the mass of the population. The 'Bawdy Courts', so named because they were particularly concerned with sexual transgressions, emerged with the rise of private confessions of sins in the late thirteenth century. With a brief inter-ruption, between 1641 and 1660, they operated at their peak between 1450 and 1640 (Hair 1972: 24–5). While the cases they dealt with often had to do with property settlements on death or divorce, the courts also heard accusations of sexual transgressions. Punishment, like the misdemeanours, was generally mild, involving some sort of personal penance, though often in public. Physical chastisement was rare. The most common sexual offence, next to adultery, was 'pre-nuptial fornication'. This aspect of sexual behaviour was a new preoccupation. In medieval times, pre-nuptial sex was an expected preliminary to marriage among the majority of the popula-tion. But the number of adultery and pre-marital sex cases brought before the courts between the fifteenth and the seventeenth century illustrates the growing importance of marriage as a public and social institution. The social standing of those called before the courts indicates another innovation: the regulation of the sexual behaviour of the 'common people'. In both respects, the Bawdy Courts marked a concern with shaping new boundaries for a common sexual morality that applied across all classes. They were to continue to do so, sporadically, till the latter years of the eighteenth century.

But adultery was not just an issue for religion. In England, the Commonwealth (Adultery) Act (1650) was expressly aimed at 'sup-pressing the detestable sins of incest, adultery and fornication' (Thomas 1978: 257). It laid down the death penalty for adultery and incest, while fornication (defined as any sex outside marriage) was punished by three months' imprisonment. Brothel keepers were whipped, branded and gaoled for three years, and executed if they reoffended. But perhaps the most significant aspect of this Act was that it identified adultery as the most serious offence. Women who expressed their sexuality within marriage under the confines of Puritan expectations were the source of harmony and peace. Women who expressed their sexuality outside of marriage, especially if they were married, were considered the most socially dangerous individuals. Adulterous women suffered the death sentence under the Commonwealth (Adultery) Act. Men who were unfaithful did not. Though 'barely put into practice for its ten years' life', this legislation was 'unique in English history, to put the full machinery of the state behind the enforcement of sexual morality' (ibid.). However, that it was passed at all again indicates the impor-tant role marriage had come to play in the taming of women's sexu-ality, and in establishing a new foundation for social as well as sexual order.

Heterosexuality, homosexuality and new
boundaries of desire

It was in the aftermath of the Reformation that binary categories of desire appeared that identified and fixed opposing categories of erotic practice and which defined their social acceptability. There were three aspects to this process. First, it was in the seventeenth century that sexual acts between men were morally as well as legally outlawed. Though sex between men and women had always been valued more highly as the norm, homoerotic encounters between men, especially in the upper classes, were tolerated. Under the Commonwealth Act, sodomitic practices were for the first time designated as a specific crime. Until this time, 'sodomy' had been more loosely defined, being a more general term for any unnatural couplings between men and women, men and men, or men and animals. Second, sexual acts became directly associated with concepts of masculinity and femininity. Boundaries between appropriate male and female behaviour were drawn, involving reference to uses of the body in behaviour and in dress. Third, the conditional promotion of marital sex renewed interest in defining a specific female sexuality.

Outside the religious framework, other voices of authority promoted the physical, emotional and social advantages of marital sex. Surgeons and physicians wrote about the necessity of sexual arousal in the woman, giving detailed accounts of foreplay and of concoctions from plants and animal organs to ensure the maximization of sexual pleasure (Laqueur 1990: 102–3). In these early stages of the modern medical profession the subject of physical pleasure was not considered undignified, as it was to become in succeeding centuries. Concern with and methods to enhance sexual pleasure in both men and women were also evident in the first published works of early modern midwives. This preoccupation may seem inconsistent with the religious ambivalence about sex and its expression. One explanation for this might be the links made in medical circles between physical health and the regular relief of sexual desire. But as the religious authorities continued their support for sexual pleasure within narrow confines, so their secular counterparts placed restrictions on how this release should be obtained. Medical tracts, for example, supported the views of religious writers that coitus *in retro* (entry from behind) was bestial and therefore unnatural. Vaginal penetration was the only acceptable means of releasing sexual tension. To do otherwise would result in deformed or deficient offspring (Matthews Greico 1993: 70–1).

In this period the view that male and female shared the same sexual anatomy and physiology still prevailed. Logically, therefore, there could be no denial of the equal potential for pleasure in both. Though the 'one-sex' understanding of physical sexuality had to recognize the need for women to experience the same pleasures as men, the conditions under which they did so undermined any acknowledgement of autonomous female sexuality. One can see examples of this in the explicit Renaissance erotica and pornography reproduced by Frantz (1989). In widely available illustrations of acrobatic couplings, the centrepiece is consistently the erect phallus whose goal is the receptive woman's vagina. In each case it is the male who is the principal actor, if not the aggressor, and the message is clear – the penis is the author of all erotic pleasure. While medical discourses on sex revolved around the benefits of sex between men and women for a healthy mind and body, Renaissance pornographers depicted sex between men and women as an exercise in erotic domination. Notwithstanding their distinct motives, both medical and popular depictions of acceptable sex in the early modern period operated to control sexual behaviour in ways that were different from the medieval period. Emphasis was on an education rather than punishment. The existence of sexual desire was accepted, even welcomed. The focus of attention was now to offer a justification for specific uses of the body, while at the same time identifying practices that fell outside this normative framework as socially disruptive.

It is commonplace now to identify the categories male and female by their possession of distinct and different genitalia and sexual anatomy, though this does not determine either sexual identity or the direction of sexual desire. In the early modern period, changing social structures, especially in relation to education of women and the meaning of marriage, intensified interest in defining distinct identities of masculine and feminine – of 'manly men' and 'womanly women'. The belief of natural philosophy that direct observation would yield truth renewed a focus on the body to establish verifiable distinctions between male and female. The one-sex model that prevailed did not recognize the fixed state of bodily sexuality. This instability of the sexual organs is illustrated in the anxiety expressed over the possibility that one sex could 'become' another, often as a result of some minor physical trauma. Across Europe, there were widely circulated cases of individuals who were born women and became men. In one, a girl 'sprouted' a penis when she began to menstruate. This may well have been a clitoris, enlarged at maturity, but this specifically female organ was not recognized as such at the time. In another case, 'a young man in Reims who lived as and anatomically seemed to be a girl until the age of fourteen when he/she, "while disporting him[/her]self and frolicking" with a chambermaid, suddenly acquired male genital parts' (Laqueur 1990: 126). The factual accuracy of these tales is not of concern here. They convey a growing anxiety about the instability of the sexual body, on the one hand, and the need for it to be fixed, on the other. Not surprisingly, given the shared sexual organs, no anatomical male, that is, with external organs, ever reverted to his lesser form, a woman. As a contemporary commentator observed, 'We therefore never find in any true story that any man ever became a woman, because Nature tends always towards what is most perfect and not, on the contrary, to perform in such a way that what is perfect should become imperfect' (Gaspard Bauhin, *Theatrum anatomicum* (1604), quoted in ibid.: 127).

Given the unreliability of the body clearly to define male and female, attention turned to forms of *behaviour* that were considered appropriate to 'manly men' and 'womanly women'. Just as accounts of sexual change focused on women who became men, so in the early seventeenth century it was women who dressed or behaved 'like men' who received the most attention (McCormick 1997: 175). The development of new printing technology early in the period had encouraged the wider circulation of popular commentary, through the circulation of handbills, or tracts. The seventeenth-century tract *Hic mulier, or, The Man-Woman* (1620) is subtitled: *being a Medicine to cure the Coltish Disease of the Staggers in the Masculine-Feminines of our times* (Henderson and McManus 1985: 265). In this as in many similar publications, there is a sense of urgency and deep unease about women who try to be men. These concerns were intensified by reference to more traditional characterizations of women. In *Hic mulier*, for example, women were described as inconstant, unpredictable and unstable. Anxiety about the changing times and the accompanying instability is clearly evident:

> For since the days of Adam women were never so Masculine: Masculine in their genders . . . from the Mother to the youngest daughter; Masculine in number, from one to multitudes; Masculine in Case, even from the head to the foot; Masculine in Mood, from bold speech to impudent action; and Masculine in Tense, for without redress they were, are, and would still be most Masculine, most mankind, and most monstrous. (quoted in McCormick 1997: 177)

These attacks were encouraged by growing evidence of women's literacy and intellectual strength. Education and book-reading increased the dangers of becoming this dangerous and unnatural 'man/woman'. Women were warned not to behave like fictional 'strong' women, especially those who opposed their husbands (Henderson and McManus 1985: 270–1). In addition to being unfeminine, 'unwomanly women' encouraged tendencies to sexual depravity. 'Keep those parts concealed from the eyes that may not be touched by the hands. . . . For those things belong to this wanton and lascivious delight and pleasure' (ibid.: 272). At the same time, women who emulated men in dress or behaviour posed a direct sexual threat to men, tempting them beyond reason. 'I think they would as nearly become men indeed, as they now degenerate from sober godly women, in wearing this wanton lewd kind of attire, proper only to man' (Stubbes 1877: 73). Even in these early stages, the modern construction of 'heterosexuality', as both category and identity, depended as much on establishing definitions of femininity as it did on directions of sexual desire.

In contrast to this preoccupation with fixing boundaries, Renaissance literature and art freely represented same-sex desire between both men and women. However, Traub has argued that this did not indicate acceptance but rather that these figures were used as 'cautionary tales', to indicate the extent to which the 'man/woman' was a social misfit (Traub 1996: 23). The most severe judgement was reserved for women who emulated men sexually. Women accused of using dildos in sexual acts suffered severe treatment: 'One of them was sentenced to be burned alive, and the other hanged, punishments dictated, not by their sexuality as such but their transvestism and the use of the dildo' (Dollimore 1993: 284). Male–male sex also came under scrutiny, but the issue was more complex. In Elizabethan times, male friendship, sometimes even openly erotic, was part of the social fabric. These were no hidden liaisons but open, explicit and even sought-after relationships of patronage between social equals. Physical intimacy between men was a necessary public sign of the stability of networks of power, grounded in the concept of 'personal service' (Bray 1990: 7). Powerful men were expected to express their protection in openly kissing and fondling their favourites at social gatherings, while indicating the degree of their emotional intimacy and trust by marking them as their 'bedfellows' (ibid.: 4).

These were transitional times, and such examples should not be interpreted as straightforward acceptance of homoerotic desire. Before the seventeenth century, the adult male who had sex with both young men and women was admired in popular texts as being the sexual essence of masculinity. But these men were not necessarily positive role models, nor were their activities sanctioned in mainstream society. Thus, while not openly condemned, such individuals were marginalized figures in the social order (Trumbach 1989: 130–1). In this period, sodomy retained its long-standing associations with bestial sexuality, but now an accusation was also seen as a weapon against political enemies. 'There was, particularly in the sixteenth and throughout most of the seventeenth centuries, a free-floating association between sodomy, religious heresy, and political treachery' (Bray 1982: 21–3). Leading sexual historians such as Bray, Katz (1994) and Davenport-Hines (1991) have argued that the Buggery Act of 1533 was more indicative of the ongoing struggle between Church and state than a direct attack on homosexuality, as it would become (Katz 1994: 47). But a significant element in this identification in statute was that 'buggery' replaced the much older vice of 'sodomy'. The term was henceforth to apply specifically to male–male sexual penetration, thus marking the beginning of its criminalization and its secular denunciation. The process of establishing sexual boundaries for 'manly men' entailed political as much as moral considerations, and reflected the difference in social privilege and power between men and women. But the urgency was as evident and the outcome the same.

Condemnation of male–male sexual activity continued through the seventeenth century in this transitional stage of modernizing sexuality. High-ranking men, including peers of the realm and bishops, were publicly arraigned and prosecuted for acts of sodomy (Bray 1990: 13–14). In 1631 the Earl of Castelhaven was executed for rape, adultery and sodomy. This case was highly controversial and remains a topic of much historical interest, since it involved sexual relationships which crossed both class and gender expectations. Accusations of sodomy were even made against James I and his companions (ibid.: 13). These accusations may well have been informed as much by political as moral motivation. But the high profile given to details of the sexual behaviour cited illustrates heightened anxiety about acceptable uses of the body among 'manly men'. During the course of the seventeenth century the political significance of the act of sodomy began to wane. Instead of being a marker of political marginality, sodomy began to be associated with the use of the body by a type of person, marked not by unnatural *acts*, but by unnatural, and often also politically seditious, *individuals*. Discourses on sexuality continued to emphasize the degree to which the sexual body could be controlled by individual will. As with women, attention turned to male dress and behaviour as indicators of the 'inner person' and their sexuality. The ground was being prepared for the exclusion of the figure of the sodomite, who would later be characterized as the fop. These were individuals who, by their dress and erotic expression, represented a threat to the successful distinction of a hetero-sexually masculine man. More so than the figure of 'the tribade', the sodomite was clearly identified and suffered more exclusion in the making of the binary norm.

The idea of 'sexuality', as we understand it today, developed within the beliefs and arguments of humanism and natural philosophy. The body was stripped of much of its mystery by being opened and its components rendered visible. The sexual force within it, formerly represented as sinful lust, was now more directly associated with parts of the body, their appearance and function. But there was another aspect of sexuality that was being fashioned in this period. Its meaning depended on clearly visible boundaries between cate-gories of desire. The emerging distinctions masculine/male, femi-nine/female, and their accompanying sexual behaviours, were the foundation of a new binary framework. In establishing the visible appearance of manly men and womanly women, the 'other' of these categories came into clear focus.

Conclusion

The early modern period was, like all historical periods, an epoch of contradictions. But it was remarkable for forward-looking energy on the one hand and a powerful nostalgia for the past on the other. The tensions between the two created, in retrospect, a focusing lens through which to examine the birth of modern ideas and values, espe-cially those associated with sex and the body. Many beliefs and prac-tices are quite alien to modern minds and experience – for example, the belief in magic and evil forces reflected in the witch-hunts. But the epoch offers a bridge between the world of the Middle Ages and those characteristics we recognize as modern in the construction of sexual desires and pleasures of modernity. And it was perhaps because the early modern period was so riven with uncertainties that the idea of self provided the foundation for a material connection between sexual desires and the sexual body. The internal mechanisms for management of these that lay at the centre of humanism and Protestantism provided the raw materials for a modern understand-ing of 'sexuality' as a synthesis of the desiring body and the conscious self. The intertwining of sexual expression in the worldly institutions of religious faith, of marriage and of medical practice began to iden-tify the importance of sexuality and its expression for the secular social order. Central to this understanding was a new division that fused sex, gender and sexuality – the binary model. In place of religious confessionals and public penance, new social rules detailed the proper use of the social body in an increasingly complex social structure. The growing distinction between private and public spheres provided secular grounds for a moral demarcation of bodily intimacies, transgressions of which were increasingly accompanied by emotions of shame and embarrassment. Spheres of intimacy were constructed in these discourses, within which new mechanisms of self-surveillance and management began to emerge underpinned by subjective feelings of shame and embarrassment. The two great movements of the period, Protestantism and humanism, in different ways, gave the body an earthly significance denied it by the medieval Church. The period marked a shift also in the modes of viewing, understanding, categorizing and managing the sources of desire and pleasure in ways that were recognizably modern.

FURTHER READING

Ramie, A. (ed.) (1988) *Renaissance Humanism: Foundations, Forms and Legacy.* Philadelphia: University of Pennsylvania Press.

McCormick, I. (ed.) (1997) *Secret Sexualities: A Sourcebook of 17th and 18th Century Writings*. London and New York: Routledge.

Stone, L. (1990) *The Family, Sex and Marriage in England, 1500–1800.* Abridged edn, Harmondsworth: Penguin.

Veyne, P. (ed.) (1987) *A History of Private Life*, Vol. 1: *From Pagan Rome to Byzantium*. Cambridge, MA, and London: Belknap Press.

5

Pleasure and Desire in the Age of Modernity

Introduction

In the city of reason, there were to be no winding roads, no cul de sacs and no unattended sites left to chance – and thus no vagabonds, vagrants or nomads. (Bauman 1992: xv)

While there has been some disagreement about the timescale of modernity (most commonly the seventeenth to the nineteenth century) there is little debate about the scope of its social consequences. Both historians and sociologists agree that modernity refers to a revolutionary shift in economics, politics, society and culture. The key features of this historical and social process are industrialization, urbanization, secularization, and increasingly complex specialization in social roles and social functions. The driving force behind these rapid developments was the emergence of capitalism. The replacement of the feudal with the capitalist epoch involved changes that encompassed political, social, economic and ideological aspects of life. Krishnan Kumar has properly called this 'the Great Transformation' (Kumar 1978). The revolutionary advances in technologies of production demanded the reorganization of the mass population – in how they worked, how they lived and, as importantly, what they believed in and valued. The mechanisms that achieved these wide-ranging changes developed at varying speeds over the centuries and across countries, sometimes quickly and sometimes slowly. But machines were not, of course, the motors of social change. It was human ingenuity and imagination that developed innovative and more productive ways to utilize the forces of nature.

Despite increases in efficiency and profitability these developments also intensified the misery of the majority of the population, for capitalism demanded a very different mode of life. The age-old source of 'cottage' income and the rights of common land were removed and people were forced to sell their labour in order to live. The shift from country villages to fast-growing cities eroded traditional family structures, modes of work and ways of life. As a result, family and community structures that had for centuries provided a framework for a relatively stable, if impoverished, existence became less effective in the maintenance of social and moral order. Individuals were no longer subject to the scrutiny and control of family traditions and relationships as they joined the mass anonymity of growing cities. Old support systems, whether involving feudal obligations or family relationships, could no longer be relied upon to protect from starvation or illness (see, for example, Dickens's *Oliver Twist*). Urbanization also eroded the moral fabric, referred to by Emile Durkheim (1858–1917) as 'mechanical solidarity'. This, Durkheim tells us, in his still relevant analysis of modernity, was a solidarity of sameness. Old moral codes were no longer as effective in the anonymous and fragmented urban setting. Differences between individuals, in lifestyles, skills and sense of identity, were encouraged by another Durkheimian concept – the division of labour in society. This referred not only to the ways in which material things were produced, but also to the means by which individual difference was produced and rendered acceptable. Modernity fostered, and indeed depended for its survival on, this new form of social bonding that recognized differences between individuals, in the workplace, in the home and in wider society. This important identifying feature of modernizing societies provided the framework for new cement that bound societies and individuals together, one based on difference, not sameness (*The Division of Labour in Society*, 1893).

Throughout the eighteenth century there were signs that these changes accelerated, and by the early nineteenth century the negative consequences of rapid social change began to be evident. The first phenomenon that caused alarm was the overcrowded and unsanitary living and working conditions for the mass population of the industrial cities. The dreadful circumstances of the urban poor, which involved children from the age of eight years working up to fifteen hours a day, continued until the last three decades of the nineteenth century, before the passing of the Factory Acts. Domestic overcrowding in houses increased the mortality rate from epidemic diseases, especially that of children. Women's health was further compromised by the lack of access to birth control, while both women and men sickened and died from work-related injury and disease. As the living and working conditions of the poor began to attract professional and political attention, so did the implication of these conditions for sexual immorality. Characterized as it was by rapid change, modernity was also distinguished by the urgent need for reorganization of mechanisms of social order, these being forced to take account of changes in social conditions as well as social relationships.

Two important preconditions for a new social order were necessary for this to be successfully accomplished. The first was 'secularization': the gradual weakening of the control of religion over the lives of the population. This did not mean, on an individual level, that people no longer held profound religious beliefs. The term refers to the emergence of a new set of moral imperatives and the transfer of authority over populations from priests to professionals and specialists – legal practitioners, administrators and medical practitioners as well as scientists of the natural world – whose authority was underpinned by particular knowledge and skills. Secularization directly equated knowledge with a new form of power: power to explore, to record, to classify and, where necessary, to educate and discipline. The second precondition was linked to the first: the rise of science as the new foundation for explaining the rights and responsibilities of humans in the world of nature. Christianity had claimed that God placed humans in a ready-made world. The rules by which they lived in this world were divine rules, unchanging and not open to negotiation.

This conception of humanity and its place in the natural world was challenged and reversed by the thinkers of the Enlightenment. The *philosophes* of the late seventeenth and the eighteenth century, building on the arguments of humanism, replaced the notion of divine order with one achieved by human ingenuity and effort. The Enlightenment project was underpinned by a new faith – that the world of nature offered the only reliable prototype of harmony and order. Observation and systematic collection of knowledge replaced unquestioning belief in the search for universal truths about humans and their world. The role of humans, as the superior constituent of this natural order, was to observe and classify the natural environment and the forces that operated within it. As an integral part of the natural order, and by virtue of their ability to interact creatively with their natural environment, they also held the power to contain and direct these forces. This conviction fuelled the expansion of the scientific study of all aspects of human existence. Though drawing on humanist traditions, the Enlightenment version laid more emphasis on the instability and unpredictability of man in the world of nature. Humanism, as we have seen, believed that the world was divinely ordered and humans merely the informed curators.

Thinkers and writers such as Rousseau, Locke and de Tocqueville claimed that the notion of a preordained order was a fiction. The world of nature must be subjected to human effort to order and thereby direct natural forces for the good of humankind. While this new approach to the relationship between humans and their world released scientific endeavours from the constraints of blind faith, it also meant an end to the former sense of security. If no divine design existed to contain the complexities of life, then one had to be made and maintained by human effort. 'The . . . conviction that order can only be man-made, that is bound to remain an artificial imposition on the unruly natural state of things and humans, that for this reason it will forever remain vulnerable and in need of constant supervision and policing is the main (and indeed unique) distinguishing mark of modernity' (Bauman 1989: xv). Effective control depended not just on empirical knowledge about human behaviour and natural forces, but also on the development of the means by which to utilize the knowledge efficiently. This objective located the acquisition of knowledge at the centre of the new social order. Whether about health, living conditions or any other aspect of social behaviour, systematic collection was an essential element in systematic application. In relation to both, education and training of those studied was an essential element. 'People were not born into their places: they had to be trained, drilled or goaded into finding a place that fitted them and which they fitted' (ibid.).

This new aspect of social order demanded and aided by modernity entailed a new approach to the social world and its inhabitants, using methods that were already being employed in the study of the natural world. There were two approaches to practising the science of society – both born in the Enlightenment epoch. The first was to gather information about the social world that could be verified by empirically observed facts rather than faith. The most significant consequence was the focus on uses of the body considered to have the most negative impacts on social life. Accordingly, health and disease, reproduction, and criminal and, especially, sexual behaviour were subject to the most detailed investigation. Through this focus an orderly body occupied a central place in the modern social order. The ordered body was attained not through constraint or undifferentiated punishment but by education, which established alternative yet equally powerful equations between uses of the body and morality. The legitimation of this connection was now science, not religion. Social as well as medical knowledge established fixed categories that increased the effectiveness of this project. This moral order depended on a binary classification said to be 'an exercise of power and at the same time its disguise' (Bauman 1989: 14). The effectiveness of this exercise lay in the understanding of all social phenomena as 'either/or', a formulation that removed any flexibility of choice or understanding. The disguise lay in the fact that these fixed categories were claimed to be naturally ordained as well as scientifically verifiable.

In both senses, the binary now runs so deeply in our collective 'states of mind' that we feel insecure in its absence. We take for granted, even expect, that every aspect of material existence will be stamped clearly in this manner. The normal depends on the abnormal for its meaning; health depends on definitions of illness; reason on concepts of insanity. It is here that the moral core of the science of society lies. For the forces of evil have been replaced by the forces of 'disorder' – unreasoned, unnatural, diseased, uneducated – all 'others', moral hinterlands that serve as a reminder of the perilous 'other' within us. Through this dichotomy of all aspects of life we are, sometimes gently, sometimes forcibly, obliged to live within these definitions and their outcome, the modern social order. For [modernity demands] 'the suppression of the "natural" drives and the imposition of patterns of behaviour which ill fit human predisposition and offer only oblique outlets for instincts and passions' (Bauman 1989: 113). The second aspect of this process was the direction of uses of the body in relation to outcome. Without a preordained pattern defined by purpose, any use of the body would be irrational. Rationality – the conscious and reasoned orientation of human action to a preordained outcome – was the 'distinctive feature of modern Western social order' (Brubaker 1984: 9). Though more familiarly associated with economic behaviour, rationality was equally applied to the sensual body, and specifically to its response to desire. Through the 'rationalizing gaze' of the new figures of authority, physical needs and wants, like balances on a ledger, would be evaluated as to predictability of outcome, not the quality of the subjective experience.

All these features of modernity provided new grounds for concerns about, as well as definitions and scrutiny of, sexual behaviour. Concerns about reproductive sex were fed by rapidly increasing size and concentration of populations. There was recognition of the importance of both romantic and sexual love in the bourgeois family unit. In the public sphere, urbanization, and the sharp increase in population density, intensified the significance of the sexual behaviour of the 'masses'. Foucault's identification of 'domains' and 'figures' in the nineteenth century locates 'the other' at the centre of modernist strategies for directing sexual desires and their forms of expression (Foucault 1984). This dynamic did not, however, originate in the nineteenth but in the eighteenth century, articulated through the 'mixed feelings' about enlightened sexual pleasure which characterizes this period.

Natural bodies and natural pleasures: the joy of Enlightenment sex

The eighteenth century was an epoch that seemed to value and promote bodily, and especially sexual, pleasures like no other since the time of classical antiquity. The long-standing teachings of Christianity had established the moral and physical dangers associated with any experience of pleasure from sex, and fostered both fear and guilt about uses of the body for pleasure. In the seventeenth century there was a high level of sexual libertinism and even, in modern terminology, sexual perversity, but this was shot through with mixed feelings of guilt and the pleasure of the forbidden. The flowering, if that is the appropriate term, of explicit and decidedly phallocentric pornography in the seventeenth century was matched by anxieties about the consequences of such sinful behaviour. The positive re-evaluation of the forces of nature in the eighteenth century neutralized many of these misgivings about the 'wages of sin'. Desire and sensuality was now seen as proof that one's body was in harmony with the world of nature. Given the conviction that humans were the pre-eminent beings in this world, to ignore sensuality was to deny one's humanity and, more importantly, the superior status of humanity in nature. Animals react instinctively to sensations that are pleasant or unpleasant, as do human infants before 'the age of reason'. But the mature and educated individual, aware of self and of others, consciously reflects on the material sensations of worldly life and, in doing so, will act (in the pursuit of more pleasure and less pain) to adjust material existence to this end. This consciousness affirmed humans' dominion over themselves as well as their material world. 'Experience was all, and experience was derived from the senses and was mediated by the highly somatic mechanisms of pleasure and pain' (Rousseau 1991: 226–7). The role of reason in this restoration of the senses lay in the argument that bodily pleasures were not the original sin but the original innocence, and it was the duty of enlightened humanity to re-establish this essential goodness through what Gay has called 'passionate naturalism' (Gay 1967: 204). This obligation underpinned the political and social optimism of the

Enlightenment and gave new urgency to the education of both mind and body.

The Marquis de Sade took to its most extreme point in the last decades of the eighteenth century the view that humans were duty bound to explore and celebrate their sensuality, (Crosland 1991). This extraordinary individual taunted both the traditional establishment and the somewhat romanticized threads of passionate naturalism in both real and, after his imprisonment, fictional explorations of the limits of human capacity for sexualized pain and pleasure. Extreme though de Sade's activities were, they nevertheless served as a warning about the negative consequences of assuming that a judicious mix of education and social control would be sufficient to ensure a positive social outcome. For de Sade's works and the audience they found indicated the presence of another aspect of human nature with more disruptive and less controllable characteristics – the imagination and its susceptibility to moral corruption. These anxieties offer a way to understand how, in the climate that encouraged sensual experience and exploration, certain modes of expression were validated while others were outlawed. Phallocentric heterosexual exploits were lauded and encouraged, while same-sex desire was increasingly stigmatized. The joys of mutual orgasm were celebrated, while masturbation was increasingly pathologized, dangerous for both mind and body (Laqueur 2003). Finally, the arguments of radical naturalism implied that men and women equally were due full citizenship rights, but the literal application of this dictum threatened gender distinctions in both private and public spheres that were becoming more and more evident.

Despite these misgivings and modifications, the use of the body explicitly for sexual pleasure distinguishes this period as no other before it. Sexual pleasure was promoted within marriage but also widely tolerated outside it. Sexual fantasy was encouraged in popular literature as well as in widely available pornography. Notwithstanding fears about the perils of dismantling growing gender distinctions at the heart of the social order, women who partook of the sexual licence were praised and admired, while the active subversion of gendered behaviour and appearance was encouraged as legitimate entertainment and leisure. The still developing medical profession figured centrally in the legitimation of sexual pleasure, though with perhaps more misgivings about unauthorized uses of the body in its pursuit. But they were to establish a tradition of sex education for adults in the widely circulated manuals that in their content straddled the divide between the professional and the popular.

The distinctive feature of the Enlightenment was that pleasure was disengaged from concerns about social order and individual morality. Sexual pleasure was also uncoupled from legitimating frameworks of marriage and of procreation. Acceptable sex could be, and often was, fleeting, devoid of sentimental attachment, as often to be found in public spaces as in private settings. Norah Smith has shown that, in Scotland, weddings and even baptisms offered opportunities for orgiastic behaviour, which were enthusiastically embraced (Smith 1982: 58), while well-attended masquerade balls in public squares deliberately flouted gender conventions as they actively encouraged sexual titillation. Although these public celebrations often did not include actual sexual contact, their libidinous purpose was certainly recognized by moralists, who, unsuccessfully, sought to curtail them (Castle 1987: 156–81). In this period the distinction between those who sold sex publicly and confidently in fashionable areas, and those who indulged in brief and spontaneous couplings in parks, was often blurred. In both fiction and reality, however, it was the upper classes that disported themselves within this erotically charged climate. Servant girls and lusty young males were the subjects rather than the active partakers of this sexual freedom. Evidence from the court reports of adultery and other sexual crimes illustrates the licence with which aristocratic men and women availed themselves of the bodies of the 'masses' by virtue of their rank and status. Notwithstanding social rank, women who were sexually available were not, Porter argues, restricted to the ranks of prostitutes or poor young female workers (Porter 1982: 9–10). Until the close of the century, when anxieties over equal sexual licence began to produce a backlash on the erotic as well as the political freedom of women, sexual libertinism was not just the domain of men. This widening of erotic spheres was visible also in the clubs devoted to such diversions as flagellation and stylized group masturbation (see Smith 1982: 47–74, and Wagner 1987: 50–2).

What individuals did not or could not do in practice they could experience vicariously, and were encouraged to do so, through the widely available range of erotic literature, verse, cartoons and caricatures. English (as opposed to European or Eastern) pornography emerged first in the eighteenth century, which before the mid-century had to be imported from Italy or France (Stone 1990: 334), epitomized in Cleland's *Memoirs of a Woman of Pleasure* (1748). Though initially prosecuted as offensive to decency, this work signalled a widening of the market for texts that combined erotic fiction with lists of available prostitutes and their respective specialities. This evidence suggests, therefore, that the populace, or at least its more affluent members, were responding to the encouragement to enjoy sexual pleasure without constraint. There was a consistent literary presentation of the male as ever ready for sex and the female as sexually irresistible. Two works by Samuel Richardson (1681–1761), *Clarissa* (1747) and *Pamela, or, Virtue Rewarded* (1740), and *Moll Flanders* (1722) by Daniel Defoe (1660–1731) remain classics of heterosexually orientated erotic literature. Peter Wagner has provided a fascinating extension of sources of eighteenth-century erotica in his examination of trial reports for 'sexual crimes', a category much wider than in modern understanding, ranging from adultery to the rape of children. The combination of the criminal with the sexual was irresistible, and offered rich opportunities for the vicarious appetite. In cases where details were lacking, considerable editorial licence was taken in filling the erotic gaps. And, for the illiterate, and to intensify the voyeuristic content, reports were often lavishly illustrated (Wagner 1987: 126). Throughout the eighteenth century these reports did not wane in their popularity or in their production. 'No book is asked for more frequently in the leading libraries and the editions, reprints and extracts from them prove their popularity' (ibid.: 130–1).

Perhaps the most clear picture of the eighteenth-century version of sexual pleasure and its social implications can be found in the medical and quasi-medical texts, which, until the latter decades of the century, enthusiastically encouraged the enjoyment of the natural pleasures of sex. The medical profession in this period was not so strictly controlled by professional rules and boundaries as today. Medical texts were written for the general (literate) public as much as for fellow professionals. The sometimes blurred distinctions between trained and untrained practitioners were evident in the medical literature, where trained physicians and self-taught amateurs alike freely engaged in offering sexual advice that was both explicit and positive. It was this sometimes frivolous tone that distinguished such texts from the quality of their nineteenth-century successors. Advice ranged from the best methods for coital orgasm to the use of dildos, life-size dolls, potions and drugs, and especially flagellation to arouse and maintain the libido of both men and women (Wagner 1987: 46–64). But there were undercurrents which modified the libertarian stance, as Roy Porter's detailed analysis of the numerous editions of the most well known of these manuals, *Aristotle's Masterpiece* and *Tableau de l'amour conjugal*, illustrates (Porter and Hall 1995: 14–33). In the early eighteenth-century editions, the experience of sexual pleasure was the primary aim, while the context (marital or extra-marital) was a secondary consideration. As the century progressed, the 'proper place' for sexual enjoyment was increasingly the private sphere of a loving marriage. Similarly the early promotion of pleasurable sex for bodily and spiritual health, and even to cure disease, was qualified in versions published in the closing decades of the eighteenth century. The English version of Venette's work, *Conjugal Love, or, The Pleasures of The Marriage Bed*, was both 'anxiety-making and victimising' (ibid.: 89), particularly in the case of women. In these later editions warnings were given about the physical dangers of 'excessive venery' – that is, too much sex for pleasure. The 1774 version of *Conjugal Love* identifies some of the visible evidence for such over-indulgence in married women. They grow 'thoughtful, dronish, their hair becomes thin and complexion yellow. Have they tasted too freely of the nuptial pleasure? They have: by which means the animal spirits are exhausted; the fibres too much relaxed; and they fall victim to their own wantonness' (quoted in ibid.: 86).

For all the celebration of sexual activity in the eighteenth century, there was one aspect that was increasingly excluded from the category of 'natural pleasures'. The sex that was being so enthusiastically promoted was that between men and women, with men, for the most part, as the active initiators. At the same time, sex between men, for many centuries viewed as an element of acceptable masculine behaviour, was being marked as effeminate and socially disruptive. In order to understand how and why this happened when it did, we have to go back to the seventeenth century and beyond. A number of historians have offered accounts of this reversal of the connections between homoerotic activity and acceptable masculinity (see, for example, Trumbach 1989; Rousseau 1991; Gerard and Hekma 1989; Beck 1997; and Weeks 1999). The key feature of this change appears to be that, before 1700, homoerotic activities, including sodomy, were not considered to be beyond the repertoire of masculine sexuality. There is no suggestion in these accounts that sodomy was not a crime; it was still, in all European countries, a capital crime, that is, punishable by death. However, as these historians argue, though men were convicted of sodomy and executed, the numbers involved were not high. One reason for this was that sexual relations between men and adolescent boys were not considered to be a serious moral or civil crime. This different valuation was due to the adult male being the active penetrator, and the younger boy being the passive recipient. In this way, the defining feature of masculinity was not threatened. Indeed the 'rake' or libertine as a male who had sexual relations with both men and women occupied the highest position on the scale of masculinity. At the other end of the spectrum of acceptable masculinity was the 'fop', distinguished by his elaborate dress and feminine behaviour, who nevertheless sought out women only for sexual pleasure.

But between 1660 and 1750, Trumbach argues, there was a series of changes in meaning of both effeminacy and the social significance of sodomy – now viewed more narrowly as anal penetration of adult males – that signalled a shift in the parameters of normal masculinity and normal male sexuality. A number of intersecting influences were involved. First, homoerotic relations were now more likely to be between adult males, not adults and adolescent boys (Trumbach 1989: 408). Social and legal attitudes towards seduction of boys became more punitive and negative. In part this had to do with the eighteenth-century view that nature scripted sexual behaviour. Attitudes to the young had also changed; formerly seen as miniature adults, now they were considered to be unformed innocents in need of protection, guidance and education. Sexually they were vulnerable to seduction, especially by the men who were now being referred to as 'sodomites', rather than by the early modern term 'libertines'. Finally, as the changes associated with the Enlightenment demanded more rigid distinctions between men and women, effeminate behaviour was increasingly seen as antithetical to 'true' masculinity. Carole Pateman argues that the Enlightenment *philosophes* provided a new foundation for the devaluation of femininity. Women by nature were unable to partake in the social contract necessary to order civil society, as they were 'incapable of transcending their sexual passions . . . and directing their reason to the demands of universal order and public advantage' (Pateman 1988: 102). This shift in the dominant cultural norms opened up a space for a new male personage, one who violated masculinity in two senses – effeminacy and the involvement in both active and passive sexual activity with other adult men. Sexual acts thus had become the marker of a type of person, rather than a mode of seeking sexual pleasure.

An understanding of this evolution can be gained by looking at changing definitions of 'effeminacy'. Trumbach tells us that from the eleventh to about the mid-seventeenth century effeminacy had been the characteristic of both the man who sexually cared too much for women; as well as the man who took the passive role in intercourse (Trumbach 1989: 134). In neither sense was effeminacy seen to disrupt the prevailing view of correct masculinity. Adult men who sought sexual relationships with other men had by 1700 formed a sub-culture – gathering in taverns that tolerated their behaviour and appearance that came to be known as 'mollie houses'. 'Molly' was the term then for female prostitutes, and the men who frequented these houses in the eighteenth century were seen, and identified themselves, as 'he-whores' – revelling in their transvestism and effeminate behaviour (ibid.: 137). In doing so they were acknowledging the increasing association between effeminacy and social marginalization. The negative relationship came, by the mid-eighteenth century, to be encapsulated in the figure of 'the sodomite'. This person was doubly stigmatized: first by being a man behaving like a woman, and second by being a man who allowed himself to be passively penetrated by another man. Within three generations, therefore, two aspects of formerly acceptable male behaviour had come to signify a new category of person who was marked as a threat to the modern sexual order.

Writings on masturbation and its negative consequences illustrate further boundaries around permissible and advisable sexual pleasures. The first to emerge was the anonymous *Onania, or, The Heinous Sin of Self-Pollution, and All its Frightful Consequences in both Sexes Consider'd &c* (1710). The content of *Onania* was terrifying in its detail. At the very least young masturbators would be stunted mentally and physically. Strangulation of the penis, epileptic fits, priapism, gonorrhoea, consumption and infertility were all common consequences for men, while women 'suffer from imbecility . . . hysteric fits, barrenness and "a total Ineptitude in the Act of Generation itself"' (quoted in MacDonald 1967: 425). The children of those who indulge in solitary pleasures would be a 'misery to themselves, a Dishonour to the Human Race and a Scandal to their Parents' (ibid.). The anxious readers of what was originally a small pamphlet more than doubled the size of subsequent editions with their confessions and cries for help. 'Onanism' now became 'self abuse' – a significant shift in terminology that reflected the increasing role played by individual responsibility for the body. This was a point made clear in the later tract on masturbation in the second half of the eighteenth century: *Onanism, or, A Treatise upon the Disorders Produced by Masturbation* (1760), by Samuel Tissot (1728–1797). The medical training of the Swiss doctor is evident in the more measured tones of the title and of the causes and treatments contained within. Both texts, though, illustrated vividly the anxieties that sat uneasily in a period of enlightenment. Perhaps it was that these were private and solitary pleasures, taken beyond the gaze of the categorizers and experts. The tracts on masturbation mentioned nothing of the associated pleasures. It was seen as an act of self-abuse, a self-destructive addiction – rather like heroin is today, with equally terrible individual and social consequences.

A key element in the medical endorsement of heterosexuality was the 'discovery' in the mid-eighteenth century of different female and male sexual anatomy. The interest in discovering these differences reflected the growing importance of gender distinctions in the wider social and political context. As Londa Scheibinger argues, 'the interests of the scientific community were not arbitrary: anatomists focused attention on those parts of the body that were to become politically significant' (Scheibinger 1987: 42). In both the eighteenth and nineteenth centuries this resexing of the body was enhanced by contemporary anxieties about the social and political equality of women. On the one hand there were growing demands from women themselves, in literature and in political activity, for equal inclusion under the banner of the 'rights of man'. On the other, affective marital relations laid new emphasis on the domestic role of women, both as wives and mothers. In an age dominated by the importance of adhering to the laws of nature for social stability, it is perhaps no surprise that the demonstrable difference of male and female bodies became the basis for establishing and fixing a hierarchy of gender difference.

Unlocking the mysteries of the female body was not a neutral undertaking. Though the Enlightenment thinkers spoke of universal political and intellectual freedom for both sexes, there was an undercurrent of male supremacy in both respects. 'Male philosophes elaborated a dual discourse: man on man, and men of women' (Crampe-Casnabet, in Duby and Perrot 1993: 319). In this period, the dissected body was not approached in the quasi-religious manner of the Renaissance anatomists. Gone was the more humble notion of learning at the knees of nature. Now the body was approached with quite specific questions to be answered, especially those that related to the 'natural' roles of men and women. The institution of a separate anatomy and physiology for women created new means by which to monitor their experience of desire and pleasure.

Passive women and pleasureless sex

Women's bodies in their corporeal, scientifically accessible certainties, in the very nature of their bones, nerves and, most importantly, reproductive organs, came to bear an enormous new weight of meaning. Two sexes, in other words, were invented as the new foundation of gender. (Laqueur 1990: 150)

'Sometime in the 18th century', Thomas Laqueur begins a crucial chapter of *Making Sex*, 'sex as we know it was invented' (ibid.: 149). A series of social transformations, which marked a decisive break from Enlightenment sexual culture, were to become the defining features of bourgeois sexuality. In nineteenth-century thought the harmony of nature was replaced by a model of society as an entity whose component parts were of less individual importance than the health of the whole. The needs of society thus conceived added weight to the review of gender distinctions and gender roles. One result of this intellectual shift was increasing state intervention in and direct involvement of the newly established medical profession with the behaviour of people. It also provided a rationale for a clear distinction to be made between the private and public spheres. In the establishment of separate sexual spheres, the erotic equality of premodernity was dismantled. The reconstruction of women's sexual bodies and the resulting disconnection of pleasure from conception gave new and more restricted meaning to sexuality at both an individual and a social level. Women were reduced to their reproductive capacity, their sexual desires silenced in a medical discourse that pathologized any active or explicitly female experiences of pleasure. In relation to all of these aspects, the social significance of sexual behaviour increased while the boundaries of acceptable sexual expression narrowed.

As women's demands for full political and social inclusion became more insistent, attention returned to an older theme of women's inherent 'irrationality'. Given these misgivings, the body was re-examined as to the purpose of the differences and their role in what was to become a new sexual as well as social order. Forceful arguments were made, supported by detailed drawings, about the natural inferiority and lack of maturity of female bone structure. The female body was represented as closer to that of children and even some animals. In both senses it was considered inferior to the model of perfection and evolutionary maturity – man (Scheibinger 1987: 53–66; Laqueur 1990: 164). Extensive dissections and experiments on animals during the late eighteenth and early nineteenth centuries provided new insights into the mechanisms of reproduction. Anatomical illustrations of the nineteenth century rejected the holistic representations of 'natural philosophy and concentrated instead on individual organs and their mechanical workings. A new kind of medicine, and the new institutions in which it was practised, made subjectively reportable states, such as pleasure, of relatively little scientific interest' (Laqueur 1990: 188). The discovery of spontaneous ovulation in animals led to the reappraisal of the importance of sexual pleasure and orgasm for women. If women spontaneously ovulated, as was proved by the examination of physical virgins, then sex, and especially orgasm, was irrelevant for fertility. Conception was disconnected from pleasure with the discovery that only men ejaculated. (The question of whether this is so remains in contention today. See, for example, Cabello 1997.) At the same time, the German anatomist George Ludwig Kobelt (1804–1857) explored in detail the morbid anatomy of the human clitoris. He concluded that the *glans clitoridis*, though analogous to the *glans penis*, was the 'passive female sex organ', the mechanical stimulation of which prepared the 'active female sex organ', the uterus, for reception of the male seed (Lowry 1978: 21). Sexual pleasure, though still acknowledged to originate in the clitoris, was an 'optional extra' for women's experience of their 'true' sexuality, that is, that defined in terms of their fecund uterus. Its classification as a passive sex organ removed the element of consciousness from clitoral pleasure, while retaining its role as a mechanistic switch for the sexual excitation necessary for successful reproductive coitus. 'Orgasm continue[d] to play a critical part in conception but now those who suffer it need feel nothing' (Laqueur 1990: 187).

The discovery of a mechanism that governed ovulation added scientific weight to a long-standing belief about women's sexuality – that it was beyond conscious control. In the new medical discourse, scientific proof was sought to revive and explain this old belief. In this endeavour, the uterus, 'women's most important sex organ [and the one which] has no analogue in man' (Scheibinger 1987: 53), became the single focus of attention. What it was to be, feel and act like a woman was determined, increasingly, by the one reproductive female organ that mattered – the uterus. All possibilities of conscious sensual experience were subordinated to the mechanics of reproduction. A woman's reproductive capacities were, quite literally, who she was. William Acton (1813–1875), a Scottish physician and disciple of Tissot, wrote many texts about female sexuality. In one he claimed, 'the best mothers, wives and managers of households know little or nothing of sexual indulgences. Love of home, children and domestic duties are the only passions they feel' (Acton, 1859, quoted in Heath 1982: 17). The certainties proclaimed from the anatomist's table did not just distinguish, but created a normative separation, between the categories of male and female. The 'discovery' of distinctive female sexual anatomy legitimated simultaneously the social role and the narrowed self-identity of women. The receptive yet insensitive uterus was the metaphor for the passive female. In the context of bourgeois patriarchy, man was the author of life and of its subsequent direction. The medical profession was a central influence in this new discourse of sexual (and political) inequality that was founded in biological functions and anatomical structures.

These medical discoveries directly reflected the strengthening bourgeois social order. The key organizing theme was social and political, and now sexual, 'separate spheres'. Increasingly divided into its functional parts, mechanically interconnected, the female body was ideologically remoulded as a machine for efficient reproduction. Within this model, any aspect of sexuality not necessary for this outcome was superfluous and therefore, formally, irrational. Invisible and therefore unmeasurable, desires were pathologized as dangerous to both individual and social order. Accordingly, a variety of physical or emotional disturbances in women were commonly associated with their levels of experience of sexual pleasure. The nineteenth-century visage of 'erotomania' was matched by the affliction of 'nymphomania', fearful labels for which there were even more fearful treatments, extending, in their extremes, to surgical removal of the clitoris or the uterus (Gilman 1989; Nye 1999).

The more the female body was open to exploration and violation in this manner, the more the same troublesome parts became associated with the internalized emotions of modesty and shame (Elias 1982). Once the proud flagship of natural joys and pleasures, the desiring body was, once again, associated with social danger. Female eroticism was removed through the cultural and medical imperatives as a source of fear and anxiety, not about sin but about disease. The civilizing process in its full maturity rendered positive pleasures 'private and secret . . . while fostering the negatively charged affects – displeasure, revulsion, distaste, as the only feelings customary in society' (ibid.: 142).

Dangerous practices and disreputable desires

A persistent presence in nineteenth-century discourses of the sexual body was what Weber has called 'the cold skeletal hands of rationality' (Weber, in Gerth and Mills 1970: 347). More than concerns about health, purpose and outcome increasingly formed the moral framework for legitimate sexuality. The preoccupation with genital structure and function in medical discourse sought to establish a positive equation between anatomy and purpose, in which purposeful sexuality was directed by biological function. The establishment of functionally distinct male and female sexual organs gave final legitimacy to heterosexual reproductive coitus. Yet in this neat formulation there were residual fears. The first related to the essential unruliness of the genitals, improperly used. The second related to female sexuality believed to exist beyond the stable boundaries of respectability. In relation to both there persisted the view that *some* sexual bodies were beyond reason or control.

For example, in premodern proscription of pleasures, masturbation was not viewed as a serious offence. The sex-positive eighteenth century nevertheless elevated 'onanism' or 'self-abuse', alongside sodomy, as the most individually and socially dangerous sexual practice. The nineteenth-century works on masturbation extended these concerns beyond the question of individual health to social order. While the masturbating individual continued to be the focus of attention, masturbation was now seen as a threat to the stability of the gendered patriarchal order and to the health of the nation. The hydraulic model of male sexuality was as insistent and effective as was the de-eroticization of female sexuality and was an equally important factor in gender socialization. Though female masturbation was acknowledged, it was located at the extreme end of perverse and monstrous sexuality. Masturbation in men and boys was not considered to be either diseased or perverse. Rather, as Lesley Hall has argued, nineteenth-century discourses on masturbation were 'discourses about male sexuality, its nature and its control' (Hall 1992: 367). Excitation of the genitals in men was an unavoidable aspect of their active natural 'drives'. The issue of concern with the male sexual body was the degree to which this excitability could be controlled. 'Nocturnal emissions' and related fears associated with excessive loss of semen (spermatorrhea) proved that, even in men, reason could not always control the sexual body and its responses. In the nineteenth century, medical regimes to manage the unruly penis were an important element in social as well as hygienic education, and the proliferation of self-help manuals bring to mind training manuals one might now purchase for domestic pets. In the context of concerns about national superiority this bodily management had wider implications. Popular medical texts, their readership ensured by increasing literacy, claimed that children of masturbators would inherit the physical and intellectual infirmities of their parents and the health of the nation would suffer.

Earlier nineteenth-century views emphasized the importance of serene reproductive sexuality in marriage, for both men and women (Mort 1987; Stearns and Stearns 1985). But in the second half of the century, despite efforts to reconstruct female sexuality as passive, there was evidence to suggest that this model was not applicable to all women. The sexuality of uneducated, working-class women, physically and morally removed from the traditional social controls of pre-industrial communities, attracted new attention. With such women living in overcrowded tenements and working in close contact

with men in factories or in mines, the possibility of female promiscuity and its negative social consequences was resurrected. The
responses could be seen in increasingly punitive treatment of 'unwed
mothers' and of women who sold their bodies for sexual gratification (see Barret-Ducrocq 1991; Walkowitz 1982; Mort 1987; Mason
1994). Prostitution had been associated with bodily pollution for centuries (Gilman 1988), but the Contagious Diseases Acts (UK) of
1866–9 made direct links between the sexuality of polluted women
and the moral and physical destruction of the nation's defences. As
the scholars listed above have noted, the Acts were applicable only
to those women who strayed within the vicinity of the sex-segregated
garrisons and ports. Moreover, in keeping with the by now institutionalized gendered sexuality, male sexual desire and its need for relief
was assumed. Females who provided, or were suspected of providing, sexual services presented a threat to the new sexual order.
Women who provided sex must have been offering erotic possibilities that in 'real' women should have been unthinkable. Men who
purchased these were indicating their lack of self-control in pursuing
and paying for pleasure.

The bourgeois model that established clear distinctions between
the inherent sexuality of men and women also established clear class
distinctions in desire. Respectable female sexuality was passive sexuality, not one that actively sought an outlet. Respectable male sexuality, on the other hand, was expected to seek relief from whatever
source. Often, this source was the women of what were then termed
'the lower orders', women who worked in factories, in mines or in
domestic service. The sexuality of such women was understood to be
qualitatively different from that of their middle-class sisters. Uneducated and uneducable in the ways of bourgeois virtue, these women
were characterized as being beyond the moral constraints both of
traditional communities and of the newly classed urban society. This
representation was far from the truth in most cases, as the work on
the foundling homes of London has illustrated (Barret-Ducrocq
1991).

Notwithstanding this, male observers, chroniclers and officials
were employed to report on the conditions of the poor to the gov-
ernments of the day. What was written about women who worked
and lived in close physical contact with men went beyond dispassionate observation. Though ostensibly aimed at providing information that would help relieve the extremes of urban poverty, the gaze
of these nineteenth-century 'social explorers' (Keating 1972) lingered
on the partially clothed bodies of female workers in factories and
mines. Factory inspectors' reports 'eroticised the cultural distance

between the observer and the observed' (Mort 1987: 49). Stephen Marcus and Liz Stanley confirm the role played by these constructions in the sexual fantasies of middle-class men (Stanley 1984; Marcus 1966). Stanley offers a first-hand account of such conscious eroticization of class difference in the relationship between the 'gentleman' Arthur Munby and his housekeeper Hannah Culwick. Similarly, Marcus's interpretation of the diaries of the late nineteenth-century libertine 'Walter' emphasizes the role played by lower-class female sexuality viewed, in pornographic fantasy, as both inevitable and irreversible. Thomas Hardy's account of a fatally erotic relationship across the classes in *Tess of the D'Urbervilles* typifies this view. In a key scene, Tess, the daughter of a local drunkard, descends the stairs to meet Angel, her aristocratic lover: 'She was yawning and he saw the red interior of her mouth as if it had been a snake's. She had stretched one arm so high over her coiled up cable of hair that he could see its satin delicacy above the sunburn: her face flushed with sleep. Her eyelids hung heavy over their pupils. The brimfulness of her nature breathed from her' (Hardy [1891] 1965: 142). Charles Dickens similarly consistently offers contrasts between contained and unconfined female sexuality that are class dependent. In less erotically charged language, Dickens marks his boundaries by physical appearance, where dark hair, dark eyes and brooding countenances convey the message of exotic otherness whose counterpart is child-like helpless and fair-skinned asexuality. (See David Copperfield's Dora compared with Rosa Dartle, his mother's passionate and fatally attractive female companion; Dickens 1861.)

This acknowledgement of the sexuality of working-class women offered a justification for the exercise of male desires outside of the respectable expectations of bourgeois marriage. But behind the façade of class difference, there was more than a suggestion that all women's sexuality was, at its centre, socially dangerous and lacking in self-control. The figure of the socially disgraced upper-class woman is a recurrent one in Victorian literature and art. The disgrace stems from a single source, the production of an illegitimate child. In the opening chapter of Dickens's *Oliver Twist*, the hero's middle-class mother, who had clearly given in to unmarried sexual desire, suffered social disgrace and ultimately death in childbirth. Undisciplined and disreputable sexuality guaranteed social exclusion and, in fiction as well as fact, social ruin and often death. This was a powerful lesson to be learned by all women about the social consequences of straying from the narrowly confined sexuality of the bourgeois model.

Anxieties about dangerous sexuality cannot be disentangled from the wider insecurities of the group who were, to use Gay's phrase, even by the close of the century, 'uneasy in their middle class skins' (Gay 1986: 31). Though the source of danger was identified in socially marginalized *women*, the urgency with which this issue was addressed suggests insecurity about the model of heterosexual masculinity essential for the wider social order. Masturbation threatened masculine self-control as much as it did the physical body. Its eradication was necessary, as well, to establish heterosexual coitus as the only acceptable outlet for male sexual desires. The eroticization of working women suggests unease about the effectiveness of the model that assigned different sexualities to men and women. By the close of the century a new weapon emerged in this struggle for containment of unruly eroticism, held in the hands of the groups who had been, throughout, the 'fathers' of the new social order – the men of medical science.

End-of-century anxieties and the science of sex

The closing decades of the nineteenth century were characterized by social and political instability. Demands for extension of the political franchise were intensifying. The massed urban working class, recognizing their collective misery and exploitation, began to organize in trades unions. Women were becoming more vocal in their assertions of difference and of equal citizenship rights. What the contemporary commentator Emile Durkheim called the 'division of labour in society' had delivered not social harmony but widening social inequality. There was a decline of the policy of *laissez-faire* political doctrines, as the need for state intervention in economic and social life became more obvious. In its earliest form this political shift dramatically reviewed 'the very idea of public and private' (Schwarz and Hall 1982: 11). Education of the masses was coming to be seen as a key element in the establishment of a more harmonious social order. In this project, moral education was as important as learning more practical life skills. Social commentators and health officials began to intrude into the homes of the respectable poor, seeking to educate them in proper hygiene and childcare. Another aspect of this public/private shift was the unprecedented attention now paid to behaviour that directly or indirectly related to sex, which had hitherto been seen as 'private business'. In England and Wales a series of parliamentary Acts illustrated this state-led moral reform (Weeks 1989: 81). The Married Women's Property Act (1882), the Divorce Acts (1856, 1878, 1884, 1886 and 1895), the Obscene Publications Act (1857), the Contagious Diseases Acts (1864, 1866, 1869), the

Offences Against the Person Act (1861), the Criminal Law Amendment Act (1885) and the Vagrancy Act (1898) (see Weeks 1989 and
1991 for details) all focused on aspects of sexual behaviour considered to be central to the establishment of a modern social and sexual
order. A central concern in many of these Acts was sexual behaviour
that called into question the main tenets of the bourgeois model of
sexuality. But there was a ranking of this behaviour with reference to
its threat to social order. The most disruptive was that which threatened bourgeois masculinity.

Acts of same-sex desire between men posed an open challenge to
the by now established definition of masculinity. Just as the sexual
act between men and women defined the 'real man', so sexual acts
between men labelled them as individuals who must be excluded from
'civilized society'. This process had begun as we have seen in the eighteenth century with the marginalization of the 'sodomite'. But in the
nineteenth century the consequences of this social stigmatization
became more dangerous for men who desired men. In England and
Wales the Offences Against the Person Act (1861) removed the death
penalty (in force since 1533) for sodomy, still legally a term which
covered bestiality as well as anal penetration of men or women. This
repeal did not signal a more liberal attitude. By the late nineteenth
century, any indication of erotic attachment between men would
render them liable to prosecution, social ruin and imprisonment.
Proof of anal penetration was not needed for the individual to be
identified as a homosexual. It was enough for police, or even
members of the public, to suspect a man of immoral intentions for
him to be marked out as a threat to society and treated accordingly.
The legal definition of the homosexual, contained within the
Labouchere Amendment and the 1898 Vagrancy Act in the UK,
encouraged the deliberate erosion of civil liberties through police
entrapment, false accusations and blackmail of men suspected of
'perverting' both nature and culture (Davenport-Hines 1991: 106).

The situation for women who desired women was less immediately perilous, but no less illiberal. Before the mid-nineteenth century,
as Martha Vicinus has indicated, same-sex desire between women
had attracted little except tolerantly amused or sometimes lascivious
attention, unless 'what women did' directly challenged male erotic
prowess (Vicinus 1989). All same-sex desire weakened nineteenth-
century claims for natural heterosexuality, but lesbian desire was
perhaps the most threatening to bourgeois constructions, as it challenged both female sexual passivity and the sexual supremacy of men.
That lesbian desire was rendered unworthy of comment was not to
mark its irrelevance to the sexual order. In the context of increasingly

organized feminism the public acknowledgement of woman-to-woman eroticism was politically rather than morally threatening (Faderman 1981). Though both contradicted assumptions behind the heterosexual norm, homosexual and lesbian desire were nevertheless treated very differently. Simultaneously acknowledging and criminalizing men who loved men as a different type of person meant that homosexuality would remain in the public consciousness as well as under individual scrutiny. Though lesbian love was likewise distinguished as socially and biologically aberrant, instead of raising public awareness, as was the case with homosexual desire, attention was directed away from this erotic alternative. The threat lesbian love posed to the male-defined norms of heterosexuality was not lesbian appearance, behaviour or even self-identity. The aspect of lesbian love that was covered with a cloak of silence was its erotic expression. The reality that women could give each other greater sexual pleasure than any man could offer meant two things: first, that women's sexuality was not dependent on that of men; and second, that women's sexuality was not, by nature, passive but active. In the late nineteenth and early twentieth century, 'mannish women' were not considered to be a threat; but an actively erotic woman who satisfied other women had gone too far in emulating men. The sexuality of lesbian women was, accordingly, denied and silenced. This unwittingly offered a relatively safe space in which women could love women providing they were discreet about what they did sexually. In the post-war period in England, an attempt to include lesbianism under the Criminal Law Amendment Act (1921) failed because of the belief that to give public recognition to this 'beastly subject' was to risk its encouragement (Jeffries 1985: 114).

The science of sex was born in this climate of social and political insecurity, and the work of its earliest figures sought to provide a reliable and scientifically verifiable foundation for 'fixing' sexual behaviour that fell outside the narrow boundaries of heterosexual coitus. This they aimed to do by first identifying the details of perverse sexuality and second providing a coherent explanation for their existence. This work by definition fell outside the usual remit of the medical profession, dealing as it did with aspects of sexual behaviour largely unknown and unaddressed outside pornography. In this sense, it could be said to be radical in its intent. However, this was tempered by the assumptions that underpinned the categories of normal and abnormal sexual acts, which, as we will see, were grounded in prevailing expectations of female and male sexuality. The first scientists of sex were also dedicated to the eradication of social ignorance and prejudice, which they saw as distorting the healthy and natural sexual impulse. This conviction moved the study of sexual behaviour beyond the bounds of dispassionate scientific enquiry. For the aim was not just to gather information about sexual behaviour, but also to provide information that would dispel the ignorance, fear and repression of sexual feelings that they believed were equally dangerous to psychological and physical health. Finally, their concern went beyond the health of the individual to the health of society. The direction of the sexual impulse, whatever form this took, had important consequences for the health of the nation and of the human race (Ellis 1899: 1.v; Krafft-Ebing 1899: 6–7; Bloch 1909: 282ff). The founding figures in the new discipline of sexology were Richard von Krafft-Ebing (1840–1902), Havelock Ellis (1859–1939), Magnus Hirschfeld (1868–1935), Edward Carpenter (1844–1929), Iwan Bloch (1872–1922) and Sigmund Freud (1856–1939). These individuals were not the first to address causes of sexual behaviour. The biological argument that the direction of sexual desire was determined by the reproductive mechanisms was first challenged by Karl Ulrichs in 1864–5, by the identification of individuals whom he called 'urnings': those with the body of one sex but the soul of the other. In 1869, the Hungarian jurist K. M. Benkhert first used the term 'homosexual' to refer to persons who desired their own sex.

One approach to the study of sex reflected the profound influence of Charles Darwin's *The Evolution of the Species* (1859) on late nineteenth- and early twentieth-century scientific thought. The Scottish biologists Patrick Geddes and J. Arthur Thomson, authors of *The Evolution of Sex* (1899), argued that male and female sexual behaviour had its origins in the reproductive mechanisms of the body, and that these characteristics had evolved for the survival of the species. The passive, larger and nurturing female ova complemented the small active male sperm. Pre-programmed mechanisms within these cells, they argued, determined not just physical sexuality but also 'intellectual and emotional differences between the sexes' (quoted in Bland and Doan 1998a: 14). These patterns were so deeply ingrained that 'to obliterate them it would be necessary to have all the evolution over again on a new basis . . . what was decided among the prehistoric Protozoa cannot be annulled by Act of Parliament' (ibid.). These differences also complemented the social organization required for successful continuation of the species. Men were the dynamic actors in biological and social evolution, women, in both senses, the caretakers of the species. Passive, with smaller brains, women were more patient and concerned with detail, not with the wide intellectual sweep that preoccupied men. 'Man thinks more, women [*sic*] feels more. He discovers more but remembers less; she is more receptive and less forgetful' (ibid.: 17). This evolutionary explanation impacted on understandings of sexual desire and was taken to justify the conclusion that non-reproductive sexual activity was, literally, degenerative: 'Degeneration is the opposite and regressive pole of progressive evolution' (Nye 1999: 115). The evolutionary explanation extended to behaviour and appearance, fixing masculinity and femininity as universal qualities derived from male and female sexed bodies. The consistency of these scientifically based arguments with prevailing social views made this volume a best-seller among both scientists and social commentators of the day.

The claims about degenerative sexual behaviour were also the basis for the work of the more critical and sociological sexologists. Though its leading figures were all medically trained (with the exception of Edward Carpenter, who trained as a cleric but retired on private means) their scientific enquiry went beyond a model that sought to diagnose and cure sexual aberrations. The early sexologists combined biological, social, cultural and clinical observations in order to collect information about, and establish categories of, sexual behaviour. Though not widely accepted among the establishment as a legitimate medical speciality, this approach made more acceptable what might otherwise have been considered prurient and perverse curiosity. As an early twentieth-century medical practitioner and popular writer on sexual matters commented, 'The public has for too long ignored as indelicate or as too intricate and mysterious to be comprehended except by those who are educated in all branches of the medical profession the subjects which lie at the very foundation of their earthly being' (Trall 1903: 5–6).

The earliest efforts to classify sexual behaviour concentrated on the extremes of abnormality – sexual acts seen as the most remote from a reproductive outcome. In 1886 Richard von Krafft-Ebing, a leading Austrian psychiatrist, published the results of his exploration of a wide variety of such sexual practices. This volume contained a great number of common and some very unusual sexual deviations – that is, sexual acts that fell outside the norm of heterosexual coitus. Biological, cultural and psychological aspects of sexual behaviour were explored, as were legal aspects of abnormal sexual behaviour, including child sexual abuse, sado-masochism and bestiality. The full title of this book was *Psychopathia sexualis, with Especial Reference to the Antipathic Sexual Instinct*. The 'antipathic sexual instinct' referred to 'congenital reversal of the sexual feeling with consciousness of the abnormality of this manifestation' (Krafft-Ebing 1998: 223). In the introduction to the 1998 edition, it is noted: 'Its author was ahead of his time in suggesting that the mental condition of the individual must be considered – not just the nature of the act' (ibid.: viii). It was this claim that challenged the prevailing view that sexual 'deviation' was a sign of moral degeneracy. Krafft-Ebing took a positive view of both sexual desire and sexual pleasure as aspects of healthy human nature. Indeed, he argued that sex lay at the centre of an ethical life. But he was adamant that this was so powerful a force that it was in danger of being distorted, to the detriment of both individual and society. If allowed free rein without education and guidance, the instinct 'may degenerate into the lowest passion and the basest vice' (Krafft-Ebing 1998: 1). The author wrote in the 1899 introduction: 'In . . . periods of civil and moral decline the most monstrous excesses of sexual life may be observed which . . . can always be traced to psycho-pathological or neuro-pathological conditions of the nations involved' (Krafft-Ebing 1899: 6–7). Thus, the origin of sexual variations, from mild to severe, was to be found in social experience as well as congenital variation. But there were also elements, especially in regard to women, that supported the bourgeois model of sexuality: 'Man has beyond doubt the stronger sexual appetite of the two . . . Women however, if physically and mentally normal and properly educated, have but little sexual desire' (Krafft-Ebing 1998: 8). While this might be interpreted as suggesting women have no sexuality, it is more accurately understood in the context of the nineteenth-century association of love with sex, especially in relation to heterosexuality. Krafft-Ebing differentiated sensual appetites (stronger in men) and the need for love that is continual and passionate rather than short-lived and sensual (stronger in women) (ibid.: 9).

The detailed descriptions of sexual acts and sexual crimes contained in this volume were not for public consumption. They were collected to help medical and legal professionals make judgements about whether sexually perverse behaviour was an accurate indicator of wider mental disease or simply an indication of consciously chosen sexual depravity. In this respect, the author sought to establish the difference between sexual perversion and sexual perversity. 'In order to differentiate between disease (perversion) and vice (perversity) one must investigate the whole personality of the individual and the original motives leading to the act' (Krafft-Ebing 1998: 53). He argued that sexual perversion was part of more generalized pathologies of the mind. Such individuals would not be subject to any sense of shame or conscience, since they would not know what they were doing was wrong. Sexually perverse acts (a term covering the widest possible range of acts for sexual gratification, from the mild to the excessively horrible) were not, necessarily, evidence of insanity. The level of perversity was important here, as was the level of insight into or conscience about the acts. In taking this approach, Krafft-Ebing was placing categorization and explanation before judgement – in other words, was being a scientist of sex.

Beyond providing a framework for treatment or legal accountability, Krafft-Ebing sought to explain more common sexually perverse acts – and here his attention focused mainly on same-sex desire, though he was also very interested in recording cases of sexual fetishism. Again, his attitude to what he called 'antipathic sexual feelings' was a mixture of the radical and the conservative. The normal trajectory of heterosexuality happened, he argued, with adolescence, as the maturing of the sexual organs was matched with desires for the opposite sex. Thus, the body and the psyche were in harmony. But in some individuals feelings are not in harmony with physical development or with the sex of the body. Instead, feelings and desires for the same sex develop. The cause of this outcome was, he argued, a 'congenital degeneration of the psyche' (Krafft-Ebing 1998: 188). The body developed normally but the psyche did not follow. These individuals were not, therefore, conscious that their feelings were in any way abnormal and therefore could not be held responsible for their sexual perversion. They were not criminals but were suffering from a congenital weakness.

But, Krafft-Ebing found, there are many individuals in whom the antipathic sexual feeling was acquired by circumstances, not by a force beyond their control. There was, therefore, an element of choice or consciousness in this activity. Sex between men, especially pederasty (the active anal penetration of a passive recipient), may, he argued, be explained in terms of an abnormally high sex drive, not an abnormal direction of the instinct. He continues, 'thus we find homosexual intercourse in impotent masturbators or debauchees, or for want of something better in sensual men and women under imprisonment, on shipboard, in garrisons, bagnios, boarding schools, etc' (Krafft-Ebing 1998: 188). Other explanations for acquired antipathic feelings include an underlying bisexual position, or the presence of a minor form of degeneration of the psyche that makes some individuals more susceptible than others to explore homosexuality given the right conditions. Krafft-Ebing's work offered a scientific foundation for challenging the prevailing view that homosexuals were vice-ridden individuals who must be punished by law. Though he explained antipathic sexual feelings with reference to the norm of heterosexuality, his clinical observations presented in medical language provided a more humane alternative explanation for what was, by now, a crime. But that he associated it with degeneration replaced the notion of homosexuality as a crime with that of homosexuality as a disease. The logic then was not to punish but to treat and reform.

It is in the work of Krafft-Ebing's successors that the studies of sexual behaviour matured as a 'social science'. Their intended audience was the educated layperson as well as their professional peers. Perhaps the most well known was Havelock Ellis. Born in 1859 in Surrey, England, he first trained as a teacher, going in 1875 to work in New South Wales, Australia, for four years (http://homepages.primex.co.uk/~lesleyah/havelock.html). After returning to England he trained as a doctor, but quickly 'became absorbed in literary work and original scientific investigation' (Stella Browne, quoted in ibid.). In 1897 the first of his eight-volume masterwork on sexual behaviour was published (*Studies in the Psychology of Sex*). Though it was to become the second volume in the final order of the series, *Sexual Inversion* was the first to appear. In the foreword, Ellis made clear that sexual behaviour would be presented and discussed in the 'cold and dry light [of science] (Ellis 1899: 1.xiv). However, his motivations went beyond that of scientific endeavour – he was passionately committed to establishing sexual feelings and acts as a positive force in human society. 'Sex lies at the root of life and we can never learn reverence for life until we know how to understand sex' (ibid.). This tension was present throughout his work.

In *Sexual Inversion* Ellis sought to extend Krafft-Ebing's framework of disease and degeneration. In order to support his view that human sex lives were more complex than was suggested by the evolutionary model, Ellis turned to historical and especially cross-cultural attitudes to same-sex desire. He concluded that, in societies most distant from European civilization, homoerotic acts attract little interest or concern. 'On the whole, the evidence is that among lower races homosexual practices are regarded with considerable indifference and the real invert . . . generally passes unperceived or joins some sacred caste which satisfies his exclusively homosexual inclinations' (Ellis 1899: 1.21). Like Krafft-Ebing, Ellis took for granted that the sexual instinct would, normally, be directed to the opposite sex. But those who desired their own sex were not in his view congenitally degenerate; rather, they were a constitutional variation of the norm. Unlike Krafft-Ebing, Ellis laid more emphasis on the influence of social circumstances in directing the sexual instinct. Some individuals might possess the inherent tendency to inversion but not be given the opportunity to express it. Others, especially those of high intelligence and creative ability, would have this tendency encouraged by favourable experiences or social contexts. Ellis acknowledged the role of urban life in this process, which 'renders easier the exhibition and satisfaction of this, as of all, forms of perversion' (ibid.: 1.63). He also argued that evidence of same-sex activity in the animal world questioned the 'naturalness' of heterosexual coitus as the only healthy outlet for sexual desire.

Havelock Ellis was a vocal supporter of women's rights. He viewed the bourgeois stereotype of female asexuality as both mistaken and damaging to women. He argued that women's sexuality was distinctively female and as such more complex that that of men. 'A woman can find sexual satisfaction in a great number of ways that do not include the sexual act proper, and in a great number of ways that apparently are not physical at all' (quoted in Bland and Doan 1998a: 115). Women possess three primary erogenous zones – the clitoris, the outer lips of the vagina and the nipples. Men, on the other hand, have one erogenous zone and one direct 'aim' of the sexual impulse. Ellis devoted many chapters in Volume 6 (*Sex in Relation to Society*, 1927) to the need for the art of love to be learned and practised. Natural urges to procreate do not teach individuals the art of love necessary for a satisfactory sex life. In other cultures and other historical periods great attention was given to learning the erotic arts, but Western Christendom had suppressed them, to the detriment of both individual and society. But bourgeois women especially have suffered from this enforced ignorance. Men learn about sex from prostitutes. Ellis points out, 'by the age of twenty-five . . . an energetic and sexually disposed man in a large city has, for the most part, already had relations with some twenty-five women, perhaps even as many as fifty, while a well-bred and cultivated woman at that age is still only beginning to realise the slowly summating excitations of sex' (Ellis 1927: 521n.). Such extensive sexual experience does not, Ellis argues, equip a man to make love to his formerly chaste and sexually ignorant wife. He gives examples of terrible physical injuries sustained by what he calls 'brutish husbands'. Such male ignorance about the art of love is, he says, endemic. 'Balzac has compared the average husband to an orang-utan trying to play the violin' (ibid.: 525). For Ellis, it is artificial civilization that has produced sexually frigid women, to the detriment of both sexes. Sex between man and woman should be mutually pleasurable and result in 'the acute gratification of simultaneous orgasm' (ibid.: 550).

Iwan Bloch's key publication was titled *The Sexual Life of our Time in its Relation to Modern Civilisation* (1909). Like Ellis, Bloch drew on both biological and social sources for his comments about male and female sexuality. Again, like Ellis, it was his view that modern civilization had blighted and distorted the positive aspects of human sex lives: 'The state in which the majority live, in which forced labour is the necessary centre of life, has introduced into sensual life a sting of pain' (Bloch 1909: 282). Reflecting more the influences of the evolutionary explanation, it was his conviction that civilisation had intensified the differences between men and women. These differences could be found in both physical and intellectual development. To support his contention, Bloch used examples from lesser developed parts of Europe and what he called 'uncivilized cultures' to illustrate that the differences between the sexes, in both behaviour and appearance, were less striking than in the civilized world (Bland and Doan 1988b: 31ff). Bloch's comments about women suggest that he was not so great a supporter of women's rights as were the other sexologists. In this volume he argued that the differences between men and women proved that women were at a lower level of evolution than men – more like children, he claimed (ibid.: 32). Women's sexuality reflected this lower position. Bloch conceded, after conversations with 'a great many cultured women', that the bourgeois norm of the sexually insensitive woman was 'erroneous'. He acknowledged that women's sexual erotic potential is more diffuse than that of men: 'They are a great sexual surface, or target; we only have a sexual arrow' (Bloch 1909: 84). But, because it is so, women's capacity for pleasure is less easily realized. It is the role of the civilized man to understand female sexuality and to aid in focusing this diffuse sexuality to more direct outcomes. Because women are at a lower level of civilization, the more animal aspects of their sexuality are just below the surface. In asylums, 'where conventional inhibitions are withdrawn, women greatly exceed men in malignancy and obscenity and in this relation there is no difference between the shameless virago from the most depraved classes in London and the elegant lady of the upper circles' (ibid.: 85).

The German sexologist Magnus Hirschfeld 'viewed homosexuality as a natural, inborn condition, not a sickness, and was deeply committed to eradicating public prejudice against homosexuals through education' (www2.rz.hu-berlin.de/sexology/ GESUND/ARCHIV/SEN/CH06.HTM). He also campaigned against the criminalization of homosexuality in Germany (paragraph 175 of the German Criminal Code) and established the first scientific journal on homosexuality in 1889 and the Institute for Sexual Science in Berlin in 1919. The services provided by this organization included marital counselling, training of professionals interested in sexual matters, an extensive library, and facilities for scientific and sociological research into sex and sexualities. The importance of Hirschfeld's contribution to sexual science was that he defined homosexuality as neither a crime nor a sickness. Desire for one's own sex was a natural variation in sexual behaviour and therefore homosexuals, lesbians and bisexuals were neither to be pitied nor punished. Hirschfeld's approach to same-sex desire differed from that of his contemporaries. The other sexologists, in claiming that homosexuality and lesbianism were congenital or acquired perversions of the sexual instinct, retained the fundamental normalcy of heterosexuality. Hirschfeld challenged the assumption that only heterosexuality was natural and that every other direction of desire was therefore an 'abnormal form'. He also believed that sexology had a more general political application. In 1993, two years before his death, he wrote: 'Only an objective study of mankind and of sex can prepare the way for the complete realisation of human rights' (quoted in Bland and Doan 1998b: 227; for an account of this man's fascinating life, see Wolff 1986).

Edward Carpenter, a member of the English upper middle class, was educated at Cambridge and ordained a curate in 1870. In this respect he cannot accurately be described as a scientist of sex, since he was neither trained nor interested in studying sexual behaviour from the point of view of science. His contribution was that of campaigner and writer, his work informed by and quoting much of the work of the first sexologists. Carpenter's writing on the 'intermediate sex' or 'urnings', both male and female, was made the more powerful because of his own courageously open relationship with his lover, George Merrill, which lasted for thirty years. (www.sbu.ac.uk/stafflag/edwardcarpenter.html). Carpenter's key writings in relation to sexual desire concerned what he called 'homogenic affection' – the characteristic of the 'intermediate sex'. Perhaps because he stood outside the dispassionate framework of science, his work on the subject of same-sex desire tended more towards the literary and even the poetic. Drawing on classical antiquity and medieval traditions of courtly love, he sought to distinguish between those who desired homogenic relationships for carnal and self-indulgent reasons and those who by constitution, identity and desire showed themselves to be 'true' members of the intermediate sex. 'Too much emphasis cannot be laid on the distinction between those born lovers of their own kind, and that class of persons, with whom they are so often confused, who out of mere carnal curiosity or extravagance of desire, or from dearth of opportunities for a more normal satisfaction (as in schools, barracks, etc) adopt some homosexual practices' (www.simondsn.dircon.co.uk/ecint3.htm: 8). Like Hirschfeld, Carpenter argued that homogenic love was neither a crime nor a disease. It was, rather, 'instinctive and congenital, mentally and physically, and therefore entwined in the very roots of individual life and practically ineradicable' (ibid.: 8). Members of the intermediate sex, for the most part, were healthy and well formed, both physically and mentally. They were not to be seen as handicapped in their life endeavours. Setting aside the prevailing social disapproval and legal constraints, Carpenter argued that homogenic males and females offered positive advantages to society. 'The ordinary love has a special function in the propagation of the race, so the other has its special function in social and heroic work, and in the generation – not of bodily children – but of those children of the mind, the philosophical conceptions and ideals which transform our lives and those of society' (ibid.: 14). To ignore, misunderstand or persecute homogenic persons is to risk 'considerable danger or damage to the common-weal' (ibid.: 16). The law in England (the Criminal Law Amendment Act of 1885) went beyond the justifiable aim of preventing 'acts of violence or public scandal' (ibid.: 18). In seeking to prevent what Carpenter calls 'a certain gross act' (sodomy), the Act extended its influence too far into the private lives of adults in ways that could never be effective beyond encouraging blackmail and further persecution. Carpenter's key concern was to argue for the 'normalization' of homogenic desires, and in this, like Hirschfeld, he placed individuals who desired their own sex outside the binary distinction between 'normal' and 'perverted' sexuality. His advocacy of equal sexual and citizenship rights of men and women aimed to remove the stigma associated with disease and degeneration. He also attached a positive social value to homosexuality, associating it in both sexes with heightened sensitivity and creativity. In all these respects, his work remains relevant to confronting homophobia more than a century later.

The science of sex was both a product and a project of modernity. In the wake of the Enlightenment rejection of any preordained social order, the puzzle of human sexuality was revisited. The aim, though, was not to forbid and punish but to examine and explain. The mysteries of the workings of the body were rapidly being removed with the progression of medical knowledge and practice. But the mysteries of human behaviour remained to be explored. We might ask, why did sexual behaviour attract such concentrated attention at a time when to speak about sex was considered unseemly? A number of related concerns contributed to this field of study: fertility and its relationship to public health and, as we have already seen, the need to redefine masculinity and femininity in line with the bourgeois social order. But another possibility presents itself, which links the science of sex in the late nineteenth century with unresolved anxieties about the instability of sexual desire and its social consequences. For sexual behaviour, more than any other aspect of humanity, stands at the intersection of the body and the mind. The view that the body was a mechanical entity, driven by natural forces, invited a new approach to the understanding of its sexual uses that explored the ways in which the sexual instinct was directed. The mechanical model of the sexual body offered a possibility of harnessing the sexual instinct that had for so long been the subject of anxiety. Scientific enquiry provided the means by which to establish a fixed and universal connection between the experience of desire and its outcome – the sexual uses of the body.

There were two important outcomes of the science of sex that were to define modernist sexuality. The first lay in the assumptions about what constituted natural sexual expression. Despite their focus on the psychological and social factors involved in directing sexual desire, the grounds for establishing 'normality' were those of biology, not society or individual choice. The sexed body was, in its normal state, the reproductive body, and thus sexual desire was linked to the reproductive instinct. It was this underlying assumption that led, inevitably, to the examination of sexual desires that would not have a reproductive outcome. Thus the focus was on degenerations, inversions or perversions of the sexual instinct. The second and related outcome was that the science of sex linked directions of sexual desire with a type of person. The erotic choice of the individual was a defining factor in establishing behaviour and individual identity. Fixing desire with identity in this manner was as determinist as the link made, in the biological argument, between reproduction and normal sexuality. The final factor was the creation of a binary model of desire that was also fixed in category and outcome. There was no place for flexibility or conscious choice. The science of sex opened up the topic of sex for discussion but in doing so closed down the possible boundaries of its expression.

Conclusion

In the eighteenth and nineteenth centuries, 'sexuality' was conceived and born. It can be seen, individually and simultaneously, as a category, a concept and an experience. In all three guises it is intrinsically linked with modernity as a process and as a reality. The features of a modernizing and secularizing society in the eighteenth and nineteenth centuries are evident in this tripartite entity. However, they were, in their differences, clearly illustrating that these centuries were, in the history of Western sexuality, perhaps the most dissimilar. It was in the eighteenth century that the bodily mechanics of sex began to be the foundation for types of people. For example, women, by virtue of their 'sex', were identified as having separate (if still inferior) characteristics of personality, behaviour and social function. The sexual immaturity of the young identified them as subjects for proper education and guidance. Through these discourses, the social supremacy of men, and of their less problematic 'sex', was strengthened and underpinned in a normalizing discourse of heterosexuality. With the birth of 'sexuality' came the creation of gender. We still accept the existence of two genders, while common sense links male and female with bodily parts. The assumption that masculinity and femininity implied mutually exclusive modes of behaviour and appearance is one that has its roots in this epoch of modernity. Masculine and feminine behaviour was the visible evidence of a healthy sexual entity – where modes of behaviour and appearance were 'correctly matched' with the body. The distinct categories thus reflected the normative conjunction between biology and society – where 'natural' was conflated with 'moral' and, of course, 'unnatural' with 'immoral'. These ideas were brought into being by the legacy of the Enlightenment and reflected in a scientific discourse about sex and desire. None of these features would have been possible without the ascendance of science over religion in relation to sex and sexuality. In this respect, the Enlightenment ideas offered release from the fear and pessimism of Christian discourses about the sexual body and its desires. This aspect of modernity should not be underestimated as we critically examine the new modes of regulation that were to follow. The eighteenth-century *philosophes* recognized the pleasure of sex as an essential and harmonious component of the natural order. Seeking pleasure was therefore the sign of a morally healthy individual, and it followed then that the pursuit of sexual pleasure had a positive value for the social order. However, this support was circumscribed by new boundaries of normality. First, the authors and primary consumers of these bodily pleasures were men. Women were recognized as intrinsically sexual beings, and, indeed, this was nothing new, even in the darkest writings of Christianity. But Enlightenment pleasures were primarily phallic pleasures, for both men and women. Pleasurable sex also became the foundation for happy and fecund marriages. The centrality of the phallus in this validation laid the foundations for a second discourse that was to wait until the late nineteenth century for full development – the normalization of heterosexual coitus. This phallocentricity was evident in the terrible warnings that began to emerge about the dangers of 'onanism', or masturbation, in the second half of the eighteenth century.

Second, and as importantly for the creation of the category of sexuality, was the significance attached to the differences between men and women in social behaviour, in appearance and especially in the ways in which they sought sexual pleasure. Attention focused primarily on men in this regard, and the effeminate man was the object of social contempt while his sexual behaviour, real or imputed, was increasingly scrutinized and condemned. What constituted Enlightenment sexuality was, by the end of the century, phallocentric, heterosexual, coital and linked directly with a healthy sexual body and a healthily gendered sexual identity. This last marked the third sector of sexuality – the creation of a type of person derived from the normative conjunction of the physically sexed body with the socially gendered self. Enlightenment thought about the positive aspects of sex elevated the importance of a properly managed physical body, but also of the properly managed social self. In keeping with the recognition of the individual as the building block of the social polity, Enlightenment understandings of 'sexuality' elevated the importance of education and guidance, rather than punishment, as the means to ensure this balance.

The nineteenth-century elements in modernist sexuality are distinct from those of the century that preceded it, most notably in the loss of the brief 'moment' of fundamental celebration of sexual pleasure. Though circumscribed, as we have seen, eighteenth-century society loved (heterosexual) sex and its pleasures and indulged in them with a minimum of guilt and anxiety. Nineteenth-century attitudes to sexual pleasure were very different. Overall, they represented the opposite of Enlightenment enthusiasm. But, though long associated with the stereotype of 'Victorian prudishness', the attitude to sex and the approach to sexuality were not those of outright denial or condemnation. If the prevailing characteristic of the eighteenth century was one of affirmation, that of the nineteenth was one of fear and distrust of excessive indulgence. In this it reflected the social ethic that drove capitalism to its maturity. There was in the nineteenth century an ethos of economy and of rationality of practice in all areas of life. Sober self-control in relation to all sensual pleasures was the defining feature of the bourgeois social order. Sexual pleasure was subjugated to considerations of individual purpose and social outcome. There were, however, similarities with the preoccupations of the previous century, which under the bourgeois influence completed the picture of sexual modernity.

The nineteenth century can be split into two parts in relation to its attitude to sex and sexuality. In the first half of the century the stage was set for a more negative approach by the increasing size and density of populations and the evidence that the overall health of industrializing societies was rapidly deteriorating as a consequence. Though the first official response was to attempt some management of epidemic disease, unofficially the sexual behaviour of the masses began to be seen as an equal threat to the health of the social body. But it was from the mid-century onwards that the connection between excessive sex and disease was made more explicit. This twinning of concerns heightened the social power and authority of the medical profession. But it also provided the rationale for a shift from sex as pleasure to sex as danger. These ideas, especially in the real context of heightened anxieties about public health, gave the medical profession a moral as well as a scientific authority. The direction of scientific enquiry into overcoming the negative aspects of sex and desire kept the Enlightenment ideas about 'natural sex' central, but rewrote them in more proscriptive ways. The gendered and embodied constructions of sexuality continued in this century, where heterosexual coitus, practised in moderation and within marriage, was accepted for its social and individual virtues. But what received more attention were the negative effects of over-indulgence, especially for women. Medical knowledge added greater authority to judgements about women's sexuality that in the eighteenth century were taken to be the dictates of nature. In these more specialized discourses, nature could not be trusted to ensure a positive social outcome. In its place, more detailed categories of normal and abnormal exercised control over undesirable aspects of sexuality. The binary model, which fixed expressions of desire into categories of male and female, normal and abnormal, healthy and diseased, played a crucial role in this new sexual order. Central to this was the focus on reproductive sexuality within rigid social bounds and a silencing of the 'joys of sex'. The corollary was the rejection of any other source of pleasure. Three sources in particular were isolated for more intense scrutiny and control: the sexual autonomy of women, autoeroticism, and same-sex desire, especially that between men. The essence of 'Victorian sexuality' was encapsulated in the ideal of the 'asexual woman'. This figure was used as a model for acceptable female behaviour in which sexuality was obliterated by reproduction. The continuation of the fixed relationships between bodily sex and acceptable social behaviour intensified the secular scrutiny of the sexuality of both men and women, while narrowing down the acceptable forms of expression of heterosexual desire.

The final refinement of the control of sexual desire represented by modernist sexuality was the complete marginalization of homosexuality. The category itself was a product of the nineteenth century, and its inception marked a more rigid and oppressive framework for the outlawing of same-sex desire between men. The beginnings of this process lay in the condemnation of the 'effeminate fop' in the eighteenth century. But with the ascendance of science as the new moral moderator, same-sex desire between men ceased to be a social *faux pas* and became instead a disease and a crime, as well as the sign of a distinctly different and sick individual. In this century, in a law linking it with the deviance of female prostitution, homosexuality attracted the first legal statutes against sexual behaviour since the Buggery Law four centuries earlier.

Just as with the law, so it was the case with science. For the final distinctive contribution of this century to sexual modernity was the development of the science of sex. This new discipline straddled the nineteenth and twentieth centuries and contained within it elements of the conservative past and the enquiring future. It was conservative in that, by focusing on 'the abnormal manifestations' of desire, it left unchallenged the question of what was normal sexuality. In this tacit acceptance of the normative categories, heterosexual coitus was more firmly entrenched at the pinnacle of sexual and social order. But its radical content lay in the commitment to overcome the squeamishness of talking about or studying sex: for the scientists of sex the greatest sin was ignorance. The medical training and scientific methods of its exponents gave respectability to this new arena of enquiry. It was radical also in its approach to the issue of 'sexual inversion'. In an indication of the mixed nature of their endeavours, the sexologists strove to explain the social as well as scientific origins of same-sex desire and thus to reduce its criminalization and pathologization. Through their work the final component of modernist sexuality was put in place. The sexologists moved an understanding of sex and desire beyond the dictates of the body to include the influence of the mind and of social forces. Though still at times uneasily balanced on the borders of medicalizing sexual behaviour, these pioneers opened up new dimensions of the sexual landscape and of individual sexual experience for more sober and less judgemental contemplation. Their work also brought into focus for the first time the issue of sexual identity – the conscious recognition and experience of the sexual self. It was this aspect which was to offer the foundation for movements of sexual liberation, perhaps the defining feature of twentieth-century sexuality.

FURTHER READING

Porter, R. (1982) Mixed feelings: the Enlightenment and sexuality in eighteenth century Britain. In P.-G. Bouce (ed.) *Sexuality in Eighteenth Century Britain*. Manchester: Manchester University Press.

Rousseau, G., and Porter, R. (eds) (1987) *Sexual Underworlds of the Enlightenment*. Manchester: Manchester University Press.

Duberman, M., Vicinus, M., and Chauncey, G. (eds) (1991) *Hidden from History: Reclaiming the Gay and Lesbian Past*. Harmondsworth: Penguin.

Weeks, J. (1989) *Sex, Politics and Society: The Regulation of Sexuality since 1800*. Rev. edn, London: Quartet Books.

6

Obligatory Pleasures and Undisciplined Desires: The Sexual Century Reviewed

Introduction

The twentieth century might justifiably be named 'the sexual century'. Since sex has been the central theme of the story so far, this may seem an odd statement. But historians looking at the twentieth century in the future will notice some distinctive features that would justify this claim. The distinction between heterosexuality and homosexuality in the nineteenth century was based on the assumption that heterosexuality was not only normal but also natural. This implied that sexual experience and identity operated independently of social influences. It also disengaged the idea of a sexual consciousness from sexuality and suggested that nature would provide all the instruction needed for successful sexual performance. But this conclusion assumed that people were immune from the pressures, anxieties or fixations of the period in which they lived. An underlying theme of this text is to illustrate the process of 'social construction' as dynamic, its effects fluctuating in linearity and intensity over time. There has also been a suggestion, which must not be read as essentialist, that there was an interplay between social forces and the individual experience of the sexual body. This interplay is especially evident in the immediate aftermath of a century of sexual prudery, where the fearsome messages about abnormal sex stifled the possibility of untroubled individual exploration of sexuality. The systematic focus on the negative consequences of desire and pleasure had distorted the experience of sex to such an extent that sexual ignorance and fear were endemic. It was ironic in an epoch that held the script of nature to be sacred that 'what came naturally' was the cause of so much misery. At the dawn of the sexual century, the price for 'being normal', it seemed, was ignorance.

At the same time as sexual ignorance characterized the grassroots of the sexual century, the medical profession was gathering knowledge about sexual behaviour. As we have seen, modernity was marked by the recognition of the social significance of the body. But it was in the twentieth century that the *sexual* body rather than the healthy, compliant or educated body was singled out for professional attention. Talking about sex has a long history, but, in the main, a disreputable one. The sexual century saw the emergence of sex specialists and the growth of sexpertise. The link between health and sexuality had in the past been derived from a holistic concept of the body, where health in one component indicated health of the whole. In the sexual century the sexually healthy body had a significance of its own, one that was directly related, on a number of levels, to social health. Sexual health is now equated directly with sexual disease in the physical sense. But in the early decades of the twentieth century it was as much ignorance as infection that was considered socially dangerous.

Yet to dispel sexual ignorance sex education had to be provided, and the century was beset with anxieties about the content and direction of this solution and especially about the tensions between sexual education and sexual incitement. This last was articulated in relation to the young and to women. Both were considered to be more susceptible to suggestion and to the drives of their as yet uneducated sexuality. The degree to which the democratized sexual knowledge was circumscribed is evident in the opposition to the provision of birth control for all women in the first three decades of the sexual century. Birth control did not mean sex control; it was feared. The removal of the age-old deterrent of unwanted pregnancy would, many doctors argued, encourage sexual promiscuity among women. Much less anxiety was expressed about the high infant and maternal mortality rate among the mass of the population. These misgivings did not last beyond the inter-war years, when alarm was expressed about the self-confidence and autonomy women had experienced during wartime. In a move that was part of the strategy to persuade women to return to their domestic private spheres, under the direction of the medical profession sex was promoted as the single most important aspect of conjugal happiness. As such, it was seen as the woman's role to provide this as efficiently and effectively as she did all other domestic services. By mid-century there was a general consensus on the 'healthiness' of sex, both physically and sociologically, and attention turned from the ethical to the empirical dimension of sexual lives. The second wave of sexologists began their studies of the sex lives of 'ordinary people' (Kinsey et al. 1948: 51).

As the century entered its second half, demands for sexual rights began to be heard. However, the voices were not those of professional experts. They were the voices of those who had been marginalized, ignored or stigmatized by the professional discourses. Thus, women, the young, gays, lesbians, bisexuals and transsexuals mobilized their sexuality and sexual identity in opposition to the heteronormative and male-prioritizing orthodoxy. Campaigners for sexual liberation began to disengage heterosexuality from traditional associations with marriage, the family, reproduction and the 'happy home'. They also claimed that sexual diversity had equal validity for the attainment of personal satisfaction and freedom of choice. This sexual politics was encouraged by the climate of wider political activism that in the 1960s flourished in the fertile soil of economic growth and full employment. Within the four key movements – second-wave feminism, radical left-wing politics, black liberation and lesbian and gay liberation – sexuality was a central dynamic. As the most personal of characteristics, sexuality offered the basis for new claims for personal freedom. Sexual politics was also informed by the commonality of experience with other social divisions such as race and class. Women's right to define and experience their sexuality independently of male sexuality was matched by the effective organization of a gay and lesbian consciousness and sensibility after centuries of oppression and vilification.

The optimism and energy that characterized these movements of sexual affirmation were in part what gave a positive feel to the experience of the sexual century. Indeed, it seemed as if the 'sex educators' had been right; eradication of ignorance did lead to freedom. But such an interpretation ignores the key theme of this book – the connection between sexual and social order. By the 1980s the climate of collective and inclusionist radicalism had been replaced by one of radical right-wing individualism. Unemployment rose as global capitalism exerted its influence on the international labour market. The optimistic ethos of the 1960s that celebrated communal action was replaced by an increasingly intense individualism. The strengths of the movements of liberation were weakened and undermined in the face of a climate of competitiveness necessary for survival in these conditions. These social expectations were driven by the needs of global capitalism, where the boundaries and allegiances that distinguished one nation-state from another were now an impediment to the viability of globalized profits. Social insecurity intensified with an increased sense of individual competitiveness. The optimistic collectivism of the 1960s and 1970s was now deemed by most a sign of weakness. The political New Right in advanced Western countries gained new confidence and proclaimed an end to 'society'.

It was into this climate that a new blood-borne virus appeared, to which, initially, young homosexual men appeared particularly vulnerable. The response to a new incurable disease might once have been the mobilization of government-led defensive public health initiatives and generous funding of research to discover a cure. In this climate of new individualism, however, it was the diseased individual who was held responsible for their condition. HIV/AIDS was seen as a punishment, a warning from nature that 'unnatural desires' and sexual promiscuity would invite destruction of the body. The depth of fear and revulsion that drove these responses illustrated the persistence of traditional distinctions between healthy and diseased sexuality, as well as fear associated with pleasure-driven sexual freedom. The older ideas were revitalized also by more modern anxieties about the permissive era of the 1960s, where what had been 'permitted' was sexual pleasure disengaged from reproductive and stable relationships. HIV/AIDS also revitalized anxieties about youthful sexual desire, however directed, as being difficult to contain and to educate. Thus, as well as being a real threat to social and sexual health, the response to HIV/AIDS illustrated the fragility of the modern sexual order. By the 1990s punitive solutions to HIV/AIDS were moderated as research revealed it to be a blood-borne virus that was not directly associated either with homosexuality or with sexual promiscuity. Indeed, by the early twenty-first century in the West, the connection between HIV/AIDS and sex appears to have been replaced by its connection with intravenous drug use. It is in the countries of the South that the connection between HIV/AIDS and socially unacceptable sexual behaviour – promiscuity, prostitution, anal sex and intergenerational sex – has been maintained.

The last feature of the twentieth century was the commodification of sex and its pleasures in ways that connected the spheres of profitability and of self-identity. In this more than any other aspect of the sexual century can be seen the foundation of a new sexual order for the new millennium. What was once considered special and mystical became mundane as the commercial world increasingly drew on aspects of sexuality to sell commodities. In this guise, sex was presented as devoid of any of the threatening and disruptive characteristics with which for centuries it had been associated. In this sphere of presentation, those characteristics once seen as threatening to the social order were now condoned and even encouraged. The sexual experience was presented as free-floating and malleable, as varied and disposable as the products that it was used to sell. Sexual desires and pleasures were disengaged from the body and offered instead as a flexible and fluid 'wardrobe' of self-expression. This chapter will argue that, though there is an appearance of choice and diversity in this erotic marketplace, it is this appearance that itself signifies new and more effective boundaries for the shaping of sexual order. For the whole of this account there has existed a single sphere of sexuality within which normative boundaries are crafted. During the sexual century this single sphere fragmented into a number of discrete yet often overlapping spheres. Each of these offered the possibility of individual self-expression, but together they formed a new model of fragmented sexual order, one that had the appearance of liberation but in reality comprised a normative network – a series of playgrounds within which to experience simulated freedom. The sexual century can thus be split into two phases. The first was characterized by the eradication of sexual ignorance through professional education of the masses, but with a focus on the domestic and marital significance of the sexually competent woman (Hawkes 1996). The second, which coincided with post-World War II prosperity, was marked by the emergence of two further discourses on sex and sexuality: sexual liberation and sexual commodification. It is in tracing the details of these interlocking dynamics that we can gain an understanding of the construction of a sexual order in late modernity. Before these are discussed, there is one body of knowledge about sex and pleasure that needs to be reviewed, as its shadow falls over much that was said and thought about sex in the sexual century.

Sigmund Freud and the instinct to pleasure

The work of Sigmund Freud on sexuality is often underestimated as an account of the social construction of desire and pleasure. Even less often acknowledged is his pronouncement that heterosexual desire was not 'natural'. He also wrote controversially about the question of infantile and childhood sexuality. It is for these three reasons that he is placed at the head of this account. For though his work may appear old-fashioned, idiosyncratic writings of one of the first practising psychiatrists, these key themes might be understood as the presentiment of the distinctive features of the sexual century. (For more on the impact of his work, see Gay 1988 and Bullough 1994.) Freud wrote three pieces in which he specifically addressed the impact of social forces on this instinct. These were *Three Essays on the Theory of Sexuality* (1905), *'Civilized' Sexual Morality and Modern Nervous*

Illness (1908) and the later *Civilization and its Discontents* (1921) (Freud 1986a, 1986b). In the first two Freud makes very particular claims. In *Three Essays*, he details his argument about the presence of the sexual instincts in the newborn infant and its development throughout the child's life to adulthood. In *'Civilized' Sexual Morality*, he identifies the specific impacts of 'civilized society' on the instinct to pleasure with which we are all born. He would later return to the destructive social and individual consequences of this relationship in *Civilization and its Discontents* (Freud 1986c).

The starting point of Freud's work on sexuality, and the aspect that is crucial for his argument, is what he understands as 'the sexual instinct' or, more accurately, 'the instinct to pleasure'. This is an instinct in the literal sense of the word, one present from birth and one that is directed towards some aspect of survival. It is related to survival since the activities most crucial to survival are the most pleasurable. Freud's 'sexual instinct' is a long way from the 'drive to procreate' that has underpinned the argument for millennia that heterosexual sex is natural. The instinct he speaks about has seeking pleasure and gratification of desire as its object. In *'Civilized' Sexual Morality and Modern Nervous Illness* (1908) Freud made it clear that the direction of the instinct neither corresponded with, nor indicated the 'naturalness' of, the urge to procreate. He argues that the original instinct does not automatically direct itself towards reproductive activities, or even sex, narrowly defined, but to pleasure. Therefore, it follows that heterosexuality, in its normative state, is not instinctive (Freud 1986b: 188). The instinct to pleasure does not demand any fixed correspondence either to parts of the body or to gender. Similarly the correspondence between masculinity/femininity and the preferred sources of pleasure are neither fixed nor predictable, he says. 'We are accustomed to say that every human being displays both male and female instinctual impulses, needs and attributes; but though anatomy, it is true, can point out the characteristic of maleness and femaleness, psychology cannot' (Freud 1986c: 106). The channelling and restricting of this instinct to pleasure within the norms of heterosexuality is the result of socializing forces, not those of nature. Freud argues that the instinct is subject to these social forces in three stages, that correspond to infancy, childhood and adulthood: 'A first in which the sexual instinct may be freely exercised without regard to the aims of reproduction; a second, in which all of the sexual instinct is repressed except what serves the aim of reproduction; and a third, in which only legitimate reproduction is allowed as a sexual aim. This third stage is reflected in our present day sexual morality' (ibid.: 189).

Thus, civilization suppresses the pleasure-seeking aspect of the sexual instinct and directs it instead towards reproduction. This, Freud argues, is a necessary part of the civilizing process and of the maintenance of social order. Children must be trained to abandon their multiple sources of sensual pleasure and focus instead on a genital heterosexual outlet. If they do not succeed they will be unable to control their sexual drives in adulthood. The social consequences are equally dire. 'Society believes that no greater threat to its civilisation could arise than if the sexual instincts were to be liberated and returned to their original aims' (Freud 1986c: 48). However, these positive outcomes are not assured, and the efforts to suppress the instinct to pleasure have even greater negative consequences for both individual and society. Individuals often cannot give up their original sensuality, and misery and neurosis result. The wider suppression of all but reproductive coitus with the minimum of pleasure leads to unhappy marriages, sexually frigid and unfulfilled women, and men who seek sexual gratification from prostitutes (Freud 1986b: 194ff).

However enlightened the writings of the first scientists of sex were for their time, they nevertheless retained heterosexuality as the normal expression of sexual desire. Sexual perversion, however tolerantly viewed, remained 'the other' to 'natural' heterosexuality, an expression of desire that resulted in the distortion of the normal by circumstance or by congenital predisposition. Freud reversed this assumption of heteronormativity. Rather, 'the disposition to perversions of every kind is a general and fundamental human characteristic' (Freud 1986b: 109) and 'something innate in everyone' (ibid.: 87). All humans are born with polymorphously perverse potentials, which are visible in the behaviour of a nursing infant at the breast, and subsequently in activities that mimic this original source from oral and other sensual sources, including, though not exclusively involving, masturbation. The variety of these activities provides an outlet for 'uncivilized' – that is to say, socially unregulated – sensory pleasures. This is the original (unmediated by social mores) definition of perversity. Thus, we are born perverse and forced to become 'normal'. However, Freud argues that social forces, especially those of bourgeois society, have redefined the meaning that remains associated with it today. He says: 'The . . . turning point of sexual life lies in it [the instinct] becoming subordinate to the purposes of reproduction. Everything which happens before this turn of events, and equally everything which disregards it and that aims solely at pleasure is given the uncomplimentary name of 'perverse' and as such is proscribed' (Freud 1974: 258; for a further discussion of this point, see Dollimore 1993: 176ff).

These arguments, published amid much controversy at the very beginning of the twentieth century, offer some explanation for the preoccupations of the first half of the century. To begin with, Freud's views on 'civilized sexual morality' were reflected in the fear and misery that accompanied many heterosexual marital relationships. Especially it offered insights into the consequences of the bourgeois dictums about the asexuality of women. Second, his analysis offered some theoretical foundation for the evident unease about the fragility of the heterosexual order that forced a reluctant commitment to adult sex education. Finally, he identified fault lines in the construction of heteronormativity, and, though he may not have been accredited with this, the key preoccupations of the sexual century reflect the contemporary relevance of his work.

Training heterosexuality, 1: containment

Birth control does not mean sex control, but unlimited indulgence without its responsibilities and consequences. (*The Practitioner* 1923)

Social purity organisations perceived a menacing tide of filth about to swamp the nation: indiscriminate circulation of undesirable literature dealing in unwholesome ways with crime, with birth control and with sexual matters. (Porter and Hall 1995: 258)

In the first half of the twentieth century the focus on education and reform of social behaviour breached the nineteenth-century divide between the private and public spheres. Public authorities in health and social planning began to involve themselves in the domestic lives of the populace, where the diets, sleeping habits, levels of parenting and conditions of housing all became legitimate spheres for official intervention. Though public health was the rationale for this development, the medical profession was only tangentially involved. But there was one aspect of private life that the doctors reluctantly incorporated in their practice: reproductive sex. This involvement was not one they welcomed. Then as now, many in the profession considered sex to be a topic unfit for their status and training (Hawkes 1991). The issue of birth control had been a contentious one for doctors since the late nineteenth century (McLaren 1978; Hawkes 1991), despite the fact that the consequences of not providing birth control were obvious. In the first decades of the twentieth century, one in four children in England and Wales died before their first birthday and up to one in four conceptions ended in physically dangerous and illegal abortions that contributed to the rising maternal mortality rate (see, for example, Elderton 1914: 136ff). For doctors with strong religious views, abortion and birth control were both seen as 'filthy expedients for the prevention of conception' (quoted in Wood and Suitters 1970: 114–15). It remained a generally held view that women who practised birth control were morally disreputable (Marchant 1916: 318). Leading members of the British medical profession saw the use of birth control as synonymous with sexual promiscuity, especially for working-class women. It was equally condemned as a threat to the stability of marriage: 'The state should not make available to women the means to deceive their husbands' (Marchant 1926: 121). The motivation for their involvement was to contain the growing tendency for the populace to take control of their own sex lives. 'We have to realise', the editor of the leading medical journal *The Practitioner* wrote in 1923, 'that [the knowledge of] contraception has penetrated deeply into the masses'. Such self-help among the working classes was more morally and socially perilous than knowledge mediated through professionals.

Marie Stopes, the leading birth-control campaigner of the twentieth century, directly confronted these attitudes. A member of the social elite in Britain and a doctor of science, she was deeply committed to improving the sexual and reproductive health of women of all classes. The key to this, she argued, was education, since ignorance was the greatest obstacle to health and sexual fulfilment in marriage. Accordingly, she advocated education in both birth control and sexual pleasure, which made her very unpopular with the members of the medical profession. She established the first birth-control clinic in London in 1921, circulated free pamphlets, and made birth-control devices available from her clinics and later from her travelling caravans. She also published a series of books about sex, birth control, marital happiness and motherhood. Her first publication, *Married Love* (1918), passionately addressed the issue of women's sexual ignorance and the importance of sexual satisfaction for their health. Her words were received eagerly by thousands of readers, and a collection of their letters to Dr Stopes gives an indication of the extent of sexual ignorance and the misery that it caused (Hall 1978). Stopes was highly critical of the medical profession for deliberately ignoring, or being unaware of, the reality of women's sexual needs. This did not endear her to male doctors, who took every opportunity to undermine her activities. She was not to be discouraged, and continued to provide birth control and sex education until her death.

The reluctance to provide birth control, even though to do so was a rational act in the context of public health, revealed a problematic aspect of heterosexuality. Though its 'naturalness/normality' was justified by its fecundity, reproductive sex could not be left in the hands of the populace to manage. Some groups and individuals were not deemed fit to carry that responsibility. The role of the medical profession was less driven by the need to improve maternal health than the need to prevent a free market in contraceptive use. The concern was not about demography but of sexual and social order. The way to contain problematic heterosexuality was to moderate the access to contraception. This was the only sensible conclusion to be drawn from the otherwise irrational opposition to its use. The compromise in the hands of the professionals managed to disengage sex from contraception altogether. Instead of the relaxed pleasure associated with sex without fear of pregnancy, the emphasis as the motive for its use was on 'family planning'. Women must be married or at least 'engaged' to attend for contraception, and stress was placed on 'scientific contraception' to 'space and limit families' and to provide advice and treatments for 'gynaecological ailments and marital difficulties' (Leathard 1980: 60). Even in the 1960s this left single young women without official support in their sexuality. The 'problem of the unmarried' remained, its severity indicated by rising rates of illegitimacy and still illegal abortions in the US, the UK and Australia (Grahame 1989).

Women's sexuality and the problem it posed for the changing social order in and outside of wartime continued to be the focus of concerns about unmediated heterosexuality. Wartime allowed women to move freely in spaces formerly occupied only by men and women of irredeemably loose morals (McLaren 1999: 10). This allowed women to experience self-expression, in dress, in creative or skilled work, in leisure activities and in being autonomous sexual beings. It was this democratization of social space that encouraged fears about the social consequences of sexual promiscuity. However, 'the rise in the illegitimacy rate during World War II resulted from many marriages not taking place (owing to conscription and general wartime dislocation) rather than from any rise in pre-marital conceptions' (Lewis 1984: 6). Even with the rise in illegitimacy rates during wartime, older and often already married women figured more prominently in these figures than did single women under twenty-five (Haste 1994: 129). Given the illegality of abortions (although they were undertaken, with often horrendous consequences, by desperate women) and the still problematic access to birth control, even for married women, these figures suggest an overreaction about sexual morality in wartime. But cross-cutting and informing this anxiety was a strong class-based element. The sexuality of the masses attracted attention in the sexual century more than in any other. Perhaps because class distinctions had such a powerful presence in the social order, class-based anxieties about intemperate sexuality were evident in the public as well as the private sphere. Raised expectations of social and political inclusiveness on the part of both women and the working class once again focused attention on knowledge and its significance for social order. Just as the increased circulation of the printed word intensified concerns about social disruption, so the increase in mass entertainment in the inter-war years and afterwards contributed to tighter control of access.

As wartime experience challenged the past assumption that sex was a necessary but vaguely distasteful part of romantic love, representations of the connection between the two changed their emphasis. In popular entertainment, especially in the key entertainment of the masses – the cinema – the 'selling of heterosexuality' was more and more evident. The focus of attention was on young women, whose beauty was directly associated with their ability to attract men sexually. Thus modified, legitimate sexual pleasures were increasingly being presented for mass consumption. Nevertheless, commentators of both inter- and post-war periods acknowledged that there had been a seismic shift in public morality. 'There has been an inevitable swing from concealment to exhibitionism, from repression to expression, from reticence to publicity, from modesty to vulgarity' (Haire 1929: 12). Alex Comfort claimed in 1940 that the public's knowledge of sex was greater than that of the reluctant keepers of this knowledge – the doctors (Porter and Hall 1995: 270). That official attention focused on the issue of mass circulation of sexual knowledge can be seen in the activities of the censors. In the UK and the US, works of great fiction were banned because of their representations of heterosexual activity disengaged from marriage and with pleasure as its sole motive. Since its inception in 1910, the British Board of Film Censors had censored material that dealt with 'prostitution, pre-marital and extra-marital sex, sex perversion, incest, seduction, [and] venereal disease' (Richards 1981: 96). As cinema attendance became the 'essential social habit of the day' (ibid.: 95), restrictions on what could be seen by mass audiences increased. Dressing and undressing, drunkenness or any reference to intimate bodily functions, prostitution, free love, bigamy and adultery were all deleted (ibid.: 102).

The first half of the twentieth century saw a delicate line being trod between the changing social mores and the need to rein in the sexual lives of the mass population. This task was made more difficult as well as more urgent, given the impact of the world wars on public expectations and experiences of sexual expression and sexual freedom. One strategy was to operate constraints around some aspects of heterosexuality, especially those that involved women and the working class. Attempts to contain sexual licence have a long history. This version entailed more subtle control mechanisms that responded to social change while retaining the primacy of institutional control. In the face of these adjustments, the claim that the first part of the sexual century was characterized by sexual ignorance may seem contradictory. Two points need to be made. First, despite this increased sexual democracy, there was a great deal of sexual ignorance among both men and women (see Ruth Hall's collection *Dear Dr Stopes*, Hall 1978). Speaking about sex had, until the late inter-war years, been avoided by all concerned. Second, sexual ignorance gave the experts a legitimate motive for intruding even more into the bedrooms of the population, where a new figure emerged, which arguably remains a feature of the sexual landscape – 'the erotic house-wife'. In the second aspect of training heterosexuality, sexual incite-ment became the new weapon against a new vice. Sexual ignorance had once been the sign of a virtuous woman. Now it was a signal that 'something was wrong' – something for which the experts had the cure.

Training heterosexuality, 2: sexual hygiene and sexual performance

To the reticent, as to the conventional, it may seem a superfluity to speak of the details of the most complex of all our functions. They ask, 'Is not instinct enough?' The answer is 'No'. Instinct is not enough. (Stopes 1918: xii)

In the early twentieth century, as increasing numbers of commentators claimed that any normal person had to experience sensual bliss, the pursuit of sexual satisfaction took on an unprecedented importance. (McLaren 1999: 111)

Many decades before the swinging sixties, the issue of sexual freedom was causing concern. Authorities were caught between two contra-dictory forces. On the one hand there was a commitment to eradi-cate damaging ignorance through the provision of advice from suitably qualified experts. On the other there was an increased level of popular exposure to sexual imagery that might encourage 'amateur experimentation'. The answer was to distinguish these discourses about sex – one deemed essential for public order, the other deemed a threat to it. This was accomplished through the emphasis laid in the 'official discourse' on 'sexual hygiene'. The latter did not refer to sexual cleanliness but to the proper use of sexual desire and of its expression. 'Proper sex' was that which performed a social function; it was not to be used frivolously by the uneducated and uncommitted, as appeared, increasingly, to be the case. The sexually competent and responsible individual was essential for harmony both in the bedroom and in society as a whole (Lewis 1984: 134; Bullough 1994: 136). Medically qualified experts were considered most suited for this serious task, and in the first four decades of the century dozens of practitioners from both sides of the Atlantic became sexperts in print. The focus on sexual hygiene linked sexual fulfilment with health, not pleasure. To do otherwise was to involve oneself in 'wasteful expenditure' of the sex impulse (Bernard 1929: 78–9). 'In general it may be said that coitus on two successive occasions thrice a week to be normal ration' (Haire 1929: 210). The optimal balance would immediately be evident: 'on the day following intercourse both husband and wife should feel perfectly fresh, vigorous and lively' (Kisch 1931: 182). However, there was a fine line to be trodden between adequate instruction and unnecessary titillation. Writing about sex was still a morally questionable activity even for respected professionals. Some, like Marie Stopes and later Eustace Chesser, found themselves defending their publications against charges of obscenity in court actions (Porter and Hall 1995: 260–2).

The regime for training heterosexuality took three related directions. First, the sexual instinct must be channelled towards penetrative sex. Second, the couple must be trained in achieving mutual orgasm. Finally it was women's sexual responses that required attention: where male sexual performance was concerned, it seemed that nature required no improvement. Attention turned first to the mechanics of penetration, as it was assumed that women would be virgins on marriage. This 'prenuptial sexual hygiene' involved a doctor instrumentally rupturing the hymen and dilating the vagina before first coitus. This 'not only removes the fear and embarrassment but if the hymen is really difficult to dilate it is better that the unpleasant memories are attached to a stranger – the doctor – rather than to the husband' (Haire 1929: 226). Alternatively, the woman herself undertook this procedure, though still under professional guidance. Following a detailed internal and external examination of the sexual organs, the woman is given a glass tube, which she is encouraged to insert into the vagina to establish that penetration is possible. Then, 'the physician directs the bride how to insert her finger, properly lubricated, into the vaginal opening. Then he will have her insert several gradated vaginal dilators ... until she can introduce a dilator 3/4" thick without wincing' (Davis 1960: 114–16).

Having established the mechanics of penetration, attention turned to sexual technique. The most explicit example, even in contemporary terms, was *Ideal Marriage* (Van de Velde 1930). This text provided a clear picture of the aim to offer erotic instruction without crossing the boundaries of 'taste and decency'. Explicit sexual detail was combined with traditional moral and gendered messages about sexual mores. Emphasis was placed on the importance of the man in erotic education, though men, too, are acknowledged to be ignorant in these matters. 'I also direct myself to married men, for they are naturally educators and initiators of their wives in sexual matters' (quoted in Bland and Doan 1998a: 125). Women are depicted like machines that the man has to learn, under expert tuition, how to operate to maximum efficiency. He must learn to 'give delight', but for this he needs 'explicit knowledge' if he is to be equipped to 'inspire desire and give joy' (ibid.: 126). However, women's erotic potential was recognized in the emphasis placed on preliminary arousal. Cunnilingus was recommended in glowing terms to aid lubrication and to prepare the woman for coitus. It is particularly useful for 'overcoming frigidity and fear in hitherto inexperienced women' (ibid.: 128), but must not be practised to orgasm.

Another aspect of training heterosexuality mixes erotic education with gendered expectations, giving 'the erotic housewife' a sphere of expertise all her own. A leading female medic of the period, Helena Wright, advises women to be mindful of their sexual responsibilities in marriage, for 'it is only through making yourself open to sexual passion can you really show your love' (Wright [1930] 1961: 3). But while the responsibility for a happy marriage lay on the shoulders of the woman, she was not 'naturally' equipped to perform this role. 'The great majority . . . are capable of passionate affection [but] that capacity has to be wakened in them by their husbands. They can feel, but they have to be *made* [my emphasis] to feel' (ibid.: 14). The use of clitoral stimulation was recommended for this purpose, to 'aid lubrication' and encourage a properly responsive vagina. In cases where 'friction in the [vaginal] passage arouses no more sensation than it would if a knee or elbow was rubbed' (Medica 1950: 58), it can be an acceptable substitute. However, care had to be taken not to overuse these alternative sources of pleasure. Over-indulgence might deflect married women especially away from the coital path. There is no denying that the clitoris is a source of pleasure, 'but if indulged in very frequently, may lead to an inability to experience proper sexual satisfaction in normal coitus' (Griffith 1938: 210).

Masturbation was not condemned outright in this discourse, since the aim was to educate women erotically (Haire 1929: 72). But, again, dangers existed in overuse. Practised too often, and especially before marriage, masturbation risked rerouting women's sexual desire away from the 'norm'. 'The sex organs may become so accustomed to responding to some particular method of self-relief that enjoyment of the normal sex act may be difficult to establish' (Wright [1930] 1961: 64). So fragile was the establishment of heterosexual coitus that any alterative source of pleasure threatened successful coital commitment. The danger in the acknowledgment and training of women's erotic potential was that she might seek alternatives to marital coitus. 'If she has used some other form of self-stimulation, breast, or thigh rubbing or wriggling on the arm of a chair it is even longer before she enjoys intercourse fully' (Davis 1960: 44).

The first half of the sexual century was one where a careful balance was struck between education, containment and incitement to pleasure. The erotic housewife is an unacknowledged figure in this process, yet her successful elevation was at least temporary evidence that a method had been found, again, to combine the extension of erotic democracy with intensified surveillance of 'natural' sexual behaviour. But the expansion of a discourse of pleasure that this entailed unwittingly provided an unprecedented development, one that characterized the second half of the sexual century. Sexual participation was to become synonymous with extended political participation.

'Liberating heterosexuality?'

It is commonplace to identify the 1960s and 1970s as 'the permissive era'. But we need to ask, what was permitted, and by whom? Second, under what conditions was this relaxation of sexual mores permitted? Third, did the changes in sexual mores of this era expand or limit the experience of sexual pleasure? Between approximately 1960 and 1970 (though the era depends somewhat on the country in question) advanced Western nations were benefiting from post-war full employment. Such a concept would now be a fairy tale, but it was then a reality that delivered unprecedented prosperity for the majority. The group that benefited most from this was unmarried young adults. Full employment meant the possibility of independent living, away from the influence of their parents and especially from their moral and sexual standards. This economic and social autonomy offered the opportunity for young people to mark their independence from the morality of their parents by challenging the long-standing condemnation of extra-marital sex. The phrase 'living together' was born in this period, as couples rejected legal marriage as the only acceptable (and lawful) basis for a sex/love relationship. But in the swinging sixties sex was also liberated from a necessary context of a 'stable relationship'. 'Making love' was an option for non-committed individuals in more fleeting physical engagements with each other. In both cases, sex provided the means not just to express a degree of personal autonomy but also to claim liberation from parental (and to a degree societal) constraints.

However, there were limitations to this licence. The sex that was disengaged from the traditional contexts of marriage or even roman-tic commitment was expected to be coital: in definition and experi-ence it served the erotic needs of men. Second, this freedom remained haunted (for women) by the spectre of unwanted pregnancy, since, although the pill was released for prescription, access was mediated through a medical profession unwilling to inhabit the front line in reversing the stigma of extra-marital sex. For single, sexually active young women, walking the gauntlet to gain access to effective con-traception was difficult, if not impossible. In the 1960s, unwanted pregnancy was still a source of shame and social disgrace. Homes for 'unmarried mothers' offered the only socially acceptable form of atonement, where the young women were persuaded, and sometimes almost coerced, to give up their babies for adoption.

Despite this, the two decades saw a series of laws passed that acknowledged the shift in sexual mores in the post-war years. These involved three key areas: family planning, abortion and homosex-uality. In the UK, all these areas were addressed in 1967, when, in three separate Acts, contraception was made available for the unmar-ried and abortion and homosexuality were decriminalized. In Australia abortion was decriminalized in all states between 1969 and 1982. The contraceptive pill was available to married women from 1961 but not for the unmarried until 1970. In the US, a landmark case, *Roe* v. *Wade* (1976), rendered the existing laws forbidding abortion except in extreme circumstances unconstitutional. As with Australia and the UK, unmarried women in the US were granted access to the pill in the context of the sexual liberation demands of the 1970s. The decriminalization of homosexuality occurred in the UK following the Wolfenden Report into homosexuality and prosti-tution. The Sexual Offences Act (1967) decriminalized same-sex activities between men over twenty-one in private. In both Australia and the US this aspect of sexual freedom took longer to be real-ized. In Australia, homosexuality was progressively decriminalized between 1981 and 1995; in the US this took place between 1981 and

1985, though there remain four states where 'sodomy' between men is illegal and a further six where it is illegal between both sexes (www.sodomylaws.org).

These legal changes in three industrialized Western countries identified some aspects of sexual expression as a matter for private conscience rather than for official intervention. But they were not clear evidence for a new sexual morality. Though they signify formal relaxation of past constraints, the real freedom they represented fell a long way short of liberation. First, they continued the normative distinction between homo- and heterosexuality. The age of consent, again varying between countries, was nevertheless lower for heterosexuality than for homosexuality. Second, access to contraception was still subject to medical approval of the request, and women's right to control their fertility was equally restricted by the rights of the doctors to grant or to refuse an abortion. Finally, Christie Davies has argued of the UK history that these relaxations did not signal positive approval of more sexual freedom, but were intended to prevent what were considered to be even less desirable consequences of the sexual revolution – unplanned pregnancies, abortions, and the sexual exploitation of minors (Davies 1980). Now to the question of whether fewer moral restrictions on sexual behaviour automatically delivers greater freedom of expression.

'Liberated sex' had a patchwork form in the 1960s and 1970s. Rather than a linear progression from restriction to freedom, there was another process that Foucault had identified in the nineteenth century – that of a proliferation of discourses about sex. The difference was that this time the discourses were not speaking of fears and dangers. These twentieth-century voices were more seductive, associating sex with indulgent pleasure, with humour and with recreation. It is easy to recognize fashions, movies, TV programmes and popular music of the 1960s and 1970s by the naïve yet confronting omnipresence of sexual references. There was a quality to this 'situational sex' that was fundamentally innocent, even childlike. The epitome of this 'persona' of sex was represented in the *Carry On . . .* films, produced in Britain from the late 1950s. The ingenuous joy with which traditional pruderies were confronted in these films was matched by a representation of women as the object of pleasure for men who had sex almost always uppermost in their minds. In a similar vein, television 'sitcoms' like *Man About the House* (ITV, UK, 1973–6) depicted the new sexual independence of young people from their parents' scrutiny. The programme featured two young women getting a single male flatmate – itself a risqué idea and providing a setting for a continuous stream of double entendre. The cross-generational difference was part of the humour, as the middle-aged married landlords observed and were suitably horrified by the sexual possibilities presented by this cohabitation. In this manner, two aspects of the contemporary sexual culture were represented – the new world of the sexually relaxed young set against the sexually obsessed and uptight older generation. The long-standing hit comedy *Are You Being Served?* (BBC TV, 1972–83) encapsulated the essence of this uneasily sexualized world in a series of unforgettable stereotypes: the young busty 'dollybirds', the sexually avaricious men, the middle-aged sexually frustrated matron (Mrs Slocum's Pussy) and the theatrically camp man, whose sexuality was the source of the greatest belly laughs. In Australia this association of explicit sexual reference to light entertainment was represented by the nightly antics of the inhabitants of *Number 96* (1972–7). This hugely popular show specialized in male and female nudity and frequent explicit sexual imagery and text. Sexual messages were less explicit in US television, where the most popular programmes of the decade were *The Mary Tyler Moore Show* and *Keep it in the Family*. In neither was sex depicted as a topic for humour. But the most popular imported comedy figure by 1979 was Benny Hill. The success of *The Benny Hill Show* in the US followed that in the UK ten years earlier: 'Smuttiness and lechery were the trademarks of this show in which tall beautiful girls are chased and ogled by Hill and a group of stereotypical males' (www.museum.tv/archive/etv./B/htmlB/bennyhilsh/bennyhil.htm). An American version of the widening of heterosexual boundaries was books directed at a young sexually experimental adult audience. *Sexual Swinging for Beginners: Who Does What to Whom and How* (1973), *The Group* (1969) and *Sex and the Single Girl* (1962) to different degrees encouraged the legitimacy of sexual experimentation for entertainment.

However, this encouragement represented more normative than challenging messages, in that they were constructing new versions of acceptable heterosexuality. In the context of wide-ranging social change, the usefulness of one single legitimate model of heterosexuality for maintaining a sexual order was limited. The picture of monogamous heterosexual sex was becoming less relevant when increasing numbers of people were exploring sexual freedom without reference to either marriage or monogamy. But the new version of acceptable heterosexuality presented sex as a confection, to be enjoyed at a very superficial level and usually once removed by humour, fantasy or fiction. Represented in this manner, the challenge posed by heterosexual licence was less disruptive to the still necessary stability of heterosexual orthodoxy.

The construction of confection sex drew on easily deployable but not especially challenging stereotypes. The decriminalization of homosexuality in the US, the UK and Australia had removed the legal stigma from men who desire men. But in popular cultural media the usually token gay man was invariably an object of humour and obliged to court this 'tolerance' through overt campness. Likewise, the sexually 'swinging' woman was represented as part-child, part desirable woman – an uncomfortable stalwart of male fantasy. The miniskirt and 'hotpants', now remembered affectionately (and resurrected in modified form in the 1990s), exposed the buttocks and emphasized the presence of women's genitalia while demoting in importance the more traditional markers of sexualized fertility – the breasts.

Sexual liberation of women was a key feature of the permissive era. At the centre of this freedom, though by no means its only cause, was the contraceptive pill. The revolutionary aspect of the pill did not just lie in its efficacy as contraception. Almost as important was its anonymity. Once obtained, it could be used by women at will, without consultation with anyone else, especially their sexual partners. This meant that they could at last avoid the stigma that for centuries had marked sexually autonomous women as immoral and socially corrupting. In principle, at least, the pill offered 'freedom to fuck' like a man. But this was only part of the story. There was another important element that from the beginning limited this revolutionary potential of the pill. For 'the pill' was until 1967 in the UK and some years later in the US and Australia only available to married women. Those single women who sought to control their fertility ran the risk of moral judgement or outright refusal by attending doctors. Similarly, the decriminalization of abortion retained the authority of medical professionals to permit a termination of pregnancy in all three countries. Access to abortion was also highly conditional on the personal attitudes of the medical practitioner and remained, for any women who chose to terminate their pregnancy, a stigmatized and deeply disturbing experience. Single women's fertility continued to be controlled by the medical profession, even though, formally at least, they were 'free to choose'. Thus the traditional spectre of an unwanted pregnancy continued to operate as a counterbalance to the sexual independence offered to women by the relaxed moral climate. As throughout history, the figure of the 'fallen woman' was retained, even if she did wear miniskirts. The terrain of sexual liberation that so centrally featured the sexually swinging young woman was one that was also inhabited by spectres of past marginal figures.

The second-wave feminist slogan 'the personal is the political' identified women's bodies as the primary site of oppression and exploitation. Feminist activists argued that the common factor that linked abortion, contraception, rape, pornography and penetrative sex was that women's bodies and experiences were the servants of male power and desire. Through these imperatives women's sensual independence was degraded and denied. Feminist scholars of the 1970s and 1980s argued that the construction of male sexual aggression and instinctive active sexuality was the key dynamic in these processes (see, for example, McKinnon 1987; Dworkin 1981; Segal 1987). They argued that medical and political discourses about the five key aspects were either lacking in commitment (contraception and abortion) or simply wrong (rape, pornography and penetrative sex). For 'ordinary' women, this primary focus on women's experience encouraged participation in personal politics at a grassroots level that was personally very empowering. The provision of a safe space within which to share experience without fear of ridicule encouraged women of all backgrounds and ages to take part in 'women's groups'. The subject of sexual experiences often waited for trust and friendship to develop, but the realization of common fears, frustrations and disappointments was to shake the foundations of the 'brave new world' of heterosexual pleasure (Millett 1970; Greer 1970).

For many women, the sisterhood that developed through common experience and activism was extended to sexual intimacy. For some this was driven by curiosity or the wish to explore the delights of their newly discovered female sexuality. For others, the end of women's oppression meant the end of heterosexual relationships and especially of penile/vaginal penetration (see the film *Sleeping with the Enemy*, 2001). Though in the early stages there were often differences in the motives for separatism, women were united in one view. Modelling women's sexuality on that of men denied both its social validity and the reality of its experience. Women's sexuality was not only different physiologically and experientially from that of men. It was, fundamentally, incompatible in the form in which 'sexuality' had been constructed over the previous two centuries. Within the safety of collective experience, women talked about their sexual as well as their political bodies. Just as sexual oppression by men was epitomized in the act of penetration, so the assertion of a female sexuality came to be epitomized in the pleasure of the clitoral orgasm.

The historical amnesia about the clitoris as the source of female sexual pleasure is a consistent feature in the modernist construction of 'sexuality' and of heteronormativity. The pleasurable consequences of clitoral stimulation were smothered under the anxiety-making discourse on masturbation. The freewheeling coupling of the 1960s and 1970s was, as with marital pleasures, based on the assumption that vaginal orgasm was the peak of erotic sensibility. But there were other voices being raised that were identifying different and challenging dimensions of normative heterosexuality. These insights came from empirical evidence of sexual lives, gathered from volunteer subjects. An unlikely individual pioneered these sex surveys, and quietly but insistently presented his findings. Alfred Kinsey, by training a biologist who specialized in the study of wasps, set out to reverse what he saw as flawed foundations for pronouncements about normal sexual behaviour. He insisted that all previous definitions rested on unproven and value-ridden assumptions about the 'normality' of heterosexual coitus. Thus all studies of sexual behaviour had been based on a value judgement. Such a foundation could not be tolerated in a scientific enquiry. For Kinsey, no sexual act of itself could be pronounced normal or abnormal. The most that science could or should do was to justify empirically a statement about the frequency of different sexual acts within a chosen population. Accordingly, in 1948 and 1953, Kinsey and his research team published the results of a detailed sex survey of a self-selected population of white male and female Americans (Kinsey et al. 1948, 1953). In general, it can be said that this study was profoundly satisfying for Kinsey's claim, for it illustrated a level of participation in 'abnormal' or 'unhealthy' sexual acts that, by his definition, rendered them normal. For example, even at a time when sexual ignorance was argued to be rife, he found that masturbation was the second most common sexual activity in women and the one from which 95 per cent of those in his study most frequently achieved orgasm (Kinsey et al. 1953: 171).

Similarly, the British sex reformer Eustace Chesser, writing about the erotic effectiveness of coitus, 'concluded from studies of British and American literature that 70% of women had never reached satisfaction' (Coote and Campbell 1982: 216). In 1954 William Masters and Virginia Johnson (a physician and partially qualified behavioural scientist, respectively) began their laboratory studies of the physiology of the orgasm in men and women (Masters and Johnson 1966). Their intention was to establish the source of and treatment for sexual dysfunction (defined as premature ejaculation in men, anorgasmia in women). Using physiological measurement techniques, these scientists established the validity of a distinct clitoral orgasmic pathway. However, though they accepted that women's primary sexual pleasure was derived from the clitoris, they claimed it was experienced in its complete physiological manifestation in the vagina. During coitus, the thrusting of the penis in the vagina produces an indirect stimulation of the clitoris in the same ways as direct stimulation in masturbation (Hite 1993: 47–50). This relocation of potentially radical findings intensified rather than alleviated pressure on women to respond successfully to this 'indirect stimulation'. Masters and Johnson's work also established the ground for a therapeutic project to promote heterosexual orgasm, which persists in much sex therapy today.

In the wake of feminism's focus on women's bodies and their experiences, a strand of feminist sexology emerged that listened to, rather than studied, women. Shere Hite, a cultural historian, published the results of a survey which 'asked women how they feel, what they like and what they think about sex' (Hite 1976: 11). In 1976, this text became an international best-seller and, for the women who bought it or lent it to friends, a revelation. In the same year the dimension of fantasy was added for the first time to mainstream sexual discourse (Friday 1976). Like Hite, Nancy Friday invited American women to tell her about their sexual fantasies. These accounts illustrate 'the endlessly fertile, eternally imaginative female fantasy world that has presumably existed, unseen and underground, ever since Eve in her Secret Garden' (ibid.: 4). These were words of ordinary women, not sexologists, feminist or otherwise, which encouraged other women to explore and validate a dimension of their sexuality that had hitherto been hijacked by male-orientated pornography. In the words of one respondent, which, Friday claimed, was a typical response, 'thank God I can tell these thoughts to someone; up till now I've never confided mine to a living soul. I have always been ashamed of them, feeling that other people would think them unnatural and consider me as a nymphomaniac or a pervert' (quoted in ibid.: 16). The media attention attracted by Hite's and to a lesser extent Friday's work made explicit talk about women's sexual pleasure big commercial business. Magazines like *Cosmopolitan* (whose founding editor, Helen Gurley Brown, had published *Sex and the Single Girl* in 1962), *Marie-Claire* and a host of others emerged in the wake of these studies over the last decades of the century. The resulting discourse of 'leisure sex' (Hawkes 1996) had two themes: seemingly inexhaustible variations of 'how to have, or more often, how to give, good (heterosexual) sex', and an absence of moralizing about promiscuity or disease. In this media-led sexual liberation it was women's responsibility successfully to achieve the 'ecstasy of ecstasies, mutual orgasm' (*Cosmopolitan*, 1992).

By the end of the twentieth century the normative boundaries between hetero- and homosexual desires began to blur. But it was, again, a limited relaxation. For it applied only to women, who in themed clubs and bars were invited to 'play bi or lesbian'. Gay sexuality was kept carefully separate (apart from the occasional celebrity bisexual man) but had become a popular source of mainstream entertainment. The popularity of *Queer as Folk* in the UK, the US and Australia suggested a lowering of anxiety about the 'contagiousness' of homosexuality that had been a strong theme throughout the century. In contrast, 'the lesbian kiss' in mainstream television retained its capacity to shock and disturb (see *Roseanne*, 1994; *Brookside*, 1993). Relaxation of boundaries cannot be read as the end of either dualistic desire or heterosexual hegemony. Instead, interlocking spheres of experience have replaced the 'either/or' binary as a dynamic for sexual order. At one level, it is the consciousness of individuals, encouraged by the rhetoric of 'self-identity', through which regulation operates. For the ideology of choice places the final responsibility for the outcome at the feet of the 'sovereign actor'. One can see this mechanism at work in the discourses of self-help, whether in relation to physical or emotional health. The existence of many 'separate spheres' for erotic expression entails also the existence of normative boundaries enforced not by shame and stigma but by 'rules of play'.

Foucault has argued that four domains in which sexuality was constructed emerged in the nineteenth century. This sexuality 'has its reason for being [in] innovating, annexing creating and penetrating bodies in an increasingly detailed [and] increasingly complex way' (Foucault 1984: 107). There is no reason to imagine that Foucault, the historian, meant us to understand that this process ended with the nineteenth century. The *process* of social construction is necessarily dynamic and, as modernity progresses, demands the inclusion of formerly excluded components.

Gays and lesbians in from the margins

The science of sex had modified moral judgement of those who desired their own sex. But though sexology encouraged a degree of toleration, for the most part their activities ensured that male homosexuality would remain an inversion of nature and female homosexuality little more than a footnote. The legal construction of same-sex desire followed the same pattern; laws increasingly policed and criminalized male homosexuality while ignoring lesbianism. This differential treatment was further evidence of the male model of all sexuality, male or female, gay or straight. Male homosexuality raised questions over what constituted natural desire in men and challenged the construction of a sexuality that was linked by nature with an essence of masculinity. Since lesbian women were considered to be emulating men in both behaviour and sexuality, female homosexuality was not seen as a threat to masculine sexuality. Indeed, it added support to this model. This was the background against which gay and lesbian desire began its journey through the sexual century and wrought changes that would be a landmark in sexual history.

The traditional masculine context of war was, paradoxically, to offer an arena within which homosexuality could challenge its social exclusion. The conditions of physical and single-sex intimacy intensified by the ever-present fear of death offered a space for homoerotic experience for gay and straight men alike. In plays and poems of the World War I period, homoeroticism was openly acknowledged (see, for example, E. M. Forster, W. H. Auden, Stephen Spender). More recently oral history has provided first-hand evidence from individuals who were young men at the time (David 1997: 53–62; see also Weeks and Porter 1998). From 1920 to 1939 in the privileged environment of the literary upper classes homosexuality was 'associated with the innocent eccentricity' of the wealthy and artistic (David 1997: 129). At the same time, 'ordinary homosexuals' began to create their own spaces in cities, where they could be relatively free of persecution. But, as Quentin Crisp recalls, these remained uneasy refuges that were always subject to police harassment. Nevertheless, they offered a resource to all men who sought alternative and forbidden pleasures. Many of Crisp's sexual liaisons were with self-identified heterosexual men, who could 'never admit to themselves or to God or to one another that they even liked the company of homosexuals – let alone that "trade" with them was a pleasurable pastime' (Crisp 1968: 65). Thus, however perilous their security and anonymity, these spaces were occupied by real people indicating the flexibility of the distinction between gay and straight sexuality.

In the first half of the century, homosexuality remained not only officially illegal but also officially a disease. Homosexuals, for example, were not allowed to join the armed forces, as their sexuality was deemed to be both disruptive and communicable. As a condition that was either acquired or inherited, homosexuality was seen as a social threat as well as an individual abnormality before World War II. In the UK and the US, police entrapment of homosexuals increased dramatically between 1930 and 1958 (Davenport-Hines 1991: 297). But just as prosecutions increased, so, with wartime, did the opportunities for homoerotic experiences. That this was the case was clearly illustrated by Alfred Kinsey, whose report on male sexual behaviour in the US (published in 1948) was nearly banned for obscenity. Kinsey's findings that 37 per cent of men in his study had experienced orgasm with another man and 13 per cent had experienced homoerotic contact confirmed that 50 per cent of men admitted to homoerotic desires in what was assumed to be the heterosexual majority where this was illegal. Homosexuality continued to be constructed as a threat to social order, but during and especially after the war it was also seen as a threat to national security. 'The focusing of hostile anxiety on a hateful minority of homosexuals first remarked during the Napoleonic Wars and revived during 1915–18 was a feature of the Second World War' (ibid.: 298). This association was further intensified during the Cold War with the discovery that the British diplomats turned Soviet spies, Guy Burgess and Donald McLean, were respectively homosexual and bisexual (ibid.: 300). Being suspected of homosexuality was sufficient to disbar an individual from the armed forces or the civil service, discriminatory practices that set the norms for wider society.

Given this increased social condemnation, why was it the case that by the end of the 1960s homosexuality had been decriminalized in the UK? One explanation was that the changed world of wartime had exposed the reality of sexual culture – that homosexuality was not restricted to a diseased and degenerate minority of men who were in every way distinguishable from their 'normal' brothers. If Kinsey's figures were representative, then nearly 50 per cent of the male population were potential criminals. Increased police entrapment had the opposite than intended effect. Far from stamping out homosexuality, it exposed the degree to which it was integrated in society. Worse, many of those entrapped were high-status and high-profile individuals with a great deal of public support: John Gielgud, Alec Guinness and Lord Montagu of Beaulieu were among them. Politically there was a growing view that the law was unenforceable and therefore to continue was further to compromise social order. As Ian Gilmore, an English Conservative MP, commented in 1954: '[The law] is unenforceable because there are too many of these people to enable the law to be enforced. We do not know how many there are but, if there are half a million and we are able to catch them, we would not have any idea of what to do with them' (quoted in Coppa 1999: 90). An unworkable law was worse than no law, since it held the judiciary up to ridicule. In August 1954 the British government's Home Office constituted a committee to investigate homosexuality and prostitution, headed by John Wolfenden. In 1957 the committee submitted its recommendations. The Wolfenden Report distinguished between 'genuine born' homosexuals and those who had acquired the taste in particular social circumstances. This latter group were considered reformable, the former not to blame for their inversion. The categories first established by the nineteenth-century sex scientists were fifty years later deployed to argue successfully for the decriminalization of adult consensual male homosexuality. The committee members, with one exception, were in favour of decriminalizing homosexuality between adults in private. The contentious question remained over the age of consent. Seven of the thirteen members were in favour of supporting eighteen years, but, in the light of Home Office pressures and anxieties about the corruption of youth, Wolfenden was successful in raising this to twenty-one. The legality of adult consensual homosexuality in the UK was to wait for another decade before passing into law as the Sexual Offences Act (1967). The restriction of legal acts to the private sphere strengthened the boundaries between homo- and heterosexual desires that had been demonstrated to be inadequate. The law thus reinstated the hierarchy of heterosexuality over homosexuality. Men who desired men were returned to a separate category, the evidence safely hidden behind closed doors. Freedom to express sexual or romantic feelings in public remained the prerogative of heterosexuals alone.

The integration of lesbian women in inter-war society followed similar patterns. Women in the artistic or intellectual elite could feel comfortable in expressing their identity without fear of condemnation. However, the scope for self-expression was limited. Popular expectations were that lesbian relationships, more so than gay ones, would mirror heterosexuality in their gender roles: that one partner would be the 'masculine' and the other the 'feminine'. Both gendered categories were marked by specific appearance and roles. Thus 'feminine [lesbian] women . . . could become recognisable only by association with their masculine partners' (Newton 1991: 291). Public tolerance did not extend to acceptance of a specific female eroticism. Even the early scientists of sex did not address the question of what lesbians did sexually. In the inter-war years, as women began to challenge traditional roles, details of their sexuality came under greater scrutiny. This was especially the case for sexual activity that excluded men altogether. In 1921 the British lord chancellor expressed the view that ninety-nine out of a hundred women had no concept of lesbian sex, nor should they be exposed to any 'noxious and horrible suspicions' of just what it did entail. Lesbianism was only acceptable under two conditions: that lesbians signalled their 'condition' by emulating men, and that details of their sexuality was hidden from the public eye.

The anxiety over explicit details of lesbian desire and its sexual expression can be illustrated in the story of a book and its author.

Radclyffe Hall (1880–1943) was an established literary and social figure in inter-war Europe and the US and a contemporary of Vita Sackville-West and Virginia Woolf. Dressed always elegantly in masculine fashions, Hall lived openly with her female lover. Her book *The Well of Loneliness* (1928) followed the life story of a young girl to adulthood as she struggles to come to terms with her identity and sexuality as a lesbian woman, not a mannish counterfeit. This text offered the first opportunity for women to recognize and identify with erotic and emotional experience separate, not derived, from male sexuality and identity. The book was notorious from its publication and was banned under the Obscene Publications Act of 1857. In the US the book was similarly banned as obscene, and it was eventually printed in France. The popular and legal condemnation illustrated the threat that certain sexual details posed to heterosexual norms. The response to *The Well of Loneliness* illustrated the dangers to heterosexuality of an autonomous female sexuality that rendered men irrelevant. In the 1950s lesbian women and homosexual men were viewed as an equal threat to stable heterosexuality. False accusations, persecution and exclusion from public life or service awaited those who visibly rejected traditional expectations of womanhood (Faderman 1981: 130ff). Such women were considered unfit for public roles, especially those that involved the young. Moreover, they were considered sick and in need of psychiatric treatment. These strategies reflected the need to reverse the economic and social gains made by women in wartime and to restore them to subordinate and marginalized domestic roles. The 'diagnosis' of lesbianism was a way to contain women's freedoms while re-establishing male dominance both in and outside the bedroom.

By the early 1960s public and especially media condemnation of homosexuality was decreasing. Though legislation passed in the UK, the US and Australia had decriminalized homosexuality between 1967 and the late 1980s, this did not necessarily ensure social acceptance and even less so equal citizenship rights. It was left to the groups, united by their sense of history and growing sense of community, to make the demands for social and political inclusion for themselves. Gay and lesbian liberation movements claimed their rights as humans to enjoy the same freedoms of sexual expression as heterosexuals without stigmatization. The sexual century offered a series of contexts within which communities of sexual identity developed, gaining social and political influence independently of the more liberalizing legislation (see David 1997: 228ff and Weeks 1999: 182ff).

Two key issues weakened widespread and institutionalized homophobic attitudes on the one hand and strengthened the political effectiveness of sexual minorities on the other. The first was the rise in gay and lesbian political activism following the Stonewall Riots in the US. In 1969 police raided a gay bar in Greenwich Village, New York. The patrons of the bar – gay men, lesbians and drag queens – refused to accept the flimsy grounds for this raid and instead demanded an end to police harassment. Popular support for this direct action related the oppression of sexual minorities with that of workers, women and people of colour. Its timing, at the end of the decade, coincided with a maturing political organization of these excluded social groups, and offered a wider foundation from which to make demands for equal human rights. The second offered a platform from which to launch lesbian experience and identity as a separate political issue. Second-wave feminism gave new meaning to erotic attachment between women while establishing the concept of lesbian experience as a social as well as sexual ideal. For radical feminists, women could neither express their own sexuality nor avoid the domination of men in heterosexual relationships. Only through lesbian existence could women be free to explore and take control of their own sexuality. This association brought lesbian desire in from the shadows for many individual women as well as in the wider social consciousness.

At the beginning of the 1980s both gay and lesbian identities and political organization had strengthened and public attitudes had begun to condemn homophobia as a parallel prejudice to racism and sexism. Deregulation of global economies and the rise of 'market forces' increased the disposable incomes of childless gay and lesbian couples. 'The pink pound' (or dollar) had become an economic force in its own right. At the same time, gays and lesbians were moving beyond the limits placed upon them by heterosexual society in their appearance and behaviour. The 'new homosexual' subverted 'orthodox masculinity' by becoming himself 'hypermasculine' in appearance and dress (Blachford 1981; Marshall 1981; Plummer 1981; and Evans 1993). Many lesbian women likewise moved beyond the 'butch-dyke' image to express themselves in markers of heterosexual femininity. But in the same decade a virus emerged that would reverse these gains in public acceptance. It would also strengthen the organization and sense of collectivity within the gay and lesbian communities for the next twenty years. Weeks has argued that 'it was an historical accident' that the virus first appeared (in Western experience) in young, sexually active gay populations of first the US and then, rapidly, of Western Europe. Its appearance coincided with the exploration of now legal sexual pleasure as well as with the public profile of a politically well-organized movement for equal citizenship rights. Though within two years of its isolation, the new virus was disassociated from gay sex and recognized as a threat to all who were sexually active, HIV/AIDS released old fears and prejudices that were only just below the surface of liberalized attitudes of the 1970s. The coincidence with the rise of conservative political administrations in both the UK and the US that actively promoted traditional family and sexual values 'shaped, and has continued to form, the social and cultural response to AIDS' (Weeks 1999: 149).

But the lack of public opposition to, and even acceptance of, these political platforms suggested that there was a significant degree of popular support for these views. In both respects, this disease, and its erroneous association with specifically gay sexual acts, offered a powerful platform from which to launch a new attack on 'abnormal and unnatural' sex. It also provided a rationale for denouncing the heterosexual freedom of the 1960s and 1970s. In both discourses the language of Christianity was never far away. 'The wages of sin' was a phrase used as often in relation to heterosexual as homosexual promiscuity in the first years of HIV/AIDS. In both official and popular discourses, ideas about pollutive sexual acts and disease, about moral corruption from degenerate 'others', immobilized any rational or scientific response. It was left to the gay community to lead the way through the darkness of fear and prejudice in more measured official responses in the coming decades. By the close of the century, the initial panic about HIV/AIDs being a gay disease had been muted by the reduction in rates in the West and a corresponding rise in sero-positive heterosexuals.

At the same time, gay and lesbian political communities expanded to include bisexuals and transsexuals. The letters LGBT came to be recognizable as the marker of this inclusion. Queer sexual politics represented the voice of this new widened consciousness. First, by identifying themselves as 'queer', those involved reversed the pejorative heterosexual meaning of the term. Second, this challenge was a statement that rejected the view, encapsulated in 'heteronormativity', that heterosexuality was superior to homosexuality. Finally, and most radically, queer sexual politics demanded the end to the binary – 'either' hetero- 'or' homosexual – whether this related to appearance, desire or self-identity. Queer politics claimed that the link between gender identity, physical sex and subjective desires was artificial, wrong and oppressive. Many radical queer practitioners refused to 'identify' as male, female, hetero- or homosexual. Their sexuality, identity and practice were flexible and subject only to their choice. Though not universally accepted among more traditional wings of the gay and lesbian community, this new challenge opened up a landscape of fluid sexual desire and identity. In many ways, it offered at the close of the twentieth century the means to dissolve the term that was just a hundred years old – 'sexuality'. It certainly challenged the notion that sexual desire was fixed in bodies by either natural or social forces. Queer sexuality offered the possibility of radical action without the necessity of a revolution. In the context of late modernity, its ideas fitted neatly with the mantra of flexible lifestyle choices in all areas of life. This was demonstrated by the ease with which it was partially expropriated by the very category it denied. The 'queering of heterosexuality' is a contemporary phenomenon, as in popular culture; in television and music videos, crossing the boundaries is the marker of 'cool'. But it remains to be seen whether this cross-fertilization signals the end of the binary that ensured the supremacy of heterosexuality and all that it entailed. First, this blurring of distinctive desires does not necessarily benefit both 'sides' equally. The strength of the LGBT community grew out of difference and the sense of a distinct identity. Second, the relationship with the wider socio-economic climate suggests that this 'freedom' could equally be reversed if circumstances changed, as they did in the late 1970s. Finally, it is of interest that this 'playing at the margins' appears from popular youth culture to be more acceptable in young women than in young men. This suggests at least that these ripples in the pond are not challenging the central core of heteronormativity.

Conclusion

Making sense of the 'sexual century' is no simple task. One interpretation would argue that there was a linear progression from repression to liberation. Another would emphasize the continuities in ideas between that century and the previous one. But in previous centuries dominant sexual discourses also contained contradictory ideas. In the eighteenth century, for example, there were mixed feelings that modified the widespread acceptance of sexual pleasure (Porter, in Bouce 1982). In the nineteenth century four key discourses developed within which knowledge was accumulated and behaviours simultaneously problematized and managed. What was being said about sex in each was self-contained, playing its own role in the maintenance of the wider social order. The sexually precocious child, the perverse adult, the hysterical woman and the Malthusian couple (Foucault 1984) were subjectively and objectively recognizable, were all connected to 'the centre' – bourgeois culture – yet were, themselves, mutually exclusive. Within the twentieth century, the professionals and experts whom Foucault identified as the key dynamic in the regulatory discourses of modernity became less visible. Like Durkheim's argument about social facts, their regulatory role was mobilized only when equally less visible boundaries were crossed. So, for example, the 'decriminalization' of homosexuality offered a sphere within which non-heterosexual desires could be experienced and become the foundation for identities and communities. But the limitations of this free choice were revealed when demands for full erotic equality were made. The age of consent still, in the twenty-first century, operates as the means by which boundaries between heterosexuality and homosexuality are reaffirmed. (In 2004 this is gradually being eroded.) The authority of the medical profession over women's bodies and the definition of their sexuality was dissolved partially in the post-liberation claims for women's sexual self-expression. Yet in the latter years of the century, young women seeking contraception experienced the regulatory force of medicine and the state because they crossed the constructions of 'youth' that attached individual and socially dangerous consequences of 'choosing' their right to sexual self-expression (Hawkes 1991, 1996).

In reviewing the sexual history of the twentieth century a complex picture emerges. It cannot be denied that arenas for sexual pleasure were widened. This entailed a process of fragmentation where a finer moral mesh was placed over sexual activity. Thus, acts or expressions in one context were considered beyond comment, while in a different context the same sexual behaviour remained problematic. For example, in work done in UK family-planning clinics, it was found that medical professionals would speak about methods of mechanical contraception but not non-procreative sexual acts (Hawkes 1991). Similarly, sexual diversity could be 'experimented with' from the 'safety' of heteronormativity. Despite the links of that century with movements of sexual liberation, there was no 'sexual revolution' – at least, not in its real sense. For the structural institutions and ideologies remained intact in Western industrial nations, their stability and legitimacy reflected in the relaxation of sexual laws in the 1960s to 1980s. These statutes did not set in law what the movements of sexual liberation had demanded. But at the same time they did not overtly repress the expression of sexual desire. The boundaries of legitimacy were widened, but not weakened. At the end of the century, as at its beginning, heterosexuality remained in its predominant position, underpinned now less by 'nature' than by the near compulsory optimization of sexual pleasure. The moral fixities of the binary model that distinguished between acceptable and unacceptable desires were 'shaken but not stirred' in the move to train heterosexuality to maximize pleasure. The difference between abnormal and normal, between acceptable and unacceptable, in the new millennium is no longer fixed. Sexual morality is no longer universal or absolute. What is right or wrong either morally or socially depends on the contexts within which actors are 'free' to choose. Yet there are echoes of disquiet in these domains. In relation to any experience of sexual desire the association between youth and sex remains disturbing. Second, there continue to be suggestions of an essence of sexual desire that predisposes it to uncontrollability in relation to young gay sex. Young men are deemed at risk from 'conversion' to homosexuality if, in adolescence, they are 'exposed' to information about homosexual desire. Finally, the power of the sexual imagination continues to be acknowledged in censorship of imagery that can 'deprave and corrupt'. These contradictions ensure that sex in all its forms is never far away from people's consciousness. They also signify that concepts such as 'freedom' and 'repression' often do not operate in a linear manner. In late modernity, the relationship between the two is, rather, reflexive and contingent. Accordingly it could be said that 'liberated confusion' has replaced 'repressed certainties' as the regulatory mechanism that continues to problematize the connection between subjective desires and the stability of the social framework within which they are expressed and against which, still, they are normatively evaluated.

FURTHER READING

Hall, R. (ed.) (1978) *Dear Dr Stopes: Sex in the 1920s*. London: André Deutsch.

Porter, R., and Hall, L. (1995) *The Facts of Life: The Creation of Sexual Knowledge in Britain, 1650–1950*. New Haven, CT, and London: Yale University Press.

Haste, C. (1994) *Rules of Desire: Sex in Britain, World War I to the Present*. London: Pimlico.

Altman, D. (2001) *Global Sex*. Sydney: Allen & Unwin.

Storr, M. (1999) *Bisexuality: A Critical Reader*. London and New York: Routledge.

Epilogue: Themes and Reflections

> What led us to show, ostentatiously, that sex is something we hide, to say it is something we silence? And we do all this by formulating the matter in the most explicit terms, by trying to reveal it in its most naked reality, by affirming it in the positivity of its power and its effects. (Foucault 1984: 9)

Foucault is identifying the profound contradiction in what 'we' in the West say about sex, and why. He is also identifying dualities: the silence and the noise; the hidden and the exposed; the willing acceptance of control and regulation. Although he was writing nearly thirty years ago, these ideas remain relevant today. This book has tried to continue this line of questioning by going backward as well as forward in the story of the ordering of sex. I began by sketching aspects of the contemporary sexual landscape to identify the coexistence of distinct yet contradictory ideas about sex and pleasure. Even from this cursory examination it was evident that sex retained its power to fascinate and cause anxiety. But it did so in ways that indicated a fragmentation of normative judgements – sex could be 'good' and 'fun' in one moment, 'bad' and 'dangerous' in the next. These, moreover, were expressed in opinions and mores rather than encased in any fixed laws. So it seemed that there was a fluidity of discourses about sex that were at the same time familiar and recognizable, yet also subtle and regulative. The second key theme has been the ongoing correspondence between sexuality and evolving modernity, in which both are understood as concepts, experiences, normalizing influences and historical progressions. The intention was to identify the ways in which ideas about sex, both positive and negative, corresponded to the key foundations of social order for each historical period. In this way, different ideas about sex and pleasure could be related to the changing social order.

I have also argued that there are specific ideas about the sexual body, desire and social order that have persisted *across* historical change. The first of these is the assumption that there are certain inherent qualities to sexual desire and pleasure that are beyond conscious control. From the beginning of Western thinking the pleasure of sex has been associated with the loss of reason and therefore with the loss of control. If ignored, this quality will deliver unpleasant and disruptive consequences for both the individual and society. Depending on the epoch in question, these may compromise individual and social health, public morality or the fate of the immortal soul. In various ways, sexual desires were seen as synonymous with animalistic tendencies that at best demanded education, at worst, complete suppression and denial. This characteristic was vividly expressed by the early Christian emphasis on the body as 'flesh', an idea that remained potent long after the decline of the power of the Church and one that remains in currency today in such phrases as 'the flesh is weak.' The ideologues of Christianity made good use of this notion of 'the enemy within' in their management of the behaviour of their growing flock. The revolutionary processes of modernity slowly secularized this mode of social control. The new figures of authority were medical, not religious, and the diseased body replaced the sinful body as the locus of fear and control. In this shift, a key idea was retained. The body continued to pose an obstacle to reason and order. The unruly sexual body could not be tamed from within, but required the efforts of external and specialized authorities – in the former case, priests, in the latter, doctors. The methods employed varied depending on contemporary understandings of the source of these dangers of the flesh. The common feature of these strategies was that 'the problem of desire' was not eradicated but perpetuated through the efforts to contain it.

Despite these recurrent ideas, dramatic changes occurred in ways of thinking about sex, desire and pleasure that coincided with the modernizing process. For example, the distrust with which Christianity viewed the sexual body fuelled the Renaissance inspiration to open the body and prove that it was the purposeful work of the creator, while replacing fear with empirical understanding. Familiarity with the appearance and function of the components of the body would foster a new foundation for order: subjected to reason, the unruliness of the body could be contained. This was the underlying principle of the modern idea of the body as machine and of the promotion of rational use of sexual desire. The new formulation broke the centuries-long association between sexual desire and sin. But it came with a price. The individual experience of desire was subject to more and more intense scrutiny by experts, especially those in the medical profession. Knowledge acquired was neither objective nor dispassionate but rather empowered a new authority to adjudicate on acceptable forms of sexual desire and pleasure. Control was now exercised through education, not punishment. Expertise had become the foundation of disciplinary power that increasingly operated through internalized mechanisms. The old 'seek and punish' modes of Christianity had been replaced by an equally effective 'education of the senses' (Peter Gay's phrase) which took account of the role of conscious subjectivity in modern social order.

The second theme was as pervasive but slower to grow: the relationship between the process of modernity and one that locked physical sex with 'gender'. Indeed it could be argued that modernity gave birth to 'gender'. There had always been character distinctions made between manly and womanly behaviour, but in premodern times these were not causally linked to either direction of desire or anatomy of the body. There were two developments that enabled this linkage. The acknowledgment of a specifically female sexual anatomy demanded a review of the question 'what is woman?' in relation to both her physical and social constitution. If the differences between men and women could be demonstrated in their physical bodies then 'nature' had designated different social roles for both. This early form of 'biological determinism' coincided with wider changes that were reflected in the growing recognition of distinctly male and female social spheres. In this context, the discourse of anatomical difference became the discourse of gender difference – one located in the material and the physical, the other embedded within social processes. In an increasingly complex and diverse society, an effective sex/gender link required the cultivation of a subjective sexual self. But the new focus on the experience of desire, however rationally directed, renewed old anxieties about the instability of the sexual body. The danger lay now not in the desires of the flesh but in the unpredictability of the 'figure' of modernity – the conscious human subject.

Under these circumstances a third theme emerged. The binary became an important ordering mechanism through which sexual desire was to be 'fixed' in its direction as either hetero- or homosexual. The significant element here was the link between sexual acts and types of sexual consciousness. In addition to fixing the distinction between homo- and heterosexuality, the binary model provided the defining framework for fixed sexual *identities*. As with gender, desires became the marker of the person, both internally and socially. However, this was not a value-free model. The binary assumed that heterosexuality was the natural default of all desires. In this Freud was the only voice unheeded, then and now, which argued that the direction of desires to even genital expression, let alone heterosexual coitus, was a fragile process in which the outcome was unpredictable. Decades later, Alfred Kinsey's research findings would support the experiential and subjective 'truth' of the irrelevance of the binary model. However, the response to this challenge was to intensify attention paid to the 'normal' form of expression – to the mechanics and the social significance of heterosexual coitus.

The nineteenth-century association with disease and social disruption had distorted the positive potentials of harmonious sex for a harmonious society. The new sexual enthusiasts now directed their gaze away from wards and clinical rooms and towards the bedroom – the private arena for 'normal' desires. In the interests of marital harmony, heterosexual pleasures were scrutinized and discussed in increasing detail by medical experts. In the eighteenth century, enjoyment of sexual pleasure was following the benign purpose of 'nature'. In the new 'sexual enlightenment' of the twentieth century, erotic education was a duty at both an individual and a social level. But the other aspect of this new discourse was to intensify the normative boundaries around sex *outside* the marital bedroom. New discourses of legitimate pleasures blurred the once clear normative boundaries. In the increasingly mandatory promotion of the 'joys of sex', once fixed distinctions between acceptable and unacceptable sources of pleasure were rendered more flexible, even permeable. Professional sexologists advised and even instructed on the use of sexual techniques once associated only with illicit public sex and the activities of prostitutes. In this new normative framework, 'illicit sex' was that which fell outside the 'instruction manuals' of the experts: those who indulged beyond the boundaries set by the professional sex reformers were, like the sex they had, labelled 'promiscuous'. These included women who pursued autonomous sex lives, homosexual men and the young, especially young women. Thus, while there was an intensification of the promotion of pleasurable sex, as with the first 'sexual enlightenment', this was accompanied by 'mixed feelings'. The relaxation of constraints in one discourse was counter-balanced by the intensification of constraints in another.

The post-war changes in the 1960s and 1970s challenged the security of this balance, managed as it was by experts from the top down. Those who were erotically disenfranchised by this model began to use its mechanisms to mould new grounds for political participation. These strategies operated within as well as outside of the heterosexual 'norm'. For example, the stigma of pre-marital sex, especially for women, was dissolved, as living together became a widespread practice among the young. Effective and confidential contraception removed the fear of unwanted pregnancy, but also the public evidence of 'illegitimate' sex. In theatre and the cinema shame and embarrassment about the naked body and sexual imagery were challenged by an emerging culture of sexual display. The obligation for monogamous marital pleasures had been extended to conspicuous sexual consumption, where the new source of shame was lack of sexual experience. The boundarie   of the binary, which clearly demarcated properly directed desires from misguided distortions of the natural, were increasingly eclipsed in discourses of self-expression and erotic consumptic . But, as the previous chapter has argued, the boundaries were not eradicated, merely adjusted.

The idea for this book began with the public debate about advertising billboards in the late 1990s in the UK, which displayed the word 'SEX' in letters 6 feet high. This might, arguably, stand as a fitting epilogue to the sexual century. Its triumphant 'attitude' made a number of statements that had relevance beyond the British roadsides on which it appeared. For it spoke of the place of 'sex' in a wider public consciousness that is the lifeblood of the advertising industry and of the economic system it supports. Sex sells, sex retains the power to fascinate and entice, even in an experience-weary world. The assumption that sex is the pleasure of pleasures perpetuates its 'specialness', while at the same time its integration into a world of commodities renders this quality 'mundane'. In both, the longstanding negative constructions that emphasized that sexual pleasure was socially disruptive appear to have been eclipsed. A century after self-conscious pruderies hid piano legs from view, and single women alone in public were forcibly examined for signs of moral corruption, whimsical experience of commodified pleasures is not now a problem for social order but operates as one of its foundations. The voices of authority have been silenced in late modernity. Experts do not maintain the boundaries of acceptable sexual practices. Instead, there has been a proliferation of erotic spheres. But the increase in these does not easily signal the decline of anxieties or strategies within which, still, to operate some form of surveillance and regulation. One example may illustrate this claim.

The advertising posters with 'SEX' displayed were part of a trilogy of experience – sun, sand and sex. These three words suggested a new social context within which sexual promiscuity was given a new and more positive value. The added aspect of such sex holidays is their age restrictions – 'Club 18–30'. Here, youth is used to legitimate rather than condemn the experience of multiple casual sexual pleasures. The contained world of the all-inclusive Mediterranean holiday legitimized sexual licence not appropriate elsewhere. In the context of another sphere inhabited by the young, encouraging sexual licence is a legitimate rationale for limiting the content of sex education in schools. In this context, talking to the young about sex is problematic, since they might just go out and 'do it'. Sex and the young in this context is a social problem, not an entertainment. Though both are dealing with specific age categories, two contradictory discourses draw on morally exclusive terms of reference. Thus the distinctions between licit and illicit sex remain, despite the inherent contradictions of this distinction. The anomaly is disguised by the non-coherence of the two spheres and of the social significance of the sex that they contain.

The sociological question therefore is not whether these different meanings, weighted normatively, exist, but what their purpose is in the ordering of sexual behaviour. I want to suggest that 'the civilizing process', which recognized differentially and normatively two spheres of sexual expression, has been replaced by 'the fragmentation process'. In late modernity, we are encouraged to explore individual desires and wants in multiple spheres that fragment their subjective meaning as well as their social significance. At one level, this proliferation of sexual spheres can be interpreted as the end of ideological 'fixities' that formed the infrastructure of modernity. In the postmodern world, this argument claims, the multiplicity of these spheres hold out unprecedented freedoms. They offer individuals the means by which they can craft their identities outside of the structural constraints of fixed social roles and expectations. The primacy of self-identity overrides the fixed moral categories of modernity and operates instead as the dynamic that allows movement between the spheres and flexible interpretation of their expectations.

But, read another way, the multiplicity of spheres merely offer an illusion of choice. More explicitly, they operate in ways that reflect the ideological infrastructure of late capitalism, as forms of manipulation rather than overt regulation. The freedom of choice suggested by the expansion of sexual spheres is limited by the contradictions between them, whose presence testifies to the persistence of a normative apparatus. The fragmentation of experience is a key motif in late modernity. Simple human functions like eating and drinking have been transformed into an arena of self-expression, undertaken increasingly under the anonymous public gaze. In glass-fronted bars and cafes, customers are not just assuaging hunger but proclaiming their right to 'choose' within purpose-built arenas where the choice has already been made for them. There is a curious disembodiedness about this 'double consumption', underpinned by an alternative discourse in which to eat when hungry is to risk physical distortion in bodily appearance. At all levels of consumption this pattern is evident, as choice becomes the new mode of regulation in the affluent West. It is commonplace now to identify the instability of the capitalist mode of production with the proliferation of choice in commodities of all types. At the heart of this connection lies the need to direct and therefore regulate patterns of consumption, while simultaneously claiming the individual sovereignty of the 'consumer'. Fragmentation of experience is central to both the mechanisms of regulation and the illusion of the 'freedom to choose'.

At its most effective, globalized capitalism has conceptually separated the spheres of production and consumption. In relation to the experience of sexual desire and pleasure, a similar process is evident. There has been a fragmentation of the modernist discourse of 'sexuality' that divided the public from the private, homosexuality from heterosexuality and stable from promiscuous desires. The conditions for this fragmentation have been provided by the proliferation of spheres within which 'sex' is packaged for consumption. In the civilizing process the management of the body offered the foundation for the fixing and managing of desires. In the fragmentation process, the body and especially its subjective experience is subordinated to the obligation to consume this pre-packed erotic experience. In place of a conscious constitution of a sexual self, a new subjectivity is thereby temporarily constructed within these multiple spheres. This plasticity of experience accounts for the coexistence of contradictory discourses without compromising regulatory efficacy.

An example of this process at work can be seen in the recent commodification of adolescent sexuality. A key factor in maintaining the viability of a consumption economy is the emphasis on individual choice. Within this sphere, young people, but young girls in particular, are encouraged to express their social 'coming of age' in sexual display and erotic adventurism. The range and content of magazines devoted to this task make no mention of ideas about 'corruption of innocence' or of the positive valuation of 'stable relationships'. Instead, the pursuit of 'the sexual' is simultaneously trivialized and kept central in the promotion of its self-evident delights. Once again, the contradiction between this discourse and that of the 'protection of the innocents' in relation to sex education and the provision of

contraception in schools, for example, is illuminating. The stability
and effectiveness of the civilizing process depended on the extent to
which the desiring population could be educated in the proper direction of their desires. The fragmentation process has replaced normative uses of the body with normatively fragmented experience that
renders redundant what in other contexts are moral prohibitions. The
problem of both very young women and young homosexual men is
that their desires fall outside existing preordained spheres of erotic
consumption, and therefore fall outside any regulatory framework.
Their existence causes unease because it points to an erotic domain
brought into being by subjective choice, not ordered fragmentations.
Like other erotic choices – for example, sexual fetishisms – they indicate a viable and challenging sensual self-consciousness that pre-
figures the social construction of its direction.

The imposition of regulatory frameworks in whatever era they
occur testifies to the presence of 'something to be contained'. The
changes in both form and content over time reflect the terms in which
this 'something' about sex is understood as well as the foundations of
the social order it confronts. That sexual desire retains this capacity
to inspire fear and mistrust over two millennia remains a subject for
enquiry. But, as Foucault has reminded us, strategies for containment
themselves open up spaces for resistance to their imposition. This is
the real dynamic of sexual history, whether at the level of ideas or
practice. The emphasis on self-expression so central to the fragmentation process might itself offer the possibility of new forms of resistance. For the one domain that has thus far remained intact is that
which links sexual desire with sexual identity. At the time of writing,
a new survey of sexual attitudes of women in two 'first world' countries has revealed a fault line in the deeply internalized binary of desire.
Shere Hite reports that 71 per cent of her British women respondents
stated that they were actively 'curious' about exploring their desires
with other women. In 2003 a major sex survey in Australia found that
8.6 per cent of men and 15.1 per cent of women reported same-sex
attraction or experience (Smith et al. 2003: 138). Those groups who
historically have been consistently associated with dangerous desires
may be the pioneers in a new landscape where erotic subjectivity is
acknowledged and valued. But another, perhaps more utopian, question was posed by Foucault; this offers an alternative to what has
been, throughout, a consistent elevation of sex, pleasure and desire as
the key domain for social regulation and order:

> We need to consider the possibility that one day, perhaps in a differ-
> ent economy of bodies and pleasures, people will no longer quite

understand how the ruses of sexuality, and the power that sustains its organization, were able to subject us to that austere monarchy of sex, so that we became dedicated to the endless task of forcing its secret, of exacting the truest of confessions from a shadow. The irony of this deployment is in having us believe that our 'liberation' is in the balance. (Foucault 1984: 159)

References and Bibliography

Altman, D. (2001) *Global Sex*. Sydney: Allen & Unwin.

Armstrong, C. W. (1936) *Paradise Found, or, Where the Sex Problem Has Been Solved*. London: John Bale, Sons & Danielsson.

Aughterson, K. (1995) *Renaissance Women*. London: Routledge.

Bailey, D. S. (1955) *Homosexuality and the Western Christian Tradition*. New York: Longmans Green & Co.

Barret-Ducrocq, F. (1991) *Love in the Time of Victoria: Sexuality and Desire among Working Class Men and Women in Nineteenth Century London*. Harmondsworth: Penguin.

Bassan, M. (1962) Chaucer's 'cursed monk', Constantinus Africanus. *Medieval Studies*, 24.

Bauer, B. (1926) *Woman: A Treatise on the Anatomy, Physiology, Psychology, and Sexual Life*. London: Jonathan Cape.

Bauman, Z. (1989) *Legislators and Interpreters: On Modernity, Postmodernity and Intellectuals*. Cambridge: Polity.

Bauman, Z. (1992) *Intimations of Postmodernity*. London: Routledge.

Baumer, F. van (1978) *Main Currents of Western Thought: Readings in Western European Intellectual History*. 4th edn, New Haven, CT, and London: Yale University Press.

Beck, H. (1997) *Where Men Meet*. Cambridge: Polity.

Becker, C. (1932) *The Heavenly City of the Eighteenth Century Philosophers*. New Haven, CT, and London: Yale University Press.

Berger, S. (1988) Sex in the literature of the Middle Ages: the *Fabliaux*. In D. Jacquart and C. Thomasset (eds) *Sexuality and Medicine in the Middle Ages*, trans. M. Adamson. Princeton, NJ: Princeton University Press.

Bernard, B. (1929) *Sex Conduct in Marriage: The Art of Maintaining Love and Happiness in Marriage*. Chicago: Health and Life.

Blachford, G. (1981) Male dominance and the gay world. In K. Plummer (ed.) *The Making of the Modern Homosexual*. London: Hutchinson.

Bland, L. (1985) 'Cleansing the portals of life': the venereal disease campaign in the early twentieth century. In B. Schwarz and M. Langan (eds) *Crises in the British State, 1880–1930*. London: Hutchinson.

Bland, L., and Doan, L. (eds) (1998a) *Sexology Uncensored: The Documents of Sexual Science*. Cambridge: Polity.

Bland, L., and Doan, L. (eds) (1998b) *Sexology in Culture: Labelling Bodies and Desires*. Cambridge: Polity.

Bloch, I. (1909) *The Sexual Life of our Time in its Relation to Modern Civilization*. London: Rebman.

Bloch, M. (1967) *The Historian's Craft*. Manchester: Manchester University Press.

Blundell, S. (1995) *Women in Ancient Greece*. London: British Museum Press.

Bocock, R. (1989) *Freud and Modern Society*. London: VNR International.

Bottomley, F. (1979) *Attitudes to the Body in Western Christendom*. London: Lepus Books.

Bouce, P.-G. (ed.) (1982) *Sexuality in Eighteenth Century Britain*. Manchester: Manchester University Press.

Bray, A. (1982) *Homosexuality in Renaissance England*. London: Gay Men's Press.

Bray, A. (1990) Homosexuality and the signs of male friendship in Elizabethan England. *History Workshop Journal*, 29, spring.

Brock, A. J., trans. (1928) *Galen: On the Natural Faculties*. London: G. P. Putnam's Sons.

Brown, H. Gurley (1963) *Sex and the Single Girl*. New York: Pocket Books.

Brown, P. (1987) East and West: the new morality. In P. Veyne (ed.) *A History of Private Life*, Vol. 1: *From Pagan Rome to Byzantium*. Cambridge, MA, and London: Belknap Press.

Brown, P. (1988) *Body and Society: Men, Women and Sexual Renunciation in Early Christianity*. New York: Columbia University Press.

Brubaker, R. (1984) *The Limits of Rationality: An Essay on the Social and Moral Thought of Max Weber*. London: Allen & Unwin.

Brundage, J. (1984) 'Let Me Count the Ways': canonists and theologians contemplate coital positions. *Journal of Medieval History*, 10, 81–93.

Brundage, J. (1987) *Law, Sex and Christian Society in Medieval Europe*. Chicago: University of Chicago Press.

Bullough, V. (1973) Medieval medical and scientific views on women. *Viator*, 4.

Bullough, V. (1976) *Sexual Variance in Society and History*. New York: John Wiley.

Bullough, V. (1982) The sin against nature. In V. Bullough and J. Brundage (eds) *Sexual Practices and the Medieval Church*. Buffalo, NY: Prometheus Books.

Bullough, V. (1994) *Sex in the Bedroom: A History of Sex Research*. New York: Basic Books.

Bullough, V., and Brundage, J. (eds) (2000) *Handbook of Medieval Sexuality*. New York and London: Garland.

Buschke, A., and Jacobsohn, F. (1932) *Introduction to Sexual Hygiene*. London: Routledge.

Cabello, F. (1997) Female ejaculation: myth and reality. In J. J. Baras-Vass and M. Perez-Conchillo (eds) *Sexuality and Human Rights: Proceedings of the XIII World Congress of Sexology*. Valencia, Spain: ECVSA, pp. 325–33.

Cadden, J. (1984) It takes all kinds: gender differences in Hildegard of Bingen's 'Book of Compound Medicine'. *Traditio*, 11.

Cadden, J. (1986) Medieval and scientific views of sexuality: questions of propriety. *Medievalia et Humanistica*, no. 14.

Calverton, V. F., and Schmalhausen, S. D. (eds) (1929) *Sex in Civilization*. London: George Allen & Unwin.

Castle, T. (1987) The culture of travesty: sexuality and masquerade in eighteenth century England. In G. Rousseau and R. Porter (eds) *Sexual Underworlds of the Enlightenment*. Manchester: Manchester University Press.

Chorlton, T. (1987) *The Gnostics*. London: Weidenfeld & Nicolson.

Clark, E. (1986) *Ascetic Piety and Women's Faith: Essays on Late Ancient Christianity*. Lewiston, NY: E. Mellen.

Clark, E. (ed.) (1997) *St. Augustine on Marriage and Sexuality*. Washington, DC: Catholic University of America Press.

Cohen, D. (1991) *Law, Sexuality and Society: The Enforcement of Morals in Classical Athens*. Cambridge: Cambridge University Press.

Coote, A., and Campbell, B. (1982) *Sweet Freedom: The Struggle for Women's Liberation*. London: Picador.

Coppa, F. (1999) A perfectly developed playwright: Joe Orton and homosexual reform. In P. J. Smith (ed.) *The Queer Sixties*. London: Routledge.

Crisp, Q. ([1968] 1985) *The Naked Civil Servant*. London: Harper Collins.

Crosland, M., trans. (1991) *The Passionate Philosopher: A Marquis de Sade Reader*. London: Peter Owen.

Cunningham, A. (1997) *The Anatomical Renaissance*. Aldershot: Scholar Press.

Davenport-Hines, R. (1991) *Sex, Death and Punishment: Attitudes to Sex and Sexuality in Britain since the Renaissance*. London: Fontana.

David, H. (1997) *On Queer Street: A Social History of British Homosexuality, 1895–1995*. London: Harper Collins.

Davies, C. (1980) Moralists, causalists, sex, law and morality. In W. H. G. Armytage, R. Chester, and J. Peel (eds) *Changing Patterns in Sexual Behaviour*. London: Academic Press.

Davis, K. B. (1929) *Factors in the Sex Life of Twenty-Two Hundred Women*. New York and London: Harper & Bros.

Davis, M. (1960) *Sexual Responsibility in Marriage*. London: Pimlico.

Delumeau, J. (1990) *Sin and Fear: The Emergence of a Western Guilt Culture, 13th–18th Century*. New York: St Martin's Press.

Denomy, A. J. (1946) 'Fin amors': the pure love of the troubadours, its morality, and possible source. *Medieval Studies*, 8.

Dickens, C. (1861) *David Copperfield*. London: Odhams Press.

Dollimore, J. (1993) *Sexual Dissidence: Augustine to Wilde, Freud to Foucault.* Oxford: Clarendon Press.

Dover, K. J. (1974) *Greek Popular Morality in the Time of Plato and Aristotle.* Oxford: Blackwell.

Dover, K. J. (1978) *Greek Homosexuality.* London: Duckworth.

Duberman, M., Vicinus, M., and Chauncey, G. (eds) (1991) *Hidden from History: Reclaiming the Gay and Lesbian Past.* Harmondsworth: Penguin.

Duby, G. (ed.) (1988) *A History of Private Lives*, Vol. 3. Cambridge, MA: Harvard University Press.

Duby, G., and Perrot, M. (1993) *A History of Women in the West*, Vol. 3: *Renaissance and Enlightenment Paradoxes.* Cambridge, MA, and London: Harvard University Press.

Duden, B. (1992) Medicine and the history of the body. In J. Lachmund and G. Stollberg (eds) *The Social Construction of Illness.* Stuttgart: Franz Steiner.

Durkheim, E. (1933) *The Division of Labour in Society.* New York: Free Press.

Dworkin, A. (1981) *Pornography: Men Possessing Women.* New York: Plume.

Edelstein, L. (1952) The relation of ancient medicine to philosophy. *Bulletin of the History of Medicine*, 26: 4.

Elderton, E. (1914) *Report on the English Birth Rate, Part 1.* London: Dulau.

Elias, N. (1982) *The Civilising Process*, Vol. 1: *A History of Manners.* Oxford: Blackwell.

Ellis, H. H. (1899) *Studies in the Psychology of Sex*, Vol. 1. Philadelphia: F. A. Davis.

Ellis, H. H. (1927) *Studies in the Psychology of Sex*, Vol. 6. Philadelphia: F. A. Davis.

Epstein, D., and Johnson, R. (1998) *Schooling Sexualities.* Buckingham and Philadelphia: Open University Press.

Evans, D. (1993) *Sexual Citizenship: The Materialist Construction of Sexualities.* London: Routledge.

Faderman, L. (1981) *Surpassing the Love of Men: Romantic Friendship and Love between Women from the Renaissance to the Present Day.* New York: William Morrow.

Foley, H. P. (ed.) (1981) *Reflections of Women in Antiquity.* New York: Goodwater.

Foucault, M. (1965) *Madness and Civilisation.* Harmondsworth: Penguin.

Foucault, M. (1984) *The History of Sexuality*, Vol. 1: *An Introduction.* Harmondsworth: Penguin.

Foucault, M. (1987) *The History of Sexuality*, Vol. 2: *The Uses of Pleasure.* Harmondsworth: Penguin.

Foucault, M. (1990) *The History of Sexuality*, Vol. 3: *The Care of the Self.* Harmondsworth: Penguin.

Fox, R. L. (1986) *Pagans and Christians.* London: Viking.

Frantz, D. O. (1989) *Festum voluptatis: A Study of Renaissance Erotica*. Columbus: Ohio State University Press.

Frend, W. H. C. (1991) *The Early Church from the Beginnings to 461*. 3rd edn, London: SCM Press.

Freud, S. (1974) *Introductory Lectures on Psychoanalysis*. The Pelican Freud Library. Harmondsworth: Penguin.

Freud, S. (1986a) *Three Essays on Sexuality and Other Works*. The Penguin Freud Library, Vol. 7. Harmondsworth: Penguin.

Freud, S. (1986b) *The Standard Edition of the Complete Psychological Works of Sigmund Freud*, trans. J. Strachey, Vol. 9 (1906–1908): *'Civilized' Sexual Morality and Modern Nervous Illness*. London: Hogarth Press.

Freud, S. (1986c) *The Standard Edition of the Complete Psychological Works of Sigmund Freud*, trans. J. Strachey, Vol. 21 (1927–1931): *Civilization and its Discontents*. London: Hogarth Press.

Friday, N. (1976) *My Secret Garden: Women's Sexual Fantasies*. London: Quartet.

Galen (1963) *On the Passions and Errors of the Soul*, trans. P. Harkins. Columbus: Ohio State University Press.

Gay, P. (1967) *The Enlightenment: An Interpretation*, Vol. 2: *The Science of Freedom*. London: Weidenfeld & Nicolson.

Gay, P. (1986) *The Bourgeois Experience: Victoria to Freud*, Vol. 1: *The Education of the Senses*. Oxford: Oxford University Press.

Gay, P. (1988) *Freud: A Life for our Time*. London: Macmillan.

Gerard, K., and Hekma, G. (1989) *The Pursuit of Sodomy: Male Homosexuality in the Renaissance and the Enlightenment*. New York and London: Harrington Press.

Gerth, H. H., and Mills, C. W. (eds) (1970) *From Max Weber: Essays in Sociology*. London: Routledge & Kegan Paul.

Giddens, A. (1991) *Modernity and Self-Identity: Self and Society in the Late Modern Age*. Cambridge: Polity.

Giddens, A. (1992) *The Transformation of Intimacy: Sexuality, Love and Eroticism in Modern Societies*. Cambridge: Polity.

Gilman, S. (1989) *Sexuality: An Illustrated History Representing the Sexual in Medicine and Art*. New York: Wiley.

Goergen, D. (1974) *The Sexual Celibate*. New York: Seabury Press.

Gosling, J. C. B., and Taylor, C. C. W. (1982) *The Greeks on Pleasure*. Oxford: Clarendon Press.

Grahame, H. (1989) *Out of the Backstreets*. London: PAS.

Graves, R., and Hodge, A. ([1940] 1985) *The Long Weekend: A Social History of Great Britain 1918–1939*. London: Hutchinson.

Greenway, J. (1998) It's what you do with it that counts: interpretations of Otto Weininger. In L. Bland and L. Doan (eds) *Sexology in Culture: Labelling Bodies and Desires*. Cambridge: Polity.

Greer, G. (1970) *The Female Eunuch*. London: MacGibbon & Kee.

Griffith, E. P. (1938) *Sex in Everyday Life*. London: George Allen & Unwin.

Gundersheimer, W. L. (1994) Renaissance concepts of shame and pocatera as dialoghi della vergogna. *Renaissance Quarterly*, 47, spring.

Hackworth, R., trans. (1952) *Plato's Phaedrus*. Indianapolis and New York: Bobbs-Merrill.

Hair, P. (ed.) (1972) *Before the Bawdy Court*. London: Elek.

Haire, N. (ed.) (1928) *Some More Medical Views on Birth Control*. London: Cecil Palmer.

Haire, N. (1929) Sex in civilization. In V. F. Calverton and S. D. Schmalhausen (eds) *Sex in Civilization*. London: George Allen & Unwin.

Haire, N. (ed.) (1935) *Encyclopaedia of Sexual Knowledge*. London: Aldor.

Hall, L. (1992) Forbidden by God, despised by men: masturbation, medical warnings, moral panic and manhood in Great Britain in the nineteenth and twentieth centuries. *Journal of the History of Sexuality*, 2, 367–87.

Hall, R. (ed.) (1978) *Dear Dr Stopes: Sex in the 1920s*. London: André Deutsch.

Halperin, D. (1990) *One Hundred Years of Homosexuality and Other Essays on Greek Love*. London: Routledge.

Halperin, D., Winkler, J., and Zeitlin, F. (eds) (1990) *Before Sexuality: The Construction of Erotic Experience in the Ancient Greek World*. Princeton, NJ, and Oxford: Princeton University Press.

Hardy, T. ([1891] 1965) *Tess of the D'Urbervilles*. New York: Norton.

Hart, C., and Gilliland Stevenson, K. (1995) *Heaven and the Flesh: Imagery of Desire from the Renaissance to the Rococo*. Cambridge and New York: Cambridge University Press.

Harvey, D. (1989) *The Condition of Postmodernity: An Enquiry into the Conditions of Cultural Change*. Oxford: Blackwell.

Haste, C. (1994) *Rules of Desire: Sex in Britain, World War I to the Present*. London: Pimlico.

Hawkes, G. (1987) *The Gillick Ruling (1984): A Study of Attitudes to Sexuality in Young People*. Manchester Sociology Occasional Papers, Department of Sociology, University of Manchester.

Hawkes, G. (1991) ' "Raucous Guests at the Feast": Young Women and Sex in Family Planning'. PhD thesis, Victoria University of Manchester.

Hawkes, G. (1995) Responsibility and irresponsibility: young women in family planning. *Sociology*, 29, 257–73.

Hawkes, G. (1996) *A Sociology of Sex and Sexuality*. Buckingham and Philadelphia: Open University Press.

Heath, S. (1982) *The Sexual Fix*. London: Macmillan.

Henderson, K., and McManus, B. (1985) *Half Humankind: Contexts and Texts of the Controversy about Women in England, 1540–1640*. Urbana: University of Illinois Press.

Hickman, T. (1999) *The Sexual Century*. London: Carlton Books.

Higgins, P. (1996) *Heterosexual Dictatorship: Male Homosexuality in Post-War Britain*. London: Fourth Estate.

Hite, S. (1976) *The Hite Report on Female Sexuality*. London: Pandora.

Hite, S. (1993) *Women as Revolutionary Agents of Change: Selected Essays in Psychology and Gender*. London: Bloomsbury.

Hunter, D. G. (ed.) (1992) *Marriage in the Early Christian Church*. Minneapolis: Fortress Press.

Ingram, M. (1985) Sex and marriage in early modern England. In B. Reay (ed.) *Popular Culture in 17th Century England*. London: Croom Helm.

Jackson, S. (1982) *Childhood and Sexuality*. Oxford: Blackwell.

Jacquart, D., and Thomasset, C. (1988) *Sexuality and Medicine in the Middle Ages*, trans. M. Adamson. Princeton, NJ: Princeton University Press.

Jaeger, W. (1961) *Paedeia: The Ideals of Greek Culture*, Vol. 3. Oxford: Blackwell.

Jeffries, S. (1985) *The Spinster and her Enemies: Feminism and Sexuality, 1880–1930*. London: Pandora.

Johns, C. (1982) *Sex or Symbol: Erotic Images of Greece and Rome*. London: British Museum Press.

Jones, A. R. (1988) City women and their audiences. In A. Ramie (ed.) *Renaissance Humanism: Foundations, Forms and Legacy*. Philadelphia: University of Pennsylvania Press.

Jordan, C. (1988) Feminism and the humanists. In A. Ramie (ed.) *Renaissance Humanism: Foundations, Forms and Legacy*. Philadelphia: University of Pennsylvania Press.

Katz, J. (1994) The age of sodomitical sin. In J. Goldberg (ed.) *Reclaiming Sodom*. New York and London: Routledge.

Keating, P. (1972) *Into Unknown England, 1866–1913: Selections from the Social Explorers*. London: Fontana.

King, M. L. (1991) *Women of the Renaissance*. Chicago: University of Chicago Press.

Kinsey, A., et al. (1948) *Sexual Behaviour in the Human Male*. London: W. B. Saunders.

Kinsey, A., et al. (1953) *Sexual Behaviour in the Human Female*. London: W. B. Saunders.

Kisch, H. (1931) *The Sexual Life of Women, in All its Physiological and Hygienic Aspects*. New York: Allied Book Company.

Koedt, A. (1970) The myth of the vaginal orgasm. In A. Koedt, E. Levine, and A. Rapone (eds) *Radical Feminism*. New York: Times Books.

Krafft-Ebing, R. von (1899) *Psychopathia sexualis, with Especial Reference to the Antipathic Sexual Instincts: A Medico-Forensic Study*. London: Rebman; new edition. New York: Arcade, 1998.

Kumar, K. (1978) *Prophecy and Progress: The Sociology of Industrial and Post-Industrial Societies*. Harmondsworth: Penguin.

Labisch, A. (1992) The social construction of health. In J. Lachmund and G. Stollberg (eds) *The Social Construction of Illness*. Stuttgart: Franz Steiner.

Laqueur, T. (1990) *Making Sex: Body and Gender from the Greeks to Freud*. Cambridge, MA, and London: Harvard University Press.

Laqueur, T. (2003) *Solitary Sex: A History of Masturbation*. New York: Zone Books.

Leathard, A. (1980) *The Fight to Save Family Planning*. London: Macmillan.

Lecky, W. (1880) *A History of European Morals from Augustus to Charlemagne*, Vol. 2. 4th rev. edn, London: Longmans, Green.

Lefkowitz, M. (1977) *Women in Greece and Rome*. Toronto: Samuel-Stevens.

Lefkowitz, M. R. (1986) *Women in Greek Myth*. London: Duckworth.

Lefkowitz, M., and Fant, M. (1992) *Women's Life in Greece and Rome: A Source Book in Translation*. London: Duckworth.

Legge, F. (1915) *Forerunners and Rivals of Christianity: Being Studies in Religious History*. Cambridge: Cambridge University Press.

Lemay, H. R. (1981) William of Salicento on human sexuality. *Viator*, 12, 165–81.

Lemay, H. R. (1988) Human sexuality in twelfth through fifteenth-century scientific writings. In D. Jacquart and C. Thomasset (eds) *Sexuality and Medicine in the Middle Ages*, trans. M. Adamson. Princeton, NJ: Princeton University Press.

Levack, B. P. (1995) *The Witchhunt in Early Modern Europe*. London: Longmans.

Lewis, J. (1984) *Women in England, 1870–1950*. London: Wheatsheaf.

Licht, H. ([1931] 1994) *Sexual Life in Ancient Greece*. London: Constable.

Lobek, G. L. (1858) The female sex organs in humans and some mammals. In T. P. Lowry (ed.) (1978) *The Classic Clitoris: Historic Contributions to Scientific Sexuality*. Chicago: Nelson-Hall.

Logan, G. M., Adams, R. M., and Miller, C. H. (eds) (1995) *Utopia*. Cambridge: Cambridge University Press.

Longrigg, J. (1993) *Greek Rational Medicine: Philosophy and Medicine from Alcmaeon to the Alexandrines*. London and New York: Routledge.

Lowry, T. P. (ed.) (1978) *The Classic Clitoris: Historic Contributions to Scientific Sexuality*. Chicago: Nelson-Hall.

McCormick, I. (ed.) (1997) *Secret Sexualities: A Sourcebook of 17th and 18th Century Writings*. London and New York: Routledge.

MacDonald, R. (1967) The frightful consequences of onanism: notes on a history of a delusion. *Journal of the History of Ideas*, 28, 423–31.

MacKinnon, C. (1987) *Feminism Unmodified*. Cambridge, MA: Harvard University Press.

McLaren, A. (1978) *Birth Control in Nineteenth Century England*. London: Croom Helm.

McLaren, A. (1999) *Twentieth Century Sexuality: A History*. Oxford: Blackwell.

McNeill, J. T., and Gamer, H. M. (1990) *Medieval Handbooks of Penance*. New York: Columbia University Press.

Marchant, J. (1916) *The Declining Birth-Rate: Its Cause and Effect*. London: Chapman Hall.

Marchant, J. (1926) *Medical Views on Birth Control*. London: Martin Hopkinson.

Marcus, S. (1966) *The Other Victorians: A Study of Sexuality and Pornography in Nineteenth Century England*. London: Book Club Associates.

Marcuse, H. (1966) *Eros and Civilisation: A Philosophical Enquiry into Freud*. Boston: Beacon Press.

Marketos, S. (1997) Origins of nephrology, Greece and Byzantium. *American Journal of Nephrology*, 17, 205–8.

Marshall, J. (1981) Pansies, perverts and macho men: changing conceptions of male homosexuality. In K. Plummer (ed.) *The Making of the Modern Homosexual*. London: Hutchinson.

Mason, M. (1994) *The Making of Victorian Sexuality*. Oxford: Oxford University Press.

Masters, W., and Johnson, V. (1966) *Human Sexual Response*. Boston: Littlejohn.

Matthews Greico, S. F. (1993) The body, appearance and sexuality. In G. Duby and M. Perrot (eds) *A History of Women in the West*, Vol. 3: *Renaissance and Enlightenment Paradoxes*. Cambridge, MA: Belknap Press.

Medica [J. G. Malleson] (1950) *Any Wife or Any Husband: A Book for Couples Who Have Met with Sexual Difficulties and for Doctors*. London: Heinemann.

Millett, K. (1970) *Sexual Politics*. London: Abacus.

Milton, J. (1974) *Poetical Works*, ed. D. Bush. London: Oxford University Press.

Mort, F. (1987) *Dangerous Sexualities: Medico-Moral Politics in England since 1830*. London: Routledge & Kegan Paul.

Murnstein, B. (1974) *Love, Sex and Marriage through the Ages*. New York: Springer.

Muscatine, C. (1986) *The Old French Fabliaux*. New Haven, CT: Yale University Press.

Newton, E. (1991) The mythic mannish lesbian: Radclyffe Hall and the new woman. In M. Duberman, M. Vicinus and G. Chauncey (eds) *Hidden from History: Reclaiming the Gay and Lesbian Past*. Harmondsworth: Penguin.

Noonan, J. T. (1986) *Contraception: A History of its Treatment by Catholic Theologians*. Cambridge, MA: Harvard University Press.

Nye, R. (ed.) (1999) *Sexuality*. Oxford: Oxford University Press.

Padgug, R. (1979) Sexual matters: on conceptualising sexuality in history. *Radical History Review*, 20, spring/summer.

Pagels, E. (1988) *Adam, Eve and the Serpent*. London: Weidenfeld & Nicolson.

Parry, J. J. (ed.) (1941) *Andreas Cappelanus: The Art of Courtly Love*. New York: Columbia University Press.

Pateman, C. (1988) *The Sexual Contract*. Stanford, CA: Stanford University Press.

Pateman, C. (1999) The sexual contract. In R. Nye (ed.) *Sexuality*. Oxford: Oxford University Press.

Payer, P. (1980) Early medieval regulations concerning marital sexual relations. *Journal of Medieval History*, 6, 353–76.

Payer, P. J. (1984) *Sex and the Penitentials: The Development of a Sexual Code, 550–1150*. Toronto and London: University of Toronto Press.

Payer, P. J. (1994) *The Bridling of Desire: Views of Sex in the Late Middle Ages*. Toronto and London: University of Toronto Press.

Plato (1951) *The Symposium*, trans. W. Hamilton. Harmondsworth: Penguin.

Plumb, J. H. (1964) *The Penguin Book of the Renaissance*. Harmondsworth: Penguin.

Plummer, K. (ed.) (1981) *The Making of the Modern Homosexual*. London: Hutchinson.

Pomeroy, W. (1972) *Dr Kinsey and the Institute of Sex Research*. London: Harper & Row.

Porter, R. (1982) Mixed feelings: the Enlightenment and sexuality in eighteenth century Britain. In P.-G. Bouce (ed.) *Sexuality in Eighteenth Century Britain*. Manchester: Manchester University Press.

Porter, R., and Hall, L. (1995) *The Facts of Life: The Creation of Sexual Knowledge in Britain, 1650–1950*. New Haven, CT, and London: Yale University Press.

Porter, R., and Teich, M. (eds) (1994) *Sexual Knowledge, Sexual Science: The History of Attitudes to Sexuality*. Cambridge: Cambridge University Press.

Ramie, A. (ed.) (1988) *Renaissance Humanism: Foundations, Forms and Legacy*. Philadelphia: University of Pennsylvania Press.

Ranke-Heinemann, U. (1991) *Eunuchs for the Kingdom of Heaven: Women, Sexuality and the Catholic Church*. Harmondsworth: Penguin.

Reeder, E. (ed.) (1995) *Pandora: Women in Classical Greece*. Baltimore: Walters Art Gallery.

Richards, J. (1981) The British Board of Film Censors and content control in the 1930s: images of Britain. *Historical Journal of Film, Radio and Television*, 1: 2.

Robie, W. F. (1916) *Rational Sex Ethics*. Boston: Goreham Press.

Rougemont, Denis de (1956) *Passion and Society*. London: Faber.

Rousseau, G. S. (1991) *Enlightenment Crossings: Pre- and Post Modern Discourses*. Manchester: Manchester University Press.

Rousseau, G., and Porter, R. (eds) (1987) *Sexual Underworlds of the Enlightenment*. Manchester: Manchester University Press.

Rousselle, A. (1988) *Porneia: On Desire and the Body in Antiquity*. Oxford: Blackwell.

Rowbotham, S., and Weeks, J. (1977) *Socialism and the New Life: The Personal and Sexual Politics of Edward Carpenter and Havelock Ellis*. London: Pluto Press.

Salisbury, J. (1986) The Latin doctors of the Church on sexuality. *Journal of Medieval History*, 12, 279–89.

Sawday, J. (1997) Self and selfhood in the seventeenth century. In R. Porter (ed.) *Rewriting the Self: Histories from the Renaissance to the Present*. London and New York: Routledge.

Scarborough, J. (1969) *Roman Medicine*. London: Thames & Hudson.

Scheibinger, L. (1987) Skeletons in the closet: the first illustrations of the female skeleton in eighteenth century anatomy. In C. Gallagher and T. Laqueur (eds) *The Making of the Modern Body: Sexuality and Society in the Nineteenth Century*. Berkeley and London: University of California Press.

Schmaulhausen, S. D. (1929) The sexual revolution. In V. F. Calverton and S. D. Schmalhausen (eds) *Sex in Civilization*. London: George Allen & Unwin.

Schofield, M. (1965) *The Sexual Behaviour of Young People*. London: Longman.

Schwarz, B., and Hall, S. (1982) State and society, 1880–1930. In B. Schwarz and M. Langan (eds) *Crises in the British State, 1880–1930*. London: Hutchinson.

Segal, L. (1987) *Is the Future Female? Troubled Thoughts on Contemporary Feminism*. London: Virago.

Segal, L. (1994) *Straight Sex: The Politics of Pleasure*. London: Virago.

Smith, A., Rissel, C., Richters, J., Grulich, A., and de Visser, R. (2003) Sex in Australia. *Australian and New Zealand Journal of Public Health*, 27, 103–251.

Smith, N. (1982) Sexual mores and attitudes in Enlightenment Scotland. In P.-G. Bouce (ed.) *Sexuality in Eighteenth Century Britain*. Manchester: Manchester University Press.

Smith, P. J. (ed.) (1999) *The Queer Sixties*. London: Routledge.

Stanley, L. (1984) *The Diaries of Hannah Culwick*. London: Virago.

Stearns, C., and Stearns, P. (1985) Victorian sexuality: can historians do it better? *Journal of Social History*, 18, 625–34.

Stone, L. (1990) *The Family, Sex and Marriage in England, 1500–1800*. Abridged edn, Harmondsworth: Penguin.

Stopes, M. (1918) *Married Love: A New Contribution to the Solution of Sex Difficulties*. London: Putnam.

Storr, M. (1999) *Bisexuality: A Critical Reader*. London and New York: Routledge.

Stubbes, P. (1877) *Anatomy of the Abuses in England in Shakespere's Youth*. London: Trubner.

Tentler, T. (1977) *Sin and Confession on the Eve of the Reformation*. Princeton, NJ: Princeton University Press.

Thomas, K. (1978) The Puritans and adultery: the Act of 1650 reconsidered. In D. Pennington and K. Thomas (eds) *Puritans and Revolutionaries*. Oxford: Clarendon Press.

Thomasset, C. (1988) *Sexuality and Medicine in the Middle Ages*, trans. M. Adamson. Princeton, NJ: Princeton University Press.

Thompson, R. (1979) *Unfit for Modest Ears: A Study of Pornographic, Obscene and Bawdy Works Written or Published in England in the Second Half of the Seventeenth Century*. London: Macmillan.

Trall, R. T. (1903) *Sexual Physiology and Hygiene: An Explication, Practical, Scientific, Moral and Popular, of Some of the Fundamental Problems of Sociology*. London: Simkin, Marshall.

Traub, V. (1996) The perversion of 'lesbian' desire. *History Workshop*, 41, 23–43.

Trumbach, R. (1989) The birth of the queen: sodomy and the emergence of gender equality in modern culture, 1660–1750. In M. Duberman, M. Vicinus, and G. Chauncey (eds) *Hidden from History: Reclaiming the Gay and Lesbian Past*. Harmondsworth: Penguin.

Turner, J. G. (1987) *One Flesh: Paradisal Marriage: Sexual Relations in the Age of Milton*. Oxford: Clarendon Press.

Utley, F. L. (1972) Must we abandon the concept of courtly love? *Medievalia et Humanistica*, new series, 3, 299–323.

Vance, C. (1991) Anthropology rediscovers sexuality: a theoretical comment. *Social Science and Medicine*, 33: 8.

Van de Velde, T. (1930) *Ideal Marriage: Its Physiology and Technique*. London: Heinemann.

Veyne, P. (ed.) (1987) *A History of Private Life*, Vol. 1: *From Pagan Rome to Byzantium*. Cambridge, MA, and London: Belknap Press.

Vicinus, M. (1989) 'They wonder to which sex I belong': the historical roots of modern lesbian identity. In D. Altman (ed.) *Homosexuality, Which Homosexuality?* London: GMP.

Wagner, P. (1987) The discourse on sex – or sex as discourse: eighteenth century medical and para-medical erotica. In G. Rousseau and R. Porter (eds) *Sexual Underworlds of the Enlightenment*. Manchester: Manchester University Press.

Waites, M. (1998) Sexual citizens: legislating the age of consent in Britain. In T. Carver and V. Mottier (eds) *Politics of Sexuality: Identity, Gender, Citizenship*. London and New York: Routledge.

Walcot, P. (1984) Greek attitudes towards women: the mythological evidence. *Greece and Rome*, 31, 37–47.

Walkowitz, J. (1982) Male vice and feminist virtue: feminists and the politics of prostitution in nineteenth-century Britain. *History Workshop Journal*, 13, 79–93.

Warnicke, R. (1988) Women and humanism in England. In A. Ramie (ed.) *Renaissance Humanism: Foundations, Forms and Legacy*. Philadelphia: University of Pennsylvania Press.

Weeks, J. (1989) *Sex, Politics and Society: The Regulation of Sexuality since 1800*. Rev. edn, London: Quartet Books.

Weeks, J. (1991) *Against Nature: Essays on History, Sexuality and Identity*. London: Rivers Oram Press.

Weeks, J. (1999) *Making Sexual History*. Cambridge: Polity.

Weeks, J., and Porter, K. (eds) (1998) *Between the Acts: Lives of Homosexual Men, 1885–1967*. London: Routledge.

Weir, A., and Jerman, J. (1986) *Images of Lust: Sexual Carvings on Medieval Churches*. London: Batsford.

Williams, M. A. (1996) *Rethinking Gnosticism: An Argument for Dismantling a Dubious Category*. Princeton, NJ: Princeton University Press.

Williams, N. P. H. (1927) *The Ideas of the Fall and of Original Sin: A Historical and Critical Study*. London: Longmans, Green.

Winkler, J. J. (1990) *The Constraints of Desire: The Anthropology of Sex and Gender in Ancient Greece*. London: Routledge.

Wood, C., and Suitters, B. (1970) *The Fight for Acceptance: A History of Contraception*. Aylesbury: Medical and Technical Publication Company.

Woolf, C. (1986) *Magnus Hirschfeld: Portrait of a Pioneer in Sexology*. London: Quartet.

Wright, H. ([1930] 1961) *The Sex Factor in Marriage*. London: Williams & Norgate.

Zweig, S. (1979) *Erasmus and the Right to Heresy*. London: Souvenir Press.

Index